White Light

Bucknell Studies in Latin American Literature and Theory

Series editor: Aníbal González, Yale University

Dealing with far-reaching questions of history and modernity, language and selfhood, and power and ethics, Latin American literature sheds light on the many-faceted nature of Latin American life, as well as on the human condition as a whole. This highly successful series has published some of the best recent criticism on Latin American literature. Acknowledging the historical links and cultural affinities between Latin American and Iberian literatures, the series productively combines scholarship with theory and welcomes consideration of Spanish and Portuguese texts and topics, while also providing a space of convergence for scholars working in Romance studies, comparative literature, cultural studies, and literary theory.

Selected Titles in the Series

Rebecca E. Biron, *Elena Garro and Mexico's Modern Dreams*

Persephone Brahman, *From Amazons to Zombies: Monsters in Latin America*

Jason Cortés, *Macho Ethics: Masculinity and Self-Representation in Latino-Caribbean Narrative*

Tara Daly, *Beyond Human: Vital Materialisms in the Andean Avant-Gardes*

Earl E. Fitz, *Machado de Assis and Female Characterization: The Novels*

Earl E. Fitz, *Machado de Assis and Narrative Theory: Language, Imitation, Art, and Verisimilitude in the Last Six Novels*

Ronald J. Friis, *White Light: The Poetry of Alberto Blanco*

Naida García-Crespo, *Early Puerto Rican Cinema and Nation Building: National Sentiments, Transnational Realities, 1897–1940*

Thomas S. Harrington, *Public Intellectuals and Nation Building in the Iberian Peninsula, 1900–1925: The Alchemy of Identity*

David Kelman, *Counterfeit Politics: Secret Plots and Conspiracy Narratives in the Americas*

Brendan Lanctot, *Beyond Civilization and Barbarism: Culture and Politics in Postrevolutionary Argentina*

Marília Librandi, Jamille Pinheiro Dias, and Tom Winterbottom, eds., *Transpoetic Exchange: Haroldo de Campos, Octavio Paz, and Other Multiversal Dialogues*

Adriana Méndez Rodenas, *Transatlantic Travels in Nineteenth-Century Latin America: European Women Pilgrims*

Cecily Raynor, *Latin American Literature at the Millennium: Local Lives, Global Spaces*

Andrew R. Reynolds, *The Spanish American Crónica Modernista, Temporality, and Material Culture*

Elisa Sampson Vera Tudela, *Ricardo Palma's Tradiciones: Illuminating Gender and Nation*

Mary Beth Tierney-Tello, *Mining Memory: Reimagining Self and Nation through Narratives of Childhood in Peru*

Alberto Villate-Isaza, *Exemplary Violence: Rewriting History in Colonial Colombia*

White Light

The Poetry of Alberto Blanco

Ronald J. Friis

Bucknell University | University Press

Lewisburg, Pennsylvania

Library of Congress Cataloging-in-Publication Data
Names: Friis, Ronald J., author.
Title: White light: the poetry of Alberto Blanco / Ronald J. Friis.
Description: Lewisburg, Pennsylvania: Bucknell University Press, [2022] | Series: Bucknell studies in Latin American literature and theory | Includes bibliographical references and index.
Identifiers: LCCN 2021008378 | ISBN 9781684483464 (cloth) | ISBN 9781684483457 (paperback) | ISBN 9781684483471 (epub) | ISBN 9781684483488 (mobi) | ISBN 9781684483495 (pdf)
Subjects: LCSH: Blanco, Alberto, 1951—Criticism and interpretation. | Blanco, Alberto, 1951—Knowledge and learning.
Classification: LCC PQ7298.12.L27 Z67 2022 | DDC 861/.64—dc23
LC record available at https://lccn.loc.gov/2021008378

A British Cataloging-in-Publication record for this book is available from the British Library.

♾ The paper used in this publication meets the requirements of the American National Standard for Information Sciences—Permanence of Paper for Printed Library Materials, ANSI Z39.48-1992.

www.bucknelluniversitypress.org

Distributed worldwide by Rutgers University Press

Manufactured in the United States of America

For Laetitia, Sophie, Hudson, and Carole

Contents

Acknowledgments

This project began in the poetry section of San Francisco's City Lights bookstore in September 1998 when I reached out and drew Alberto Blanco's bilingual collection *Dawn of the Senses* off the shelf and into my hands. Over the next two decades my fascination with those poems evolved into the writing of this book thanks to the support and encouragement of a large number of colleagues, students, administrators, family members, and friends.

For more than twenty years I have had the good fortune to work at Furman University, a liberal arts college that has loyally supported and encouraged my research and given me more opportunities to grow as a teacher, student, and scholar than I can mention here. Furman's Research and Professional Growth Committee, Humanities Center, librarians, and, especially, a Furman Standard Research Grant provided generous funding without which this study would not have been possible.

I am especially appreciative of Furman's Department of Modern Languages and Literatures, my chairs Linda Bartlett and Bill Allen, and the colleagues who have listened to versions of these ideas at conferences, in hallways, and over meals, especially Lourdes Manyé, Angélica Lozano Alonso, and Jeremy Cass. I thank Eunice Rojas and my retired mentor David Bost for reading drafts of these chapters. Many Furman students have contributed in different ways to this project, but none more than my Furman Advantage Research Fellow and co-translator of *Medio Cine/Cinemap*, Maria Bartlett (2018).

I am grateful as well to many colleagues at other institutions for their help over the years, particularly to Cecelia Cavanaugh, for our conversations about surrealism and science in Madrid, to Susan Carvalho, for her inspirational invited lecture on space theory at Furman, and to Emily Hind, for organizing a panel at the MLA Convention in New York that took my research into new directions. I am also thankful to those who provided feedback on my work in conference panels over the years at MIFLC, SECOLAS, NeMLA, and the KFLC. Furthermore, I thank the editorial board of Bucknell University Press, series editor Aníbal González, and the anonymous reviewers of this book for their thoughtful and thorough comments and suggestions.

Personal thanks go to Hudson Friis for providing the soundtrack for this project and to Sophie Friis for helping shape the ways I think about poetic language. Carole Salmon has taught me new ways of seeing that have influenced both this study and everything else I have done since we re-met. My final thanks go to Alberto Blanco. Your email to me in 2013 started the conversation that has changed the course of my scholarly life. Your generosity, intellectual curiosity, and poetics of empathy are simply inspirational.

Chronology

Selected Poems

Giros de faros [*Circling Beacons*] (1979)
El largo camino hacia Ti [*The Long Road to You*] (1980)
Antes De Nacer [*D.N.A.*] (1983)
Tras el rayo [*Afterglow*] (1985)
Cromos [*Sticker Album*] (1987)
El libro de los pájaros [*A Book of Birds*] (1990)
Materia prima [*Prime Matter*] (1992)
Cuenta de los guías [*Account of the Guides*] (1992)
Amanecer de los sentidos [*Dawn of the Senses*] (1993)
Este silencio [*This Silence*] (1998)
El corazón del instante [*The Heart of the Moment*] (1st ed., 1998), containing:

1. *Giros de faros* [*Circling Beacons*]
2. *La parábola de Cromos* [*The Parable of Cromos*]
3. *Paisajes en el oído* [*Soundscapes*]
4. *El libro de los animales* [*A Book of Animals*]
5. *Tras el rayo* [*Afterglow*]
6. *Materia prima* [*Prime Matter*]
7. *Este silencio* [*This Silence*]
8. *Trébol inverso* [*Counter Clover*]
9. *El corazón del instante* [*The Heart of the Moment*]
10. *La raíz cuadrada del cielo* [*The Square Root of Heaven*]
11. *Antipaisajes y poemas vistos* [*Anti-landscapes and Seen Poems*]
12. *Antes De Nacer* [*D.N.A.*]

Más de este silencio [*More of This Silence*] (2001)
El libro de las piedras [*A Book of Stones*] (2003)
Medio cielo [*Midheaven*] (2004)
Música de cámara instantánea [*Instant Chamber Music*] (2005)
La hora y la neblina [*Time and Mist*] (1st ed., 2005), containing:

1. *Pequeñas historias de misterio* [*Little Mysteries*]
2. *Poemas vistos y antipaisajes* [*Seen Poems and Anti-landscapes*]
3. *Poemas traídos del sueño* [*Poems from Dreams*]
4. *Paisajes en el oído* [*Soundscapes*]
5. *Romances de ultramar* [*Ballads from Overseas*]
6. *Medio cielo* [*Midheaven*]
7. *El libro de las piedras* [*A Book of Stones*]
8. *Relámpagos paralelos* [*Parallel Lightning Strikes*]
9. *El libro de los animales* [*A Book of Animals*]
10. *La hora y la neblina* [*Time and Mist*]
11. *Album de estampas* [*A Portfolio of Prints*]
12. *Tiempo extra* [*Overtime*]

Paisajes en el oído [*Soundscapes*] (2012)
Todo este silencio [*All This Silence*] (2013)
Medio cine [*Cinemap*] (2014)
El libro de las plantas [*A Book of Plants*] (2014)
Poesía visual [*Visual Poetry*] (2015)
La raíz cuadrada del cielo [*The Square Root of Heaven*] (2016)
Contratiempos [*Contretemps*] (2016)
El corazón del instante [*The Heart of the Moment*] (2nd ed., 2018)
La hora y la neblina [*Time and Mist*] (2nd ed., 2018)
A la luz de siempre [*In Constant Light*] (1st ed., 2018), containing:

1. *A la luz de siempre* [*In Constant Light*]
2. *Duermevela* [*Halfsleep*]
3. *El libro de las plantas* [*A Book of Plants*]
4. *Piedras rodantes* [*Rolling Stones*]
5. *Relámpagos paralelos* [*Parallel Lightning Strikes*]
6. *El tacto y la mirada* [*Touch and Sight*]
7. *La Edad de Bronce* [*The Bronze Age*]
8. *Cuenta de los guías* [*Account of the Guides*]
9. *Música de cámara instantánea* [*Instant Chamber Music*]
10. *Amherst Suite* [*Amherst Suite*]
11. *Contratiempos* [*Contretemps*]
12. *Metapoemas* [*Metapoems*]

Selected Major Collections of Essays

Las voces del ver, Ensayos sobre artes visuales [*The Voices of Vision, Essays on the Visual Arts*] (1997)
El eco de las formas, 64 ensayos sobre artes visuales [*The Echo of Forms, 64 Essays on the Visual Arts*] (2012)
El canto y el vuelo [*Song and Flight*]
 El llamado y el don [*The Calling and the Gift*] (2011)
 La poesía y el presente [*Poetry and the Present*] (2013)
 El canto y el vuelo [*Song and Flight*] (2016)

White Light

Introduction

LIGHT IS BOTH WAVE AND PARTICLE

On November 28, 2018, Fondo de Cultura Económica's expansive exhibit booths at the Feria Internacional del Libro in Guadalajara, Mexico, featured three brand new releases by Alberto Blanco: the second edition of *El corazón del instante* [*The Heart of the Moment*], the second edition of *La hora y la neblina* [*Time and Mist*], and the first edition of *A la luz de siempre* [*In Constant Light*]. Each of these three thick volumes contains a poetic movement composed of twelve individual books. Taken together, the trilogy itself forms one large body of poems, a cycle of cycles written over forty years and appearing together in public for the very first time in the chaotic blur of Latin America's most important and best attended annual literary festival.

At the FIL, bundles of Blanco's books were wheeled to the showroom floor on dollies where they were then cut free from their white shipping paper and arranged into geometric piles on crowded display tables with the other new releases. Each five-hundred-plus-page paperback had been carefully re-edited and reworked, and each appeared with a new cover designed by the poet. *El corazón del instante* features the image of a large drop of mercury against a deep red background and is enveloped by a horizontal strip of burgundy paper identifying its author and title. *La hora y la neblina*'s cover is a close-up photograph of a stone walkway scattered with the distinctive red and green leaves of the *colorín* [coral tree] and *A la luz de siempre* is in a bamboo-textured earth tone, wrapped in a bold navy band.

Upon picking up *La hora y la neblina*, the informed reader will immediately notice differences from the book's first edition. There are more *Poemas vistos* [*Seen Poems*] in this new printing, for example, than the last, and the entire sixth section, *Medio Cielo* [*Midheaven*], has been replaced by the book *Medio Cine* [*Cinemap*]. Here we find the poem "La ciudad blanca" ["The White City"]. While certainly not a template poem for the poet (how can there possibly be a template for any poet, much less one as prolific as Blanco?) "La ciudad blanca" contains many of the prominent characteristics of the poet's work that this monograph explores.

"La ciudad blanca"
Blanca
luz de todos
en la suma prevista
de la ausencia y el color

Blanca
en el centro
mismo de la noche
donde cristalizan las lágrimas

Blanca
en el límite
donde pactan silencio
los contingentes contrarios

Blanca
de las sílabas
que fueron convocadas
para darle sonido a una imagen

Blanca
una extensión
sin traza ni huellas
donde a pesar de la nieve hay vida

Blanca
de cada hueco
intermedio de las cosas
brillando siempre por su ausencia

Blanca
de la pantalla
inmensa de la mente
donde los sueños nacen y mueren

Blanca
de la punta
insumisa de la pluma
que más que escribir quiere despertar[1]

["The White City"
White
collective light
the expected blend
of absence and color

White
in the very
center of the night
where tears crystallize

White
on the border
a truce of silence
between warring tribes

White
from syllables
summoned forth
to give voice to an image

White
a virgin expanse
free from footprints
but alive beneath the snow

White
from each
suspended hollow
of shining absent things

White
on the vast
screen of the mind
where dreams are born and die

White
from the pen's
rebellious point that
more than writes awakens][2]

To begin with, "La ciudad blanca" is a visual poem, one that asks us to engage its content through a deliberate concrete design on the page. Blanco is not only a poet and designer of book covers but also an accomplished maker of collages whose poems are replete with images such as "cada hueco / intermedio de las cosas" [each / suspended hollow / of shining absent things] that, like the text's concrete form, participate in a creative interplay of positive and negative spaces. "La ciudad blanca" questions language's capacity for representation through speech and writing and then takes this inquiry to a deeper level by situating the text in the literary and, ultimately, ontological tradition of questioning life as a dream. This is accomplished in the seventh and eighth stanzas through the triple-voiced metaphor of "la pantalla / inmensa de la mente / donde los sueños nacen y mueren" ["the vast / screen of the mind / where dreams are born and die"]—life is perceived in the mind in much the same way that film is seen on a screen or a dream is enacted in our subconscious as we sleep. The reference to a screen connects with the poem's context since *Medio cine* is a collection of forty texts inspired by influential film directors. This particular poem is linked in the book's index to Alain Turner, the Swiss director whose work includes 1983's *Dans la ville blanche* [In the White City]. Blanco calls his poems that dialogue with other artists "*vasos comunicantes*" [communicating vessels], a term that reminds us of his training as a chemist, and he insists that although they are inspired by their "*hacedores*" [inspirational creators], these poems are neither dedications nor examples of stylistic pastiche. Instead, like the use of a concrete form, the presence of an *hacedor* functions as a conversation starter by posing an open question between text and paratext.[3]

The writer's background in science appears again in the poem's charged poles, "los contingentes contrarios" [contrary contingents] of silence and sound that form the kind of dialectical relationship that is so familiar in his work. In the end, though, "La ciudad blanca," like so much of the poetry of Alberto Blanco, is about light, specifically the kind of white light that is formed by the combination of complementary colors. Light is at the heart of our greatest mysteries, from the biblical *fiat lux* [Let there be light!] to contemporary methods of measuring our distance from the stars. As the first stanza reminds us, when refracted, a seemingly invisible beam of light displays a whole spectrum of colors. Nearly four hundred years ago, Sir Isaac Newton used a prism to show that light can be both invisible *and* multicolored, while more recent discoveries in quantum physics teach us that light, whether visible, ultraviolet, or infrared, exists as both wave *and* particle. The paradoxes of light in "La ciudad blanca" reflect other main questions the poem asks of its readers: How do we interpret poetry that is so deeply intertwined with other artistic genres? Or how does the form of a concrete poem affect its content? Or, finally, how do we resolve the complex connection of a text to its epigraph or dedication?

Image, space, sound, reading, writing, science, faith, and being . . . in the poetry of Alberto Blanco, these key concepts weave together in and out of relationships of complementarity that together transform into something more than the sum of their parts, "an arrangement in a system to pointing."[4]

Alberto Blanco

Born in 1951 and raised in Mexico City, Blanco turned seventeen and started his university studies a few months before the October 1968 slaughter of student protesters at the Plaza de las Tres Culturas (Tlatelolco). As a student he specialized in chemistry at the Universidad Iberoamericana (1968–1973) and philosophy at UNAM (1971–1972) and then pursued a master's in Asian Studies (1974–1976) at the Colegio de Mexico. In addition to publishing his first poems, during these same years Blanco also designed and coedited the literary journal *El Zaguán*

(1975–1977), apprenticed with master print makers (1974–1976), and wrote songs, toured, sang, and recorded with the rock band La Comuna (1969–1975).[5]

It's hard to imagine anyone with a wider range of scientific and cultural interests and accomplishments before the age of twenty-five, and the impact this diverse bundle of experiences had on Blanco would be decisive in shaping the future directions of his poetry. As we shall see, Alberto Blanco speaks the languages of many disciplines as a native and creates poems whose radically interdisciplinary roots run deep.

In the late 1970s, after the breakup of La Comuna and in the heyday of the Mexican countercultural movement, the poet took a series of influential trips "on the road" to Tijuana and Southern California and came across mentors such as Juan Martínez, who would encourage and shape his writing. With the publication of the critically acclaimed *Giros de faros* [*Circling Beacons*] in 1979 by Fondo de Cultura Económica, Blanco began a remarkably productive period of work that resulted in the appearance of a new book of poems about once every two years for the next four decades. According to his personal website, as of 2019 the sum of his published works of poetry, literary and scientific translations, art and art criticism, children's literature, essays of poetics, and other books and articles totals more than fifteen hundred.[6]

In terms of his main publications, in the 1980s we find Blanco's most dense, hermetic, and formally experimental poetry in *El largo camino hacia Ti* [*The Long Road to You*] (1980), the structurally radical *Antes De Nacer* [*D.N.A.*] (1983), and the subtle and esoteric *Tras el rayo* [*Afterglow*] (1985).[7] In 1988, *Cromos* [*Sticker Album*], Blanco's first book of poems inspired by visual artists, earned him the Premio Carlos Pellicer. These years also produced a second edition of *Giros de faros* [*Circling Beacons*] (1985) and interartistic collaborations with renowned Mexican artist Francisco Toledo.

In the 1990s Blanco brought out landmark books with important publishing houses: *Cuenta de los guías* [*Account of the Guides*] with *Ediciones Era* in 1992; the first part of his trilogy of poetic cycles *El corazón del instante* [*The Heart of the Moment*] (1st ed., 1998) with Fondo and the anthology *Amanecer de los sentidos* [*Dawn of the Senses*] (1993) with CONACULTA. These books drew both national and international attention in the 1990s as witnessed by the writer's first of many entries into the Sistema Nacional de Creadores [National System of Creators] (1994), a Fulbright Grant to live and work in Irvine, California (1991), and the 1995 appearance of the bilingual anthology *Dawn of the Senses* with City Lights Publishers.[8] Among his many other publications in these years is the lengthy collection of essays on art *Las voces del ver* [*The Voices of Vision*] (1997).

Blanco's main book from 2000 to 2010 is the second part of his poetic trilogy, *La hora y la neblina* [*Time and Mist*] (1st ed., 2005), which groups together a number of smaller individual collections along with new work. In addition to four other *poemarios* that reflect his interests in nature, music, the visual arts, and Asian literatures, in this decade Blanco continued writing literary translations, children's books, and even a television series based on *Las voces del ver* (2001–2002). His international readership kept growing too, through numerous translations of individual poems and the publication of entire bilingual books in Dutch, French, and English. Finally, during these years, the writer was also awarded the Beca Octavio Paz de Poesía (2001–2002) and a Guggenheim Grant (2008–2009).

Amazingly, Blanco accelerated his literary production in his sixties, with, at the time of this writing, the publication of eight shorter books of poems and, as mentioned earlier, the third installment of his poetic trilogy, *A la luz de siempre* [*In Constant Light*] (2018). It's hard to imagine how the poet was able to write and publish so much new work while also re-editing and proofing his three largest and most important collections so they all could make the deadline to appear at the 2018 Feria Internacional del Libro. Let's remember that the trilogy contains thirty-six individual books housed in more than fifteen hundred total pages. If that were not enough, in 2011, 2013, and 2016 Blanco published important collections of essays on poetics that, like *A la luz de siempre*, each contain twelve chapters. In 2016 this essayistic trilogy, *El canto y el vuelo* [*Song and Flight*], earned him the prestigious Premio Xavier Villaurrutia, and in December 2019, the poet accepted the Premio Nacional de Poesía Ramón López Velarde.

Since Blanco's musical, artistic, literary, and essayistic production is simply too large to consider here in its entirety, our study focuses on the poetic trilogy (*El corazón del instante*, *La hora y la neblina*, and *A la luz de siempre*) and makes frequent references to the essays of poetics (*El llamado y el don* [*The Calling and the Gift*], *La poesía y el presente* [*Poetry and the Present*], and *El canto y el vuelo* [*Song and Flight*]). (Note that the title of the third volume of both trilogies is also the title of the trilogies themselves.)

Regardless of his more than seventy published books, Blanco has been and still is something of a literary lone wolf. Unlike other poets of his stature, he has never held governmental or diplomatic positions, and besides accepting occasional visiting writer-in-residence positions at universities in the United States, he has never held a permanent teaching position.[9] Furthermore, he does not write journalism, short stories, or novels, all of which appeal to broader audiences than poetry. While Blanco maintains personal relationships with many of Latin America's most influential poets and critics, he has always remained intentionally apart from Mexico City's notorious literary cliques. Like the speaker of José Emilio Pacheco's "Una defensa del anonimato" ["In Defense of Anonymity"] Blanco believes that poems are more important than poets and he flatly rejects "el circo literario" [the literary circus].

Simply put, Alberto Blanco has dedicated his entire professional life to nothing other than passionately, humbly, and prodigiously creating and writing about art.

One possible consequence of avoiding the literary spotlight is the surprisingly quiet academic and critical response to Blanco's large and theoretically sophisticated body of work. Essays by Evodio Escalante and Sandro Cohen provide thorough contextualization for Blanco's early poetry, which, it should be noted, differs in significant ways from his work since the mid-1990s. Escalante identifies Blanco as "un autor cuyo registro poético es uno de los más ricos, intensos y variados" [an author whose poetic register is among the richest, most intense and varied] but also takes *Antes De Nacer* to task for its dense hermeticism.[10] For his part, Cohen highlights Blanco's mastery of form and, like all of Blanco's critics, notes the intentionality of the images and systems in his work: "La regularidad o irregularidad del verso; el hecho de que las estrofas contengan dos, tres o cuatro versos; la disposición de las estrofas, etcétera; en la poesía de Alberto Blanco, todo esto tiene *sentido*" [The regularity or irregularity of the verses; the fact that the stanzas have two, three or four lines; the placement of the stanzas, etcetera; in the poetry of Alberto Blanco, everything *makes sense*].[11] Jesús Gómez Morán, for example, equates Blanco's poetics with the work of a sculptor or blacksmith,[12] and Julio Ortega praises his "trabajo artesanal con la palabra" [craftsmanship with words].[13] Balancing his hermeticism, Escalante, Guillermo Sheridan, Juan Armando Rojas, and others have alluded to the minimalism of some of Blanco's poems and their connections to the characteristically light brushstrokes of Asian art.[14]

Based on his birthdate, Alberto Blanco is sometimes included in the Mexican "Generación del '50" or "Generación del Medio Siglo" [Generation of 1950 or Midcentury Generation], and samples of his early work appear in the most important anthologies that employ that label (Acosta, Cansigno, Escalante, Mondragón, Monsiváis, Ortega, Ulacia y Mendiola, Zaid). Some critics refer to these same writers as "la Generación del '68" [Generation of 1968] because of their active participation, during their formative teenage years, in Mexico's counterculture and student movement. Still, as Juan Armando Rojas notes of the writers in Gabriel Zaid's influential *Asamblea de poetas* [*Assembly of Poets*], "Una de sus particularidades mas sobresalientes fue la de no estar unidos bajo ninguna bandera ideológica, corriente literaria o manifiesto" [One of the most notable characteristics of this group was their lack of ideological or literary manifestos or unity].[15] Samuel Gordon calls this diverse group "una generación de soledades" [a generation of solitudes][16] in part because of their tendency to favor smaller presses and journals other than *Vuelta*, *Taller*, or *La espiga amotinada*.[17] Furthermore, Gordon notes three prominent currents in the Mexican poetry of the mid- to latter half of the twentieth century that are useful in grouping these poets: "la poesía conversacional, la neobarroca y la confesional" [conversational, Neo-Baroque, and confessional].[18] Blanco, at different moments, participates in the first two styles while mostly shunning the third. Of the major Mexican poets born between 1940 and 1979, Gordon writes:

> La mayoría ha trabajado e incidido en el panorama poético de manera individual. No han lanzado manifiestos ni proyectos de grupo, tampoco proclamas estéticas ni etiquetas o banderas de corte político o social como muchos de los grupos de poetas precedentes. Se trata de un universo caracterizado por su dispersión geográfica y de intereses culturales, su variedad de estilos, su pluralidad ideológica y estética, sus temáticas y estilísticas caleidoscópicas que abarcan desde la poesía urbana a la mística y de las letras de rock al radicalismo experimental mas exacerbado.[19]
>
> [The majority have lived and engaged the literary scene solely in an individual manner. They have neither launched manifestos or group projects, nor made aesthetic, political or social position statements like many preceding generations. Instead, this group is characterized by its geographical dispersion, its diversity of cultural interests, its ideological and aesthetic plurality, its kaleidoscopic thematics and stylistics that embrace everything from urban poetry to mysticism to rock lyrics to the most exaggerated forms of experimental radicalism.]

In general, Blanco is most often considered in the company of David Huerta, Coral Bracho, Vicente Quirarte, Elsa Cross, Carlos Montemayor, Francisco Segovia, and Gerardo Deniz—a grouping whose work tends to be highly interdisciplinary and more interartistic than the generations of Octavio Paz and José Emilio Pacheco. La generación del '68 came of age under the fading influence of the American Beats and entered their teens as the homegrown La Onda (The Wave) and jipiteca (Mexican hippie) movements spread. They read and wrote novels like Gustavo Saínz's *Gazapo* [*Gazapo*] (1965) or José Agustín's *De perfil* [*In Profile*] (1966) and grew up with access to television, where they saw events like the moon landing and censored news coverage of the 1968 protests. They read Carlos Castaneda and the Bhagavad Gita, listened to the Beatles, and threw the I Ching. They opened the "doors of perception" with marijuana and hallucinogenic drugs, and like their counterparts in Prague, Belgrade, Paris, and elsewhere, Mexico's youth marched energetically through the streets of their city, held signs of protest in the Zócalo, and faced the shields and Billy clubs of riot police. Finally, they witnessed firsthand the population explosion and ecological deterioration of the booming Distrito Federal. Taking all of these factors into account, it's not hard to understand why Jaime Moreno Villarreal and Teresa Chapa opt for the term "generación del desengaño" [Generation of Disillusion] to describe these poets.[20]

David Harvey notes that the transnational countercultures "explored the realms of individualized self-realization through a distinctive 'new-left' politics, through the embrace of anti-authoritarian gestures, iconoclastic habits (in music, dress, language, and lifestyle), and the critique of everyday life."[21] As protestors, Mexico's teens fought the hegemonic excesses of *priismo* [PRI-ism], experienced the bitter end of the economic "Miracle," and tasted disillusionment with the hypocrisy of the Olympic games. The transnational countercultural movements of the late 1960s straddle what some critics see as a transition period within modernism toward postmodernism. Harvey writes: "Though a failure, at least judged in its own terms, the movement of 1968 has to be viewed, however, as the cultural and political harbinger of the subsequent turn to postmodernism. Somewhere between 1968 and 1972, therefore, we see postmodernism emerge as a full-blown though still incoherent movement out of the chrysalis of the anti-modern movement of the 1960s."[22]

The 1970s were the time of "happenings," those spontaneous, interartistic experiences that blur conventional lines of genre by combining music, visual arts, poetry, and performance art and focusing on the transcendent importance of the present moment (*Be Here Now!*). *El largo camino hacia Ti* [*The Long Road to You*], *Antes De Nacer* [*D.N.A.*], *Tras el rayo* [*Afterglow*], and *Cuenta de los guías* [*Account of the Guides*] were written under these influences and represent Blanco's most indeterminate and highly fragmented poetry through their "postmodernist" disjointed narratives, linguistic play with signifiers, and intertextual fluidity. *Cuenta de los guías* [*Account of the Guides*], in particular, celebrates chance, contains plural metanarratives, and reveals a parodic revisiting of Dante and Paz's *Blanco* [*Blanco*] and *Piedra de sol* [*Sunstone*]. Like other "postmodernist" poetry, Blanco's books from the early 1980s focus squarely on form and process and are open-ended, more reader-centered, and less author-centered than much of his later work.

El largo camino hacia Ti, *Antes De Nacer*, and *Cuenta de los guías*, however, mark the high-water mark for this kind of poetry for our writer whose work after about 1990 tends to be less radical in form and image. Like Walter Benjamin's famous essay, Blanco's later poetry is apt to be nostalgic for "aura," that is, the phantom of original, nonreproducible art. One might say that "a fear of the conditions of postmodernity haunts these texts."[23] Through his *hacedores*, the poet rewrites the Western canon in poems that revel in the avant-garde aesthetic of "creative destruction" we associate with European cubism and surrealism after the First World War. Blanco's poems display an awareness of the limitations of "master narratives" such as science and religion but often do so from the inside, through a sustained process of skeptical inquiry by a deeply committed student of life.

The Poems

Broad statements about a body of work as large, diverse, and evolving as Blanco's are necessarily reductive, though there are a few stylistic consistencies that appear, disappear, and reappear throughout his trilogy. Before panning out to survey the structure of the poetic cycles, let's first zoom in and examine some characteristics of the form, voice, and themes of the poems since, as Luis Cortés Bargalló notes, Blanco's work celebrates "la multiplicidad y sabiduría de las formas" [the multiplicity and knowledge of forms] and is characterized by "un amplísimo registro de valores y recursos artísticos así como de temas" [a wide array and inventory of artistic resources and themes].[24]

Indeed, the presence of all manner of conventional and avant-garde poetic forms is part of the fresh individuality of the poetry of Alberto Blanco. Jesús Gómez Morán notes: "Dentro del estiramiento que el poeta realiza tanto del lenguaje como de su oficio, sería difícil pensar en alguna vertiente a desarrollar que no pasara por el tamiz de su enunciación poética" [Due to Blanco's broad definitions of language and his calling as a poet, it would be hard to think of a style of poetry that does not find itself caught in his expansive poetic net].[25] In an anachronistic way, Blanco practices traditional stanzas and meters from the Spanish canon such as rhymed *coplas* [four-line verse], *cuartetos* [quatrains], *romances* [ballads], and *sonetos* [sonnets]. Evodio Escalante sees this as part of a generational tendency toward "conformación modélica" [conformity to established poetic patterns].[26] As in the work of José Juan Tablada, Octavio Paz, and others, the poet's background in Asian cultures informs his many collections of haiku and *tankas* such as *Este silencio* [*This Silence*]. Blanco cultivates poems and verses of all lengths, from light epigrams to philosophical prose poems to the 260 hermetic cantos of *Cuenta de los guías*. The variety of forms in his work is simply dazzling.

In "La ciudad blanca" we saw another important if also anachronistic practice—Blanco's *poesía visual*, that is, his visual or concrete poetry in which a text's words are displayed graphically for visual effect on a page. This technique finds its extreme in *Antes De Nacer*, the forty-page formal tour de force in which tercets are internally divided by blank spaces of strategic lengths to create the visual impression on the page of the braided strands of deoxyribonucleic acid (DNA). Even when visual poetry does not marry form and content so closely, a quick flip through any Blanco book immediately shows that the visual impact of line length is of great import to this poet/collage maker.

As we will explore in chapter 3, Blanco's experiences as a songwriter and performing rock and jazz musician inform the rhythms of his lines through creative patterns of stress, innovative lengths of line, and original play with rhyme—both within as well as between verses. Together with timbre and lexicon, these sounds help create a poem's unique voice. Once again, Blanco shows great range here, though, a few notable exceptions aside, the kind of clear, conversational poetic voice we hear below is typical. In visual poems, clarity of tone allows the reader to focus more on experimentation with length of line and stanza.

"Las piedras del espacio"

Las piedras de la luna
se han hecho un nido
al fondo del océano

De visos azules
en tus pupilas
iridiscentes

Y en la noche blanca
de nuestras vigilias
me han dado la llave

De la certeza y la forma
para la joyería íntima
de la reconciliación.[27]

["Stones from Outer Space"

Moon stones
nest
in the depths

of the shining
blue sea
of your pupils.

In our white
sleepless nights
they give me the key

to the certainty and form
of the delicate chains
that will bring us back together.]

Here, the poetic voice spins traditional metaphors through familiar nouns and adjectives. The subtle visual slant of the first two stanzas complements the thematic descent of the moonstones into the eyes of the beloved and initiates the change in line seven that ushers in the poem's closing thoughts. This text from *La hora y la neblina* does not have a fixed rhyme scheme or meter, but it does intentionally employ near-rhyme and near-consonance (*luna/océano*; *forma/íntima*) in an intriguingly irregular pattern that contributes to the flow of its one long, enjambed verse. The verses themselves have between five and ten syllables and grow shorter, then longer in the last stanza reflecting the consolidation of the poem's message. Perhaps the most endearing melodic and visual element of "Las piedras del espacio," however, is that repetition of the letter "o" after consonants in the second, third, and fourth lines (*hecho, nido, fondo, océano, visos*) [made, nest, bottom, ocean, sheen] that both creates an audible rhythm and reflects, visually, the circular form of the speaker's partner's pupil.

For the purposes of contrast, let's consider "Las piedras del espacio" beside the first line of *Cuenta de los guías:* "Con la luna entre las cejas, con su paciencia, con las ágatas que guiñan y lo saben: una vez más, río de peces, árbol del cielo, son hojas que nunca volverán . . . criaturillas que encuentran su destino en el borde anaranjado del mantel" [With the moon between eyebrows, with its patience, with quartz that winks and knows: one more time, river of fish, tree of sky, are leaves that won't return . . . little creatures meeting their destinies at the orange border of the tablecloth].[28] Both poems start with lunar imagery, but one uses a tame and pretty personification to create a unified visual image, while the other's fragmented style leaves us on uncertain lexical and syntactic footing. The sheer length and breadth of the later poem give it room to allow space between signifiers and signifieds in ways a shorter poem simply cannot. In this manner, a long poem uses both its form and its language to search for communion across wide divides.

For all of its verbal pyrotechnics, *Cuenta de los guías* is, perhaps primarily, a spiritual journey. Like much of the international countercultural movements of the 1950s to 1970s, Blanco's work shows a sustained interest in meditation and Eastern imagery and philosophies. His poems long for spiritual connection outside of Christianity—a tradition that remains, nonetheless, an important thematic point of reference in his work, from the early poem "Un escéptico Noé" ["A Skeptical Noah"] to the climactic last lines of *A la luz de siempre*. Another thematic inheritance of the hippie movement is the individualistic streak we see in "Pensando sin pensar" ["To Think Without Thinking"], which is as much about meditation or writing poems as what might be called a Zen attitude toward life:

Pensando sin pensar
me abstengo de hacer comparaciones:
ni las flores son como el sol
ni el mar es como el cielo.
Me abstengo de los comos . . .[29]

[To think without thinking
I abstain from comparisons:
neither the flowers are like the sun
nor the sea is like the sky.
I abstain from the hows . . .]

As we explore in chapter 5, the spiritual quest of Blanco's work is balanced by his poems about science, and some of his most engaging and persuasive work is written in the style of logic puzzles or scientific hypothesis.

With very few exceptions, the poetic trilogy is neither confessional nor overtly autobiographical. Critics such as Rojas and Escalante have noted a didacticism in Blanco that may be related to what Christopher Domínguez Michael has termed his "mestizaje de los misticismos." Surprisingly, Blanco, like many of the Mexican poets who participated in the student movements of the late 1960s, swerves away from protest poetry in his work. Returning again to Samuel Gordon, we read:

> No plantean un compromiso político quizá porque ya no creen que la poesía pueda o deba cambiar la sociedad y, además, lo consideran irrelevante. En cambio, meditan muchísimo en torno al lenguaje y se inclinan, cada vez más, por escribir textos autorreferenciales cuyos sujetos son, por igual, el poeta y la poesía.[30]
>
> [Perhaps they don't make political pronouncements because they no longer believe that poetry can or should change society and, in addition, the consider such things irrelevant. Instead, they meditate deeply on language and are more and more inclined to write self-referential texts whose subjects are, equally, the poet and poetry].

In a similar vein to Gordon, Escalante sees Blanco as part of a "vanguardia blanca" [a white avant-garde], that is, avant-garde poetry written by Mexican poets in the wake of Octavio Paz: "una vanguardia introvertida, ensimismada, que vierte hacia adentro, hacia la soledad modélica del lenguaje" [an introverted, self-centered and self-absorbed avant-garde that dives deep inside, toward the exemplary solitude of language].[31] Escalante includes David Huerta, Gerardo Deniz, and Coral Bracho in this group of "nuevos radicales, desvinculados a lo social" [new radicals, unattached to social issues].[32] To clarify, Blanco rarely employs his poetry to deliver a political message, but as we read in the powerful poem about September 13, 1968's Silent March through Mexico City, "no es lo mismo guardar silencio / que quedarse callado" [being silent is not the same thing as not saying anything].[33]

Two final distinctive qualities of Blanco's poetry are his tendency to group poems into sets and his texts inspired by other artists. The former seems to connect with the poet's training as a scientist due to its desire for precision. In the words of Jorge Fernández Granados, "las series de todo tipo . . . le seducen como estructuras y como posibilidades inagotables de contenido" [all manner of series seduce him with their structure and unending possibilities for content].[34] As we shall see, the poems in each segment of the books of the trilogy are almost obsessively grouped into families or visual clusters of animals, metals, minerals, precious stones, the compass rose, the four seasons, the signs of the zodiac, and so on. For instance, within *La hora y la neblina's El libro de las piedras* [*A Book of Stones*], we find four sections: "Metales," "Minerales," "Rocas," and "Piedras preciosas" [Metals, Minerals, Rocks, and Precious Stones]. "Metales" contains poems called "El hierro," "El cobre," "El oro" ["Iron," "Copper," "Gold"], and so on. Reminiscent of Pablo Neruda's odes in scope and tone, these sets are sometimes playful, sometimes earnest attempts to find connections amid difference.

As we have noted and will explore at length, Blanco's poetry is interartistic in many senses. One of the more prominent examples of this is found in his "creaciones paralelas" [parallel creations], or series of poems that are linked, in appendices, to specific writers, musicians, or artists, his "*hacedores*" [inspirational creators]. These are not incidental pieces for Blanco but rather large and important sections of his books. All in all, the trilogy contains over seven hundred poems of this kind.[35] For ease of expression we may sometimes speak of these poems as being "dedicated to" or "inspired by" artists, but Blanco insists that his poems are placed "in dialogue with" his *hacedores* or that, quoting Stravinsky, they use other works as "un excitante para la 'facultad creadora'" [stimuli for the powers of creation].[36] The rules for these games are explained in the "Notas preliminares" [prefatory notes] of the books of the trilogy and we will examine the implications of reading through paratexts at length in the pages to come. Blanco's *hacedores* give us a glimpse into his personal library, as it were. His is an international canon—mostly, but not exclusively, European, Latin American, North American, and Chinese. While some of the *hacedores* are Mexican, Blanco is not an overly nationalistic poet in the sense that he makes some references to his country's pre-Columbian heritage but certainly does not privilege Mexico's culture or legacy over others.

The *hacedores* are, in a sense, a list of hundreds of influences, but if this list were to be narrowed down to a pantheon of Blanco's most influential precursors, one would have to mention the interdisciplinary brilliance of Leonardo da Vinci, the spatial and conceptional revolution of Mallarmé's *Un Coup de Dés . . .* [*A Throw of the Dice . . .*], the surrealism of André Breton and Paul Éluard, the cerebral elegance of Fernando Pessoa, the freewheeling adventurousness of the American Beat Generation, and the mysticism and resistance to representation of Juan Martínez. Blanco's work also reflects and recalls the concrete innovations of Haroldo de Campos, Mário de Andrade, and Vicente Huidobro, Chinese and Japanese poetry's connections to nature, the verbal eloquence of Octavio Paz, John Cage's work with silence and music, and the Beatles, Bob Dylan, and Pink Floyd.[37]

One of the innovations of Blanco's poems about influence and the advantages to the placement of the list of *hacedores* in his appendices (rather than on the same page as his poems) is that it allows the reader to experience the *vasos comunicantes* for the first time, if they choose, without knowing with whom the texts are connected. After this first pass, a reader may then choose to return to a poem again after consulting the appendix. We will explore the variety of genres of *hacedor* poems and the kinds of reading strategies they invite in our different chapters, but one of the main outcomes of this kind of poem deserves to be mentioned here.

Among the large number of his poems dedicated to visual artists, only a small number engage in ekphrasis, that is, the re-creation with words of specific scenes from pictures. There are, however, elements of ekphrasis in a more general sense in many of Blanco's interart poems. In *Picture Theory*, art critic W. J. T. Mitchell calls ekphrasis "a curiosity" and, in doing so, puts his finger right on an important impulse that drives Blanco's use of *hacedores*.[38] Mitchell notes that ekphrasis is powered by a hope of overcoming "otherness" and thus reflects the need for communion that undergirds the poetry of Alberto Blanco.[39] The interartistic nature of Blanco's poems and, it should be noted, his essays, share the goals of ekphrasis by piquing his readers' curiosity to experience the enormous world of art, literature, and music out there. It is only through going out and looking and listening compassionately to the world that one can receive the kind of inspiration and connection that is the ultimate goal of poetry. We will at times refer to this drive as Blanco's poetics of empathy.

Cycles

Along with his sets of related poems and *vasos comunicantes* another key concept in Blanco's universe of verse is the "ciclo poético" [poetic cycle]. The poet uses this term in two ways—first, to describe the internal architecture of the books *El corazón del instante*, *La hora y la neblina*, and *A la luz de siempre* and, second, to define the poetic trilogy itself.

Each volume of the trilogy contains a *nota preliminar* [prefatory note] by the poet explaining its division into twelve cycles that we will alternately refer to as "chapters," "sections," or "books." Most chapters present previously published books, but some do not. As the first entry of the trilogy, it makes sense that *El corazón del instante* would mostly contain older poems (1973 to 1993), but the next two books are much less tied to chronology. A prominent example is the important *Cuenta de los guías*, written during the late 1970s and early 1980s but not finding a home in the trilogy until 2018's *A la luz de siempre*. Addressing these anomalies, Carlos Zamora notes: "¿Qué significa toda esta reordenación? Para Alberto Blanco, el tiempo convencional no le sirve para establecer sus ciclos" [What does this kind of reorganization mean? That conventional notions of time do not work for establishing Alberto Blanco's cycles].[40] Zamora elaborates that one intention of Blanco's reordering of poems is to explore their possibilities of cohabitation, both as new chapters and as part of one long new, book-length poem.[41]

Always the visual artist, Blanco sees his cycles as wheels. He knows they are complete, he says, by "seeing how they roll." He also sees a thematic progression from his first to his third book. All three titles reference time and refer to the movement from the moment of poetic inspiration to the creation of something that lasts. In the poet's words:

> *El corazón del instante*: una sola realidad: el centro. Sólo en el centro no hay conflicto. Atención: creatividad . . . *La hora y la neblina*: el tiempo y el espacio. La dualidad. Y donde hay división, hay opuestos, contrarios . . . hay creación y siempre hay conflicto. Es el mundo relativo . . . *A la luz de siempre*: una dedicatoria y una invocación.[42]

> [*The Heart of the Moment:* a single reality: the center. Only in the center is there no conflict. Being present: creativity . . . *Time and Fog*: time and space. Duality. And where there is division, there are opposites, opponents . . . there is creation and there is always conflict. That's the relative world . . . *In Constant Light*: a dedication and an invocation.]

The overall internal structure of the trilogy is like an expansive coral reef, both structured and not—"not unordered in not resembling," as Gertrude Stein once wrote. At times, Blanco's sets and chapters have the feel of *cantos* in the tradition of Dante or Ezra Pound. While each volume of the trilogy has three sets of twelve chapters, there is great structural variety within those thirty-six books. Some are just one long poem, while others are broken into thematic subsections. As should be expected from a maker of collages, the number and order of poems and verses in the trilogy are meticulously mapped.[43] In his analysis of the structure of *El corazón del instante*, Zamora draws on the work of Neil Fraitstat and Earl Miner to assert that first and last poems form the "columna vertebral del libro" [spinal column of the book].[44] As in any collection, first and last poems occupy privileged positions, and Zamora adds that poems can open or close when read within or apart from the context of their larger cycles.[45]

In the pages to come we will explore at length Blanco's deep personal relationship to numbers. This comes, in part, from his training in mathematics, geometry, and the "hard sciences," but also, the poet insists, from studying his own poems. The order of that last statement is crucial for Blanco—a poem is written and then, when examined later, the text reveals its dominant numbers and connections to other stories to the poet. In addition to numbers with traditional significance in numerology (1, 3, 4, 7, 9, 11, 13, 18, 36, 81, 108, 1008, etc.) many of the verse and stanza counts of Blanco's poems contain correspondences or "acuerdos" with the poet's personal life and context. One small example is the seventy-seven poems in the seven sections of *Giros de faros*, conceived of and written in 1977. Numbers associated with natural cycles, such as quaternities, are especially important to Blanco, particularly when it comes to structuring his collections. This is why we find groups of twelve books and twelve essays that mirror the sense of completion we see in the twelve hours on a clock's face or the twelve months of the year. In our coda we will study the poem “El canto y el vuelo” [“Song and Flight”], Blanco’s *ars poetica*, that, like his books, has three stanzas of four lines each for a total of twelve verses. Drawing from pre-Columbian traditions, five and fifty-two also play important ritualistic roles in books such as *Cuenta de los guías* and one hundred eight, a magic number par excellence, is a major structuring element in the one thousand eight double verses of *Antes De Nacer.*

Regardless of their internal architecture, in the most basic sense the three tomes of *A la luz de siempre* are, if nothing else, large . . . so large that one has to ask, *who reads five-hundred-page books of poetry in the age of Twitter?* When posed this question in an interview, the poet answered simply, “¿Quién lee los libros grandes de poesía? . . . Los grandes lectores” [Who reads great big books of poems? Great readers].[46]

Polarities

One of the primary motives in Blanco’s poetry is the presentation and resolution of binary oppositions. In this section we will lay out a few useful metaphors for understanding these relationships, metaphors we will then use later in our reading of the poems. Blanco’s work returns again and again to the dance between two different but related ideas or textual elements. These tensions might appear as thematic opposites like day and night, as visual counterparts like the left and right justified stanzas of “La ciudad blanca,” or as the intertextual push and pull between a poem and its *hacedor.* Complements in search of communion function in both literal and figurative levels for the writer.

Irma Chávez Robinson calls Blanco’s paired opposites “palabras antípodas” [antipodean words], while the poet himself draws on his experiences in the chemistry laboratory by calling them “charged poles” or “polarities.”[47] In his essays on poetics, he terms the tension between complementary forces an “anhelo polar” [“polar longing”]:[48]

> Ya me he referido a muchos de estos pares opuestos, complementarios, alternos, antagónicos y/o contradictorios: imagen y música; espacio y tiempo; Apolo y Dionisio; vida salvaje y vida domesticada; atracción y repulsión; calidad y cantidad; tradición e innovación; poesía escrita y poesía oral; aspiración y espiración; lo incondicionado y la causalidad; y un larguísimo etcétera . . . su cristalización en la poesía implica—como en la vida—un milagro de equilibrio, una suerte de iluminación.[49]

> [I have already referred to many of these opposite, complementary, alternating, antagonistic and/or contradictory pairs: image and music; space and time; Apollo and Dionysus; wild life and domestic life; attraction and repulsion; quality and quantity; tradition and innovation; written poetry and spoken poetry; inhaling and exhaling; the unconditional and the causal; followed by

a long etcetera . . . their crystallization in poetry—as in life—implies the miracle of balance, a sort of enlightenment.]

Chávez Robinson's study of Blanco focuses on that last point, finding enlightenment through a process of balancing opposites inspired in Zen Buddhism. In reality though, the poet's treatment of polarities draws on many traditions from Hegelian dialectics (thesis-antithesis-synthesis) to Mikhail Bakhtin's dialogism by putting terms into conversation without necessarily pulling the strings of synthesis too tightly. Blanco's work tends to reject hierarchical dualism (one element dominating the other) for the more Taoist concept of mediated and intertwined pairs of complements in what might be called a "dialectical monism" in progress or under interrogation. Here we find a particularly strong set of convergences and divergences with Octavio Paz's dialectical vision of the world. In "Los signos en rotación" ["Signs in Rotation"] Paz writes, "No me preocupa la otra vida sino aquí. La experiencia de la otredad es, aquí mismo, la otra vida. La poesía no se propone consolar al hombre de la muerte sino hacerle vislumbrar que vida y muerte son inseparables: son la totalidad" [I am not worried about the other life, only this one. The experience of otherness is, right here, the other life. Poetry does not console us about death but rather reveal that life and death are inseparable: a totality]. "Los contrarios no desaparecen, se funden por un instante" [adversaries do not disappear, they meld for a moment].[50]

As the quotation from *El canto y el vuelo* above shows, Blanco has many synonyms for his poetic polarities and multiple modes of synthesizing these concepts.[51] Opposites sometimes coexist in his poems by weaving in and out against each other like competing melodies in musical counterpoint. In an analogous way, Linda Hutcheon's examination of irony describes how working with paired complements permits and requires a "simultaneous perception of more than one meaning in order to create a third composite (ironic) one."[52] A more complex metaphor for the coexistence of a duality comes from the field of particle physics and Niels Bohr's theory of complementarity. In 1928 Bohr explained that "the behavior of such phenomena as light and electrons is sometimes wave-like and sometimes particle-like; i.e., such things have a wave-particle duality (q.v.). It is impossible to observe both the wave and particle aspects simultaneously. Together, however, they present a fuller description than either of the two taken alone."[53]

Opposites can also be imagined as complementary colors of light—the pairing of hues like red and green or yellow and violet that face each other on a color wheel. When placed next to each other, complementary colors create an uneasy and dissonant sensation in the viewer through the strength of their contrast. Paradoxically, though, when complements are combined, they cancel each other out to "produce white or colourless light."[54] To "complement" is to "make complete or perfect, to supply what is wanting." Similarly, in the field of optics, a complement is "that color which, mixed with another, produces white" and "that which completes or makes perfect." Understood in the contexts of the wave/particle duality and color theory, white light, with its traditional associations with purity and divinity, is thus a much more complex phenomenon than at first meets the eye—its wholeness is a function of its diversity and its harmony a result of its dissonance.

In this vein, Irma Chávez Robinson has identified a key visual metaphor of duality for our poet: "Blanco nunca deja desbalanceado un poema, sino hay un constante equilibrio utilizando las palabras antípodas para llegar al término medio en la unión del yin y yang" [Blanco never leaves a poem unbalanced, but rather in a state of constant equilibrium by using antipode words to find the middle ground of union between yin and yang].[55] In a basic sense, the *taijitu* or yin/yang symbol is a visual depiction of a Taoist philosophy stating that all things in life, even those that appear contradictory, are connected through a process of inseparable coexistence. Like the ancient Nahuatl concept of *teotl*, yin/yang represents a "sign in rotation," which, like poetry, is "una red de relaciones . . . un proceso" [a network of relationships . . . a process].[56] Art historian E. H. Gombrich notes that a concrete symbol like the yin and yang "conveys relations more quickly and more effectively than a string of words," has great "arousal potential," and can therefore be the "focus of meditation."[57] For this reason, Carl Jung used the *taijitu* as a metaphor for his concepts of animus and anima. The movement implied in this useful visual metaphor contains a temporal element as well since it focuses on the present moment, which, like the construction of our identities, is always evolving and growing.

In addition to his deep readings of Eastern philosophies and Octavio Paz, another source for this kind of imagery in Blanco is Mexican poet Juan Martínez. Notice the parallel imagery in Blanco's analysis of his friend's "Conocer":

> Como se puede ver, los polos formados por el hombre y las cosas, el pensamiento y el sentimiento, el blanco y el negro, el día y la noche, la razón y la pasión, el más y el menos, la vida y la muerte, lo que está arriba y lo que se encuentra abajo, se abren y se cierran formando un círculo que no cesa de girar: "la rueda del sinfín" que tantas veces le gusta citar a Juan y que en tantas y en tan diversas ocasiones me ha mostrado en las mas inesperadas circunstancias.[58]
>
> [We can see that the poles formed by people and things, thoughts and emotions, black and white, day and night, reason and passion, more and less, life and death, things up above and things down below open and close to form a circle that never stops spinning: the "ever spinning wheel" that Juan mentions time and again and that he has shown me in the most unexpected settings.]

Invoking the visual metaphor of the constellation Libra, Blanco calls "la justicia de los platillos" [the balanced scales of justice] Martínez's main theme, and we find the influence of this way of thinking in the opening essay of *El canto y el vuelo*:

> Y es que si hablamos de composiciones por matrices y series, quiere decir que seguimos operando en función de pares opuestos: uno centrado en el espacio—las formas visuales, el ojo, la imagen—y el otro centrado en el tiempo—las formas sonoras, el oído, la música—como polos inevitables de nuestra práctica. He aquí la balanza: en un platillo, en un mismo tiempo una forma poética ocupa el espacio de muchos modos distintos; en el otro platillo, una misma forma poética y un mismo modo de ocupar el espacio, desarrolla sus múltiples variaciones en el tiempo. El fiel de la balanza es, como siempre, el misterio del lenguaje.[59]

> [And if we talk about compositions in terms of source and series, this means we are still working with opposite pairs: one centered in space—the visual forms, the eye, the image—and the other centered in time—the sonic forms, hearing, music—as the inevitable polarities of our practice. Picture a scale: on one plate, in one moment, one poetic form occupies space in many different ways; on the other plate, that same poetic form and same way of occupying space develops its many variations in time. The needle of the scale is, like always, the mystery of language.]

As we shall see, Blanco systematically conjugates different ways of synthesizing the charged poles of his poetry throughout the decades. Each chapter of our book examines poems on a different subject (such as music) and then explores the tensions between that main idea and a complement (such as silence). As theme and form dictate, we will employ different metaphors such as the *taijitu*, color theory, white light, or positive and negative spaces to read Blanco's "anhelo polar" and study his many modes of synthesis.

In *El llamado y el don* the writer posits one possible answer for how to synthesize poetry's charged poles:

> ¿Y si más de tratar de componer una pieza musical utilizando la vieja técnica del contrapunto, en un intento artístico por conciliar estos dos viejos polos aparentemente irreconciliables, existiera una tercera opción que fuera más allá de cualquiera de las dos? Sí, una tercera opción múltiple, abierta, potenciada . . . una tercera vía imantada hacia todos los polos imaginables?[60]

> [And what if instead of trying to compose a piece of music using the ancient technique of counterpoint, in an attempt to reconcile these two old and apparently irreconcilable poles, there were a third option that went beyond both of them? Yes, a third, multiple option, open, powerful . . . a third magnetic path toward all the imaginable poles?]

This is the question that undergirds his self-termed "transformalismo" [Transformalism] that is, a poetics able to "superar el dualismo de la razón y la inspiración en busca de una objetividad con conocimiento de causa que niegue la tiranía del discurso racional lo mismo que de las pulsaciones inconscientes, la facilidad complaciente de la auto-expresión y la sucesión causal del mundo dividido en objetos individuales" [overcome the duality of logic and inspiration while looking for objectivity with causal knowledge that denies the tyranny of both rational discourse and instinctual urges, the complacent ease of self-expression and the causal succession of a world divided into individual objects].[61]

To put it in more concise but certainly not more simple terms, he writes:

> El Transformalismo es el reconocimiento de que en la poesía—como en todo el arte—la forma es un medio, y el fin es trascender la forma. En este sentido, el poema es sólo un vehículo, una herramienta, una hipótesis de trabajo. La meta es la transformación del artista y de quién disfruta del trabajo artístico: el creador lo mismo que el recreador.[62]
>
> [Transformalism is the recognition that in poetry—as in all forms of art—form is a means, to the end of transcending form. In this sense, a poem is only a vehicle, a tool, a working hypothesis. The goal is the transformation of the artist and of the person who appreciates a work of art: the creator, the same as the recreator.]

Blanco's work thus transforms the poet's inspiration into the inspiration of its readers.

White Light

This book explores images, space, sound, reading, writing, science, and spirituality in Blanco's poetry and how these concepts interact with their complements. Our chapters are inspired by the poet's many vocations, from being a maker of collages and art historian to a musician, chemist, reader, student of meditation and religious traditions, translator, and, of course, writer.

Chapter 1, "Image," proposes the collage as a metaphor of reading and then explores representations of visual images in the poems. Here we analyze Blanco's *poesía concreta* [concrete poetry] and calligrams as well as his poems about visual art and texts that rely heavily on verbs of perception. We will examine a few variations on ekphrasis and conclude with a study of two images that figure prominently into the structures of *Cuenta de los guías*. Since the later book is such a large and assertive statement of Blanco's early poetics, we will return to it often throughout our chapters. In fact, many of Blanco's techniques, such as his *hacedor* poems, will be examined in more than one section of this book.[63]

Chapter 2, "Space," explores the "exergue effect" caused by time and place stamps and other spatial paratexts in Blanco's poems. It also considers travel narratives and the movement from two dimensional to more multidimensional spaces and forms such as cinematic montage. The chapter concludes with analyses of how Blanco negotiates borders in his work, particularly in "Mapas" ["Maps"] and in the spatial and temporal metaforms of *Cuenta de los guías*.

"Sound," chapter 3, examines music and silence—from the poet's innovative use of alliteration and other forms of rhyme, to the silence of textual white spaces, to poems dedicated to rock and roll. "Texture," chapter 4, is about reading and writing. It examines metapoetry, the act of addressing readers in the second person through directives and, of course, poems inspired by other writers. Here we look at polarities from the metaphorical perspectives of brain lateralization and the *taijitu* and conclude by considering Blanco's desire for poetry to reveal a hidden dimension. Indeed, cognitive poetics will inform our approach to many aspects of Blanco's poetry throughout this study.

"Metaphysics," chapter 5, explores Blanco's use of scientific and mathematical discourse, particularly in poems about the sacred. The chapter closes with an analysis of "Credo" ["Creed"], the poet's climactic meditation on faith. Our coda considers the poem "El canto y el vuelo" in the light of Blanco's creative work and essays about poetics. "El canto y el vuelo" uses the metaphor of a bird in flight to embody the synthesis of complements of his transformalist poetics. The way the poet presents and metaphorically balances relationships of complementarity demands and ultimately bestows new interpretative techniques to his readers.

CHAPTER 1

Image

Les "blancs," en effet, assument
l'importance, frappent d'abord
—Stéphane Mallarmé

In 2015 El Museo de las Californias at the Centro Cultural de Tijuana held a forty-year retrospective of visual works by Alberto Blanco. In an interview with the magazine *Zeta Tijuana*, the artist shared many of his ideas on the history and importance of what Walter Benjamin called the artistic technique par excellence of the twentieth century: the collage. When asked to define what collage means for him, Blanco answered, "Podría responder de 10 mil maneras esa pregunta, en este momento lo que me viene a la mente es que el collage es una manera de ser feliz" [While I could answer that question in ten thousand different ways, at this moment the answer that comes to mind is that the collage is a way to be happy]. A little later, in response to the question "¿Qué busca lograr en el espectador con sus collages?" [What effect do you want to achieve in the viewer of your collages?] he repeated simply "Que sea feliz" [To be happy].[1]

Two aspects of this interview call our attention. First, the artist's acknowledgment that there are thousands of replies to the interviewer's question reflects both his deep knowledge of art history and his inescapable connection with the technique of collage. Blanco's answer, as he explains, was mentally selected or "cut" from dozens of preexisting definitions and then "pasted," as it were, into the context or surface of the interview. Second, rather than offer a collaged answer lacking innovation, Blanco selected an unconventional and unexpected response, happiness, to the question of what he wants those who view his work to feel. His justification for this idea is to say that it is easy, perhaps too easy, to create monsters through collage and that he wants his visual work to serve as a hopeful counterpoint to the chaos and ugliness of today's world.

This same exhibit at the Centro Cultural de Tijuana was accompanied by a handsome catalog. In its introductory preface, Blanco offers numerous perspectives on the connections between visual and verbal representations. Each paragraph of "El *collage*: una historia sin nombre" ["Collage: A Nameless History"] features one or more definitions of the technique and is followed by a number in parenthesis:

> El *collage* es un instrumento súper sensible y escrupulosamente exacto, semejante a un sismógrafo, que es capaz de registrar la cantidad precisa de posibilidades que el ser humano tiene de ser feliz en cualquier momento. (1)[2]

> [A collage is an ultra-sensitive and scrupulously exact instrument, similar to a seismograph, that is able to register the precise quantity of possibilities that a human being has of being happy in a given moment (1)]

The bracketed numbers lead the reader to a works cited section ("Referencias" ["References"]) on page 9 that discloses the often uncited sources of the essay's numerous definitions. The quotation above, for example, is from Max Ernst. It also happens to be the same definition Blanco gave the *Zeta Tijuana* reporter.

I refer to the online interview and the exhibit catalogue because they reveal the centrality of the visual image in the work of Alberto Blanco. Not only are they both texts *about* the visual arts, but both the interview and the catalogue essay *are themselves* verbal collages. In the interview, Blanco pastes an uncited quote from Ernst, an artist he greatly admires, into his own thoughts and thus shows the intertextual tension at the heart of contemporary poetry. Similarly, in the catalogue he collects, extracts, and repositions clippings of the voices that inform his work onto a new surface. As we shall see, spatial manipulation and the tension between citation and originality is a recurrent motif in many moments of Blanco's work.

This chapter uses collage as a starting point to read aspects of visual representation in Blanco, from the concrete interplay of black-and-white marks on the page, to the limits of creating three dimensional spaces through language. In our introduction we proposed white light and the *taijitu* or yin/yang symbol as metaphors for Blanco's poetic project since, for him, the visual image is nothing less than "un verdadero centro magnético" [a true magnetic core].[3] While definitions of the visual image vary greatly in different contexts, here we will occupy ourselves with how and through what means the poet represents objects and concepts through words. In Blanco's *poesía visual* [visual poetry], words help form pictures in our mind (one kind of imagery) and also make graphic forms on the page that add layers of symbolic depth to a text. These two planes of meaning work both with and against each other in a relationship of push and pull for our attention. Cognitive theorist Peter Stockwell calls this process a competition between "figures" and "grounds" in which certain elements of a text are "thrown into relief in the course of reading."[4] Such is the case particularly with concrete poetry and calligrams, which we will examine along with texts that communicate with visual artists and their specific works through ekphrasis. But, as the Tijuana exhibit shows, collage is the most important artistic medium for our poet, so we will begin there.

Collage

The word "collage" is derived from the French verb *coller*, to glue, since collage, in its most common form, involves the cutting, repositioning, and pasting of papers, textiles, or other premade materials onto a new surface. In his book of art criticism *Las voces del ver* [*The Voices of Vision*], Blanco quotes Ernst once again by writing that collage is "el encuentro de dos realidades lejanas en un plano ajeno a las dos" [the encounter of two distant realities on a plane that is foreign to both of them].[5] He also adds "se puede ver el *collage* como una forma de ecología: reciclar viejas imágenes para nuevos usos" [collage can be envisioned as a form of ecology: the recycling of old images for new uses].[6] Collage is the celebration of the "objeto azaroso" [random object], and as anyone who has taken more than a superficial glance at *ready-made* art can attest, collage, like still lifes or certain sculptures, involves difficult decisions with regard to the relationship between forms. The distance between figures, what are often called positive and negative spaces, is crucial to composition. As Blanco writes, "Si las imágenes visuales se combinan con creatividad, es posible que su impacto se amplifique notablemente. Es de este juego que se establece entre los contenidos simbólicos que emerge una nueva propuesta, una reflexión, un reflejo de la propia psique" [If the visual images are combined creatively, it is possible to amplify their impact notably. From this interplay between symbolic contents a new project emerges, a reflection of the very psyche].[7] So the creator of collages relies on three main skills: the selection, extraction, and repositioning of foreign fragments into new contexts. And there must be balance of the type Blanco sees in the art of Joseph Cornell, who, he writes, establishes "un diálogo delicado y justo entre las cualidades narrativas y visuales de su obra, de tal forma que ninguna de ellas domina a la otra" [a delicate and fair dialogue between the narrative and visual qualities of his work, in such a way that neither dominates the other].[8] The act of placing an object on top of a surface or another object challenges traditional understandings of dimensionality, as does the use of textured papers, fabrics, or other materials that give depth to a piece. As the cubists knew, collage also has its temporal aspect. Their use of newspaper clippings, for example, highlighted how objects inserted into a collage come from different time periods. In the way that Picasso's cubist portraits simultaneously show us, for example, a front and side profile, collage's play with time contributes to the sense of estrangement we get upon viewing perspectives we are not accustomed to seeing both at once and in the same place.

The process of collage is also a rich metaphor for many of the main artforms of the twentieth century, from a way of dealing with the pieces of a shattered

Europe after the first World War, through cubism, theories of intertextuality, film editing, or the pervasive use of sampling in rap and hip-hop music today. In a sense, collage is the ultimate avant-garde technique in that it embodies creation through destruction and celebrates the "no." Some collages contain shocking juxtapositions, others do not. Some artists, for example, lay bare their cuts in order to draw attention to the foreignness of the objects on their surfaces, while others blend and conceal those edges. Just as in poetry, some collages cite, while others simply steal.

On the macro level, the three poetic cycles of *A la luz de siempre* [*In Constant Light*] are themselves large collages composed of recycled sets of visual images, intertexts, and the parodic revisiting of traditional poetic forms such as sonnets, *cuartetos* [quartets], or *romances* [ballads]. As we saw in the poet's clever response to the *Zeta Tijuana* interviewer, everything about his work is intentional. His insistence that the chapters in his poetic trilogy are not chronological contributes a temporal aspect to their artistic effect: to extend the comparison, they are like collages of collages arranged by a poet/compiler rather than collections ordered by an editor or by their date of publication. The essays on poetics of *El canto y el vuelo* [*Song and Flight*] follow a similar pattern to the catalogue preface from the Tijuana exhibit by quilting together scraps of quotations by other writers at a rate of two, three, or more to a page.[9]

Each subdivision of the poetic cycles are also collages: in *A la luz de siempre*, for instance, the sections "Flores" ["Flowers"] and "Árboles" ["Trees"] create arrangements of similar objects displayed in new relationships and "Tarjetas postales" ["Postcards"] brings together disparate thoughts and images that are time-stamped from trips. Furthermore, these poems contain seemingly autobiographical information—whether or not this is the case, the paratexts certainly suggest that reading.

As on a canvas, a poetic collage, taken broadly, can simply be a collection of fragmented images on a new surface. It can be explicit or subtle. Poems like Eliot's *The Waste Land* or Blanco's texts based on rock music create an overt collage effect through intertextual citation while other texts simply feature odd juxtapositions of forms or the insertion of foreign objects in unexpected contexts.

As an example, the poems of *La edad de bronce* [The Bronze Age] from *A la luz de siempre* lend themselves to being read as poetic collages due to their disconnected visual images set up in surprising spatial and temporal perspectives. Most of the poems open with references to light, distance or seeing. "Puertas" ["Doors"], for example, directs us to pay attention to its negative spaces ("Ve el vano / de la puerta / ¡Qué limpio / el puro vacío" [Look at the hollow / of the doorway / Such a clean / and pure emptiness])[10] and then highlights the fact that its visual images, such as its flag, are all mental: "Es la conciencia / que se agita / Con la luz / puedes hacer cualquier cosa" [Consciousness / is what waves / With light / you can do anything].[11]

The first stanzas of "Raíces" ["Roots"] set up dialectical relationships (distance/proximity, day/night, above ground/below ground, light/darkness) and thus draw our attention to the negative space where roots grow. From the first verse we know that "todo esto es muy extraño" [all of this is very strange].[12] Next, the text deploys a chain of visual images that function much as collage through relationships of space and time:

De los días a donde van a dar
las calles vacías
los caballos al vapor
que sacuden el árbol de monedas[13]

[From the days where
the empty streets end
the steamy horses
shake the money tree]

"Raíces" ["Roots"] then spaces out its images and conjugates the signifying possibilities of the preposition "de" by presenting it as a locative ("al pie de las hilanderas" [at the feet of the weavers], "a través de la ventana" [through the window]), a simple modifier ("la isla de astillas" [an island of splinters]) and, most importantly, in reference to time ("la línea intermitente del futuro ferrocarril" [the intermittent line of the future railroad], "el pesebre de siempre" [the customary manger], etc.). The innovative use of the same preposition helps create visual and conceptual difference between images, so we have not just "basura" [garbage] but "la basura del domingo" [Sunday's garbage]. Furthermore, Blanco uses anaphora to create and then break rhythms with "de" thus adding more punch to metaphors such as, here, "los espejos ahumados" [the smoky mirrors]:

la línea intermitente del futuro ferrocarril
tres clavos y un manojo de huesos
la isla de astillas
los espejos ahumados[14]

[the intermittent line of the future railroad
three nails and a bunch of bones
an island of splinters
the smoky mirrors]

The temporal referents of the images in "Raíces" contribute to the feel of an avant-garde collage since syntax, perspective, and time are all interrupted and put into play in new relationships of space. This feel also permeates the highly metapoetic "Círculo del horizonte" ["Horizon's Circle"] which opens with a spray of scattered images of presence and absence, past and future: "una semilla" [a seed], "embarcaciones" [embarkations], "palabras puntuales como pupilas" [words as punctual as pupils], etc.[15] The collection of indeterminate images in new temporal contexts makes us recall Max Ernst and the technique of collage making, as do the lines "La omega de las especulaciones / acerca de la profundidad de la mina / la posibilidad de ser feliz / y la energía que implica" [The omega of speculations / about the depth of the mine / the possibility to be happy / and the energy that implies].[16]

"Pirámides" [Pyramids] is a strong poem in this vein that picks up and synthesizes themes from other texts that precede it in *La edad de bronce*. "Pirámides" [Pyramids] is about creating through seeing, but only under certain conditions. Like "Tótems" ["Totems"], "Naguales" ["Shamans"], or "Puertas" ["Doors"], it is quiet, airy, and meditative and features longer verses that give it more authority in the collection. Its first stanzas, too, are long, and the reader following the text's direction to observe carefully will notice that the stanzas form an inverted pyramid (from eight verses down to one). This inverted pyramid reflects the text's message about presence and absence that is expressed through positive and negative images and verbs: *decir/silencio, futuro/sol quemado, altura/pozo* [saying/silence, future/burned out sun, heights/well], etc. To read "Pirámides" is to move through time by constructing and then deconstructing pyramids with our eyes:

"Pirámides"

Ya no queda nada por decir
más allá de este silencio
que se convierte en piedra
ni queda ya otro futuro
que este viejo sol quemado
por más que exista siempre
la claridad del acto creativo
y el puro anhelo del porque sí

Un pozo que se yergue
desde el dolor extremo
donde se reúnen a pactar
los colores encendidos
del ancestral arcoiris
hasta llegar a un acuerdo
con respecto a la altura

Un templo que se hunde
en sus cavilaciones y da
justamente en el blanco
negrísimo de nuestra pupila
que se constela en silencio
para poder reconocer al fin

Que afuera el tiempo se mueve
en lentos círculos concéntricos
que solicitan de los presentes
la más absoluta complicidad
para llevar a cabo su tarea

Y construir ese segundo cielo
que no es más que una fuente
de construcciones fugaces
ardiendo bajo las estrellas

Las pirámides desaparecen
como las nubes en el cielo
hasta convertirse en nada

Se necesita ser un niño
para ver con estos ojos

Las pirámides no existen[17]

[Nothing is now left to say
beyond this silence
that turns into stone
there is no other future
than this burnt out sun
that despite existing forever
the clarity of the creative act
and the pure longing for a because I say so

A well dug up
from deep pain
where the flaming colors
of the ancient rainbow
meet and conspire
until finding agreement
about the heights

A temple that sinks
into its own worries and strikes
the dead dark center
of our eyes and makes
silent constellations
in order to be able to recognize at last

That outside time goes by
in slow concentric circles

that demand full cooperation
from the present moments
to do their job

And making that second sky
that is no more than a fountain
of fleeting constructions
burning beneath the stars

The pyramids disappear
like the clouds in the sky
until converting into nothing

We need to be children
to see with these eyes

The pyramids don't exist.]

The complex verses of "Pirámides" rely primarily on the dialectic of positive and negative imagery that powers their visual and verbal collage making, that is, the accumulation of unanticipated objects from diverse times and places ("una fuente de construcciones fugaces" [a fountain of fleeting constructions]) into new spatial relationships in the present-tense surface of a poem.

Absence and Negation

The negation that powers the last verse of "Pirámides" ("Las pirámides no existen" ["The pyramids do not exist"]) is a frequent technique in the work of Alberto Blanco. Along with simple negation, Blanco's poetry is replete with tropes that present ideas *sous rature* through rhetorical devices such as *litotes* ("affirmation by the negative of the contrary")[18] or *apophasis / paralepsis* ("a speaker emphasizes an idea by pretending to say nothing of it even while giving it full expression").[19] Proof of the ubiquitous nature of this mode is found in the very first words of the book *A la luz de siempre*:

No la flor
ni el florero
sino el espacio vacío
donde sucede el milagro del color.[20]

[Neither the flower
nor the vase
but rather the emptiness
where the miracle of color takes place.]

The creative possibilities of negation are also found in the essay "La poesía y la imagen": "la única manera de hablar de lo que no se puede hablar es hablar de lo que no conocemos en función de lo que sí conocemos. Éste es el mecanismo que gobierna los símbolos. Como dijo Platón: 'aquello que es perceptible a los sentidos no es sino la reflexión de lo que para la mente es inteligible'" [the only way to describe what we cannot describe is to describe what we do not know in terms of what we do know. This is the mechanism that governs symbols. As Plato said, "that which is perceptible to the senses is only the reflection of what is intelligible in the mind"].[21] As in his work with making collages, Blanco's poetry constantly experiments with new ways of creating poetic images through negation. Haiku "XVII," for example, from the series "Haikus de primavera" ["Spring Haiku"], gives a clear example of absent presence: "Es de mañana / y las estrellas brillan / más por su ausencia" ["In the morning time / the stars shine even brighter / in their absence"].[22]

In this vein, Blanco's trilogy features two sections of "Antipaisajes" [Anti-landscapes]. In the one from *La hora y la neblina* [*Time and Mist*], we discover a cluster of poems that conjugate the possibilities of absence and presence in explicit ways. "Más que un antipaisaje" ["More than an Anti-landscape"] and "Los abuelos" ["Grandparents"], for example, wonder at how ghosts of the dead can move among the living, while a text like "La séptima botella" ["The Seventh Bottle"] uses the image of an unopened bottle of wine to tell the story of a hypothetical opportunity not acted upon:

> "La séptima botella"
>
> De las siete botellas de vino
> prefiero la que no compramos,
> la que no descorchamos nunca,
> la que jamás nos bebimos . . .
>
> La que nos embriagó serenamente
> con la bondad de su ausencia
> y nos dejó volver a casa temprano
> en la ilusión renovada de la amistad.[23]
>
> ["The Seventh Bottle"
>
> Of those seven bottles of wine
> my favorite is the one we never bought,
> the one we never uncorked,
> the one we never drank . . .
>
> The one that made us glow serenely
> in the kindness of its absence

and allowed us to go home early
in the renewed comfort of friendship.]

Reading with an eye for the absent, like that unopened seventh bottle of wine, takes many forms in Blanco. A missing sound in the night drives "Las ganas de creer" ["Wanting to Believe"] and takes the reader to a deeper, more ontological level of inquiry than the previous poem by exploring dreaming as another reality:

"Las ganas de creer"

Vuelve la noche
y no escucho el ruido.

Me quiero concentrar
y sólo sueño, sueño . . .

Mis sueños son
polvo en el camino.

Sombras de sombras
mientras no son reales.

Y yo sólo quiero
la realidad . . .

Éste es mi sueño.[24]

["Wanting to Believe"

Night returns
and I don't hear the sound.

I want to concentrate
but I only dream, dream . . .

My dreams are
dust on the road.

Shadows of shadows
since they are not real.

And I only want
reality . . .

This is my dream.]

As in the introductory essay to his art exhibit, Blanco delights in presenting positive and negative concepts together in poems. "Año nuevo sin poema" ["New Year Without Poem"], for example, is an uncommon case of anti-metapoetry, that is, a poem about not writing a poem:

"Año nuevo sin poema"

Si tuviera que escribir un poema
sobre esta madrugada gris de año nuevo
poco tendría que decir.

Es cierto que el viento sopla,
levanta las hojas y mueve las nubes . . .
es cierto también que está a punto de amanecer.

Pero estas observaciones
—por demás evidentes—
no hacen un poema.

Tal vez habría que inventar algo
—mentir, embellecer, exagerar—
pero eso tampoco hace un poema.

Mejor dejar el año que comienza así: gris
con viento, a punto de amanecer
y sin poema.[25]

["New Year's Day Without a Poem"

If I had to write a poem
about this gray New Year's morning
I wouldn't have much to say.

It's true that the wind is blowing,
it stirs the leaves and shifts the clouds . . .
it's also true that day is about to break.

But these observations
—besides being evident—
do not make a poem.
I guess I would have to invent something
—lie, embellish, exaggerate—
but that also wouldn't make a poem.
It's better to just let the year begin as it is: gray
and windy, with dawn about to break
but without a poem.]

As in "La séptima botella," the first verse establishes a hypothetical situation—*if I had to write a poem about this moment, there would be little to say. . . .* The speaker then makes a few observations about the setting and then suggests that exaggerating or making something up would provide a poem. The text concludes with a decision to not write and to just let the day unfold, gray and windy, in the poem-less predawn. In the end, though, we do have a poem, the very poem the speaker just described the process of *not writing*. This text's technique is intriguing and consistent in our writer: creating a poem from a series of observations combined with their negatives: dawn + predawn, image + anti-image, poem + no poem. The connection between these positive and negative poles gives each element of this rather sparse poem added depth by drawing our attention to the process of writing. As in collage, a new experience is created by what is both *there* and explicitly *not there* on the page.

Poesía visual

Blanco begins an essay on literary translation by drawing a biblical analogy: "todo poema a traducir es una construcción—la Torre de Babel" [every poem to be translated is a construction—the Tower of Babel].[26] Next, he extends the metaphor by stating that if a source poem is a tower, then its translation is its inverse or complement: "toda torre en la tierra es un pozo en el cielo" [every tower on the earth is a well in the sky].[27] Blanco names this art of translation the well of "Lebab" ("Lebab" being "Babel" spelled backward). We have seen how the interplay of positive and negative spaces (such as tower and well) attracts the eye of our poet but clearly so do visual images, both those composed of words as well as those that feature what Kim Knowles calls "the conceptually significant deployment of spaces between units of meaning."[28] Blanco calls these poems, which make up a significant part of his work, his "poesía visual" [visual poetry].

Following in the tradition of Guillaume Apollinaire, Stéphane Mallarmé, Vicente Huidobro, José Juan Tablada, Octavio Paz, the Brazilian Noigandres group, Eugene Gomringer, and others, Blanco's *poesía visual* [visual poetry] explores the limits of spatial representation by experimenting with typography (almost always of the same size and font) and line length to create forms on the page. As Knowles notes, in visual poetry "verbal signs perform pictorial tasks: they signify both by referring to an external signified and via their topographical position on the page and their structural interactions with other elements."[29] Visual poetry is a hybrid genre, one that calls into question the powers of representation of both language and image. In terms of time, the Noigandres group insist that concrete poetry is a simultaneous form in which both word and image represent at the same time, while recent cognitive studies suggest otherwise.[30] A related point, articulated by E. H. Gombrich and others, should be repeated here—language is far more abstract and rich than visual representation due to the participation of the viewer—when asked to think of a cat, for example, we all visualize a different one.[31]

Blanco's poetry is especially multidisciplinary and, as we discover in his essays, the poet's passion for Mexico's pre-Columbian civilizations and his academic formation in Asian Studies inform his hybrid perspective on the connections between art forms and, more specifically, letters (graphemes) and ideas. As it was for the ancient Greeks, the pre-Hispanic *tlacuilo*, Mayan *ah ts'ib*, and Mixtec *tay huisi tacu* were names given to artist/scribes that do not make any distinction between the two crafts or genres.[32] The same held true for the Chinese, as explained by Ezra Pound's "ideogrammic method" based on Ernest Fenollosa's work on Chinese ideograms.

Given the popularity of Eastern philosophies in the countercultural movements of the 1960s and 1970s, it's easy to imagine how the relationship between form and content inherent in Chinese characters could be so alluring for a young visual artist and poet. "Canto XL del Tao" ["Canto XL of the Tao Te Ching"] from *A la luz de siempre*, for example, is visual in the sense that it imitates the spatial layout of the Tao Te Ching (five rows, six columns). While this text does not creatively manipulate space in order to produce an original visual form (it is simply mimetic) the poem's white spaces enhance the mysterious and hermetic imagery of the text and create pauses where the reader can stop and reflect while considering alternative phrasings. Interestingly, the poem has strong alliterative notes ("o" in the first line, "a" in the second) that weave together its words across the blanks:

Retorno   es   camino   suyo   movimiento
ternura   ala   frágil   ave   mismo[33]

[Returning   is   path   its   movement
affection   wing   fragile   bird   same]

Blanco's poems manipulate space with the same precision he brings to his piano playing or collage making. He is a master of forms, both traditional and original, and in his collection *Poesía visual* we see examples of countless styles of visual poetry.[34] In addition to its sound and sense, all poetry has a visual element but here we will consider texts that privilege the interplay of positive and negative space on the page for both conceptual as well as purely aesthetic ends. "La forma visual" [Visual forms], Blanco writes, "es un vehículo de alto poder al escribir un poema" [are high powered vehicles for writing poems].[35] Accordingly, readers must recognize and adjust to "una lectura y una manera de ver distintas" [a different way of seeing and reading].[36]

Poems like "Elogio de la luz" ["Elegy of the Light"] and "Teatro de ausencias" ["Theater of Absence"] use spacing in concrete ways to insert light, absence, or air into a poem. "Caminando en el aire" ["Walking on Air"], inspired by British progressive rockers King Crimson, suspends its verses between anchor words justified right and left to slow the reader down and create an almost physical response of breathlessness:

Cierra   los   ojos   y   mírame
como   si   estuviera   dentro

de un sueño
en blanco y negro

Sin más defensa
ante los misterios de
la noche que tú

Y sin otra vía de escape
Que la puerta sin puerta
De la música[37]

[Close your eyes and look
at me as if I
were in a dream
in black and white

As defense less
from the mysteries of
the night as you

And with no other way
out than the door -less
door of music]

The vertical columns provide a sense of strength that contrasts with the unpatterned and tenuous placement of long and short words in the verses. The vertical slants, random dispersion, and delicate form of words like "si" [if] and "y" [and] create a precarious feeling in the reader that reflects the poem's title and creates associations of falling through the air.

The concrete effect of "Caminando en el aire" is even more literal in poems such as "Toledo" ["Toledo"], whose verses imitate the winding streets of the hilly Spanish city, or "Lluvia" ["Rain"], which uses slashes to imitate rain falling through the white spaces of its verses.

"Lluvia"

No//////para///////el///////olfato//////
///sino///////para/////el/////recuerdo///
/////////////el//////////////olor//////////
/////de///////la///////tierra//////mojada
///en///////aquella///////estación//////
no//////para///////////la//////vista/////
/////sino///para///la///imaginación/////
//los/////tonos////////de///////gris/////
//////de////las////cambiantes//////nubes
///en///el///////escenario/////del///cielo

no//////para/////////el////////oído//////
//////sino//////para/////el///////sueño//
////el//////estruendo/////del/////rayo///
///y////el////ritmo////de////las////gotas
//////sobre//////el//////pavimento//////
no///////para//////el////////paladar/////
//sino////para////el////////entendimiento
//////////el////////////sabor/////////////
////////dulce////////y////////triste//////
/////de////////la/////////lluvia//////////[38]

[*"Rain"*

Not//////for///////the//////nose//////
///but///////for/////the/////mind///
////////////the/////////////smell/////////
/////of///////the///////wet//////earth
///in///////that///////season///////
not//////for///////////the//////eye/////
/////but///for///the///imagination//////
//the/////shades////////of///////gray/////
//////of////the////changing//////clouds
///on///the///////stage/////of//the///sky
not//////for/////////the////////ear//////
//////but//////for/////our///////dreams//
////the//////thunder/////of/////lightning///
///and////the////rhythm////of////the////drops
//////on//////the//////pavement//////
not///////for//////the////////tongue/////
//but////for////the////////mind
//////////the///////////sweet/////////////
///////and////////sad//////taste///////
/////of////////the/////////rain//////////]

"Lluvia" is much more than a visual sleight of hand. First, it offers us a modern version of the kind of typographic experimentation typical of the midcentury avant-garde. It also harkens back much farther, to the medieval traditions of the *carmina figurata* (pattern poetry) and *versus intexti* (message embedded in patterned poetry). Thanks to Blanco's background in art, the words of "Lluvia" are arranged with an eye to composition through the downward visual pattern that imbues the text with three competing streams of energy (horizontal, diagonal slashes, and vertical streams of words). Finally, the fact that the poem acknowledges inspiration from the English band Traffic (in the appendix) might cause the reader to pay special attention to the unique rhythm created by the irregular placement of its words from left to right though downpours of oblique downstrokes.

Paz, skeptical of the capacity of expression of this kind of poem, once wrote "pocas veces se ha logrado una verdadera fusión entre lo que dice el poema y su disposición tipográfica en la página" [very rarely has a true fusion between what a poem says and its typographic form on the page been achieved].[39] Despite the possible limitations of "Lluvia" (for one, it describes a free-form natural phenomenon but its form is rigidly rectangular), the message of the text does not suffer at the hand of its daring visual flourishes. Instead, it is a complex poem about the five senses (smell, sound, taste, sight, and feel) that uses innovative patterns to cue our sensorial awareness and deliver a reading experience more rich in dimension than a more traditional poem might.

Strategic line length and dynamic spaces in motion power *Antes De Nacer*, Blanco's forty-page poem from 1983 that can be read from left to right, from top to bottom (in either column), or even backward:

Antes De Nacer reconocemos verdaderamente nuestra vida
de nuevo Adán como ese niño del aire que sólo vino a dar
nombres de luz al claro mundo de la segunda concepción

de materia densa recién coronada es la forma que ha de ser
nutrida por el poder de una idea por la raíz de la acción
ala de cada vida en medio humano doble sol del que vela

en el largo camino desde los ínfimos detalles anunciados
desde ese perdón que no encuentra el momento de darse
hasta las gracias que generosamente comunican su silencio

vida y vuelta involución prevista en la primera escritura
domo laureado nace el sol de los cuatro pilares del sueño
pasan los aviones trazando con su ruido lentos números

hay una niebla solvente que no responde a los fototropismos
y una hipótesis planteada sin preguntas sobre nuestra vida
el enfermo que acepta su convalecencia de los calendarios

Este viaje y el otro los hombres del aire conocen la pobreza
conocen la herencia con el cielo de cinco siglos relacionados
nómadas en la rueda hénos aquí completando nuestra labor[40]

[Before being born we truly recognize that our life
like a new Adam like that child of air that only came to give
names of light the clear world of the second conception

of dense matter recently crowned   is the form that has to be
nourished by the power of an idea   through the roots of action
wing of every life half human   double sun of those not asleep

on the long road   from the minimal details announced
from that pardon   that can't find a moment to give itself
even thanks   that generously communicate its silence

life and return   foreseen regression in the first writing
head crowned in laurel   the sun is born from the four pillars of dreams
airplanes pass   tracing slow numbers with their sound

there is a cloud solvent that doesn't respond   to phototropisms
and a hypothesis created without questions   about our lives
the patient that accepts his convalescence   of calendars

This voyage and the other   men of air know poverty
know the legacy   with the sky of five related centuries
nomads on the wheel   this is us finishing our work][41]

The verses are arranged in the form of the double helix of amino acids that make up our DNA (or "*A.D.N.*," the abbreviation for *ácido desoxirribonucleico*). Blanco, being a trained chemist, chose double tercets to reflect the protein's tertiary structure. "En realidad" [In reality], he notes in an interview with Kimberly Eherenman "la estructura de este poema es como la estructura de un zíper: se abre y se cierra. Dos largas ristras de versos que se hablan y callan; se abren y se cierran" [the structure of this poem is like the structure of a zipper: it opens and closes. Two long wreathes of verses that talk to each other and then are silent, that open and close].[42] *Antes De Nacer* met with mixed critical reviews even though it is a bold attempt to forge a new poetic form from the building blocks of all life.[43]

The verses of *A.D.N.* manipulate the reader's eye through their form, but, as in *Rayuela* [*Hopscotch*] or Paz's *Blanco* [*Blanco*], they do so in a way that competes for our attention and, paradoxically, empowers the reader with choices of interpretative paths that traditional verses simply cannot offer. Another part of the achievement of *Antes De Nacer* lies in its use of longer and shorter verses, a combination that contrasts with the sparse nature of much of Blanco's later concrete poetry.

In an essay on Haroldo de Campos, Marjorie Perloff reminds us that the Brazilian poet's work also features such contrasts. In opposition to *Galaxias* [*Galaxies*], in his early concrete poems, Haroldo "replaces 'richness of vocabulary' with '*richness of structure*,' severely reducing the language field so as to avoid all excess and hence redundancy."[44] Similarly, João Adolfo Hansen notes that mid-century Brazilian Concretist painting "eliminated representation as a mediation interposed in the plastic form; in a homologous way, Concretist poetry claimed that it was surpassing what it called the 'old formal syllogistic and discursive foundation of the verse.'"[45] Blanco taps into these iconoclastic theories in poems such as "Surco," dedicated to Haroldo de Campos:

"Surco"

quizá alguno ha de guardar silencio
siembra alguno ha de llegar a vivir
poco a poco alguno ha de llegar
alguno ha de ver alguno ha de ser
alguno ha de llegar poco a poco
alguno ha de llegar a vivir siembra
alguno ha de guardar silencio quizá[46]

["Furrow"

Maybe one must come to keep quiet
Sowing one must come to live
little by little one must come to
one must see one must be
one must come to little by little
one must come to live sowing
one must come to keep quiet maybe]

In "Surco," the visual negative space of the furrow takes the place of traditional line breaks in verses that comment on creation through natural metaphors of growth ("surco," "siembra," "vivir" [furrow, seed, live], etc.). Form further reflects content as the seeds of poems planted in this furrow grow and then fade away much as the lines themselves go from shortest to longest and then symmetrically and rhythmically back from longest to shortest. In this way, the poem's words (which, in verses four through seven have the uniform vertical quality of mature crops) pass through a growth cycle or season of their own.

"Textil" ["Textile"] is more audacious in terms of form by dividing words into individual letters, or in this case threads, to create a textual textile patterned with both horizontal and vertical stripes:

f. . . . . f. . . . . f. . . . .
ibr. . . . . ibr. . . . . ibr. . . . .
adehe. . . . . adehe. . . . . adehe. . . . .
nequén. . . . . nequén. . . . . nequén. . . . .
plástico. . . . . estropajo. . . . . plástico. . . . .[47]

[f. . . . . f. . . . . f. . . . .
ibe. . . . . ibe. . . . . ibe. . . . .
erofh. . . . . erofh. . . . . erofh. . . . .

enequen. . . . . enequen. . . . . nequen. . . . . . .
plastic. . . . . scrubber. . . . . plastic. . . . .]

"Textil" is both a concrete poem and, in a sense, a calligram. Calligrams can be either referential in the sense that the shape of the poem reflects its meaning, or they can be abstract, like Mallarmé's constellations, by having a strong visual form unrelated to their message. Haroldo de Campos insisted upon the later technique and stressed that concrete poetry is nonmimetic and the "product of a critical evolution of forms"[48] that "shares the advantages of non-verbal communication without giving up the word's virtuality."[49] For Haroldo, concrete poetry "does not aim at a faithful description of objects" but instead creates its own objects.[50] We might assume that, as a visual artist, Blanco would line up with Haroldo on this point, but in reality almost all of Blanco's concrete poems and calligrams are mimetic, like this half-moon from "El oro azul":

luna
pájaro
luna[51]

[moon
bird
moon]

"Ver Tikal" ["Ver Tikal"] uses both an auditory (*ver+ Tikal=vertical*) and a visual rhyme to mimic the form of the Guatemalan pyramid and create a calligram in the sense of Apollinaire's classic texts. Within the verses, the visual vertical orientation is reinforced by showing us the sun in the first verse and then slowly panning down to clouds, then shadows:

"Ver
Tikal"

sol
nubes
sombras
de fuego
velas en
el espejo
y los días
más largos
que las largas
conversaciones
de la selva y el viento

Guatemala
Marzo de 1979[52]

["Ver
Tikal"

sun
clouds
shadows
in flames
candles
in the
mirror
long days
and longer
conversations
of the jungle and wind

Guatemala
March 1979]

Haroldo de Campos has called concrete poetry a "tension of word-things in space-time."[53] Visual poetry frames a text in much the same way museums display art objects on their walls—by removing them from everyday life and literally inserting them into the context of art. Similarly, Blanco's visual poems, taken together, create an especially striking form in the metacollage of his work. They test the visual and verbal representational limits of language by rebalancing charges of visual/conceptual and verbal/nonverbal. As with the poetic trope *litotes*, visual poems convey feelings or emotions that are bigger than the words themselves. Their emphasis on white spaces is a gift to readers, since these blanks open up texts to interpretation, even if they are part of a larger metapattern.

"*Donner à voir*"

In the essay "La poesía y la imagen" ["Poetry and the Image"], Blanco stresses "Y es que en el arte, como decía Edgar Degas, 'no es cuestión de lo que puedes ver, sino de lo que puedes hacer ver.' '*Donner à voir*,' como lo quería Paul Éluard" [Art, as Edgar Degas would say, "is not a question of what you can see, but rather of what you can make seen." "Making things visible" as Paul Éluard wished].[54] Blanco dedicates a large number of poems to exploring metaphors of perception, especially sight. His poems based on artists multiply the visual effect since in them the poet shares his visions (given to him by the art he references) with readers who will hopefully go out and do the same.

"Teoría del lenguaje" ["Theory of Language"], one of many types of visual poems, recounts the unlikely genesis of Ludwig Wittgenstein's picture theory of language in 1914 while serving in the Austro-Hungarian army. According to the story, the philosopher arrived independently at a critical understanding of the radical changes in perspective that were happening in avant-garde painting and collage and, in a related field, linguistics, all while manning a searchlight on the battleship *Goplana* cruising the Vistula River. Notice how many images of seeing populate this stanza:

> En medio de la masacre
> de la Primera Guerra Mundial
> y al mismo tiempo
> que el arte abstracto
> hacía explosión en toda Europa,
> Wittgenstein consiguió ver
> con absoluta claridad
> en ese desmadejado
> enjambre de reflejos que flotaba
> en las oscuras aguas del Vístula
> lo que De Saussure llamó
> "la red de trazas del lenguaje."[55]

> [In the midst of the massacre
> of the First World War
> and at the same time
> that abstract art
> was exploding across Europe
> Wittgenstein was able to see
> with absolute clarity
> in that ragged
> tangle of reflections that floated
> in the dark waters of the Vistula
> what Saussure termed
> "the web of traces of language."]

As in Wittgenstein's picture theory, Blanco's poem has "correspondencia / entre todas y cada una de sus partes" [correspondences / between each and every one of its parts] because its family of images is organically visual, being based primarily on verbs and images of perception: *faro buscador, discernir, reconocer, ver, describir, representar, escribir* [searchlight, discerning, recognizing, seeing, describing, representing, writing], etc. These ways of representing lead Wittgenstein, and the reader, to understanding ("ver / con absoluta claridad" [seeing / with absolute clarity]), as do the poem's clean, conversational, and prose-like verses.

The quote above about Paul Éluard from "La poesía y la imagen" ["Poetry and the Image"] finishes "Éste es el secreto del arte: dar a ver. Dar a escuchar, dar a sentir y dar a pensar; dar a imaginar, dar a entender y dar a soñar" [This is the secret of all art: to make things visible. To make things heard, to give things up to be felt and thought, imagined and understood, to make things we can dream about].[56] Just as this quote skips easily from sight to sound to thinking, so too does the long, gorgeous "Cuando la tierra sueña" ["When the Earth Dreams"] from *La hora y la neblina*, inspired by Mexican ceramicist Gustavo Pérez. Interestingly, the poem morphs vision into fresh new instances of interartistic synesthesia: "Cada vasija de Gustavo Pérez es una semilla, una página en blanco, un anhelo. El dibujo en el barro es un lenguaje, pero dibujar con barro es otra cosa: es una canción. La mano es al corazón lo que la sombra es a la forma, los ojos a la visión" [Each vessel Gustavo Pérez crafts is a seed, a blank page, a wish. Drawing on clay is a language, but drawing with clay is another thing: it's a song. The hand is to the heart what the shadow is to the form, the eyes to sight].[57]

"Cuando la tierra sueña" ["When the Earth Dreams"] is a narrative poem of more than one thousand words beginning with long, prosey stanzas that distill down, through a technique borrowed from concrete poetry, to tell us that vision is the one key element uniting poetry and the visual arts. The poem's first stanza has one hundred seventy seven words, while its last strophe has just two:

> La visión de la forma es la semilla del trabajo de Gustavo Pérez. El dibujo es la palabra, pero el silencio es la canción.
>
> Vasijas de barro en el corazón de la semilla de la forma.
> Desde la semilla de la vasija de la forma.
> Hasta la pura forma.
> La visión.[58]
>
> [Vision of the form is the seed of Gustavo Pérez's work. The drawings are the words, but silence is the song.
>
> Clay vessels in the heart of the seed of form.
> From the seed of the vessel of the form.
> To pure form.
> Vision.]

The way the Gustavo Pérez poem shuffles different artistic genres yet keeps returning to seeing is a good example of the primacy of light in Blanco's poetics. In his essays and poems he returns insistently to the idea that the poet must listen and watch their surroundings and then give both the gift of vision and the gifts of their visions to readers. "Cuando la tierra sueña" focuses on how a sculptor shapes these images to represent seeing itself while a poem like "Principio de incertidumbre" ["Uncertainty Principle"] resorts to rhymed *cuartetos* to muse about ways of looking at visual art:

"Principio de incertidumbre"

Al mirar un cuadro
realmente . . . ¿qué veo?
¿Lo que está pintado
o lo que yo creo?

¿Estoy viendo un mundo
o estoy viendo un plano?
¿Miro algo profundo
o no estoy mirando?

¿Y es que sólo miro
o realmente veo?
¿Creo lo que miro?
¿Miro lo que creo?

¿Lo que dice el cuadro?
¿La voz del pintor?
¿Lo representado?
¿Lo que pienso yo?

¿Y de dónde parte
lo que está pintado?
¿De las obras de arte?
¿De algún otro lado?

¿Y cuál es el juego
que juega el pintor?
¿Es tan sólo el ego
o el arte no es yo?

Fuere lo que fuere . . .
¿qué quiere el artista?
¿Saber lo que viene?
¿Seguir una pista?

¿Colores y formas?
¿Conceptos? ¿Anhelos?
¿Serán sólo historias?
¿Serán sólo velos?

¿O será otra cosa
lo que dice un cuadro?
Un mundo de formas
que canta callado . . .[59]

["Uncertainty Principle"

When viewing a picture
what do I really see?
What is painted
or what I believe?

Do I see a world
or a flat plane?
Do I see something deep
or am I not looking?

And am I only looking
or can I really see?
Do I believe what I see?
Do I see what I believe?

What the picture says?
The voice of the painter?
What is represented?
What I think?

And where does
what is painted come from?
From works of art?
From somewhere else?

And what is the game
the painter is playing?
Is it only ego
or is art not I?

Be that as it may . . .
What does the artist want?
To know what is coming?
To follow a clue?

Colors and forms?
Concepts? Desires?
Could they be only stories?
Could they be only veils?

Or is what a picture says
something else entirely?
A world of forms
that silently sings . . .]

The poem's antiquated form and tone are at odds with its plainspoken line of inquiry about some of the fundamental questions of art criticism: the intentional fallacy, a piece's openness to interpretation by a viewer, intertextuality, representational versus nonrepresentational art, and so on. Even though seeing is primary here, in the end, sight is paired inescapably with a complement from music in an interartistic *litotes* that highlights the unsung nature of painting: "Un mundo de formas / que canta callado" [A world of forms / that silently sings].

"Principio de incertidumbre" is from *Materia prima* [*Prime Matter*], a collection of Blanco's "relámpagos paralelos" [parallel lightning strikes] that pairs and compares poems with specific visual artists (his "*hacedores*" [inspirational creators]) listed in an appendix. Carlos Zamora likens these collections to museums or galleries that invite a reader to create a narrative between poem, *hacedor*, and neighboring text.[60] The connections between poem and *hacedor* are often not apparent to the reader, and Blanco insists that these texts "dialogan de muchas formas y en muchas formas con una serie de obras" [converse in many ways and by many ways with a series of works].[61]

No matter the intended or perceived connection between poem and musician, visual artist or other writer, Blanco's marginalia functions much like a title that undeniably tells us "what to see" as James A. W. Heffernan puts it.[62] We come across an interesting variation on this technique in "La abeja en el taller" ["Studio Bee"] in which title, dedication, and point of view compete for our attention. Here, the reader's eye bounces between reading the poem, looking for references to the work of Danish painter Lis Zwick, and sharing in the visual perspective, albeit it in the third person, of a flying bee.

"La abeja en el taller"

Una abeja en el taller de Orkelljunga
recorre la historia del color
en la superficie
de un trapo pintado
donde Lis limpia sus pinceles

huele violeta
mira rojo carmín
palpa rosa flamenco
escucha azul añil
siente verde manzana

cada color
en todas sus dimensiones
es un paisaje distinto en cada tono
una vegetación diferente en cada matiz
un recuerdo único en cada flor

Y paso a paso
la abeja reconoce
el laberinto de los sentidos
en la sinestesia total
de la ilusión[63]

[A bee in a studio in Orkelljunga
runs through the history of color
on the surface
of a paint stained rag
where Lis cleans her brushes

it smells violet
sees carmine red
feels flamenco pink
hears indigo blue
feels apple green

each color
in all its dimensions
is a distinct landscape in each tone
a different vegetation in each hue
a unique memory in each flower

And step by step
the bee recognizes
the labyrinth of the senses
the total synesthesia
of the illusion]

Interartistic synesthesia dominates once again as the poet questions the representational capacity of visual images. Just as poetry for Blanco can be understood as a transcendental synthesis in which complements come together to form a whole that is greater than the sum of their parts, here the bee, and thus the reader, is also able to experience a synesthetic moment from reading about viewing art.

Ekphrasis

W. J. T. Mitchell notes that ekphrasis is "a curiosity: it is the name of a minor and rather obscure literary genre (poems which describe works of visual art) and, of a more general topic—the verbal representation of visual representation."[64] Mitchell goes on to note that ekphrasis contains elements of hope, fear, and indifference. The goals of "ekphrastic hope," he writes, are the goals "of achieving vision, iconicity, or a 'still moment' of plastic presence through language."[65] It is worth noting that if we take ekphrasis as an attempt of the verbal to re-create the visual, this definition is based on an a priori assumption of difference between the verbal and visual arts. Mitchell's notions of fear, hope, and indifference come into play when we consider the relationship between different art forms: "thematizing 'the visual' as other to language," Mitchell writes, can be viewed in one of three ways: (1) The visual can be seen as "a threat to be reduced" (ekphrastic fear), (2) it can be considered for its potential of similarity and union (ekphrastic hope), or (3) poetry can regard the visual arts as something that simply can never be fully re-created (ekphrastic indifference).[66] Mitchell terms this the "social structure" of ekphrasis, which he notes is triply inscribed by the writer, the visual artist, and the reader.

Although ekphrasis is not very common among contemporary poets, as we have seen thus far, Blanco's *hacedor* poems cause the reader to be on high alert for verbal re-creations of specific scenes from known works of visual art. Interestingly, most of Blanco's *hacedor* texts are not ekphrastic and many of his most vividly descriptive poems are not connected to specific *hacedores*. "La mesa puesta" [The Set Table], for example, is a verbal still life, but not a reference to a known work of art. The first stanza's coffee cup and loaves of bread are framed by bright white walls and a window's natural light. This simple scene contrasts positive and negative space by focusing on the relationship between the objects as much as on the objects themselves:

> Reunidos al calor del buen café,
> los panes resplandecen con la calma
> de las paredes blancas, encendidas,
> rebosantes de luz por la ventana.[67]
>
> [United by the warmth of good coffee,
> the loaves shine with the calmness
> of the white walls, lit up
> and flooded in the window's light.]

In the second stanza, our eye strays out the window and then back in as the poet plays with the verb *formar* [to form] and creates visual and verbal rhyme between the circular opening of the jug and both the form and sound of *ojo* [eye] and *espejo* [mirror]:

> Ya la paja se extiende entre los pinos,
> crece la claridad y la forma del cielo,
> forma una habitación, forma una jarra
> profunda como el ojo del espejo.[68]
>
> [And the straw extends between the pines,
> the form and clarity of the sky grows,

forms a room, forms a jar
as deep as the eye of the mirror]

The poem concludes with new colors, new forms, and more play with positive and negative space in the contrast of hills and islands:

Es este mismo mar, el mar de siempre,
llano rectangular de cada cosa,
donde flotan los montes y las nubes
como islas de quietud entre las horas.[69]

[This same sea, the sea that's always there,
a rectangular plane where mountains,
clouds and everything floats
like islands of stillness between the hours]

From its very first word this poem invites us to join the poet at the table of the text and to share what Mitchell calls ekphrasis's "gift to the reader."[70] Here, that gift is not a re-creation of a known work of art (even though it might be) but rather poetry's power to evoke a visual image. Each of the poem's three stanzas emphasizes images of light and contains metaphors of a painter's canvas or surface (*las paredes blancas*, *el cielo*, and *el llano rectangular del mar*). Wendy Steiner writes that "ekphrastic poetry signifies motion through a static moment. This signification, moreover, is usually not a mere symbolic reference but often an attempt at an iconic embodying of stillness."[71] "La mesa puesta" embodies such stillness through gentle verbs like *resplandecer* and *flotar* that emphasize descriptions of states over actions.

Synecdoche is an important trope for ekphrasis since a poet can evoke the central images of a painting through a few well-selected keywords—individual parts that help the reader recall a whole. In "Climas interiores" ["Interior Climates"] Blanco activates images from many different interior paintings by Pierre Bonnard to describe feelings of nostalgia brought about by the interplay of in and out seen in the characteristic tables, windows, and doors of the French painter's late interior paintings and still lifes. Interestingly, the text ends with the synesthesia "el son de la mesa puesta" [the song of the set table]—a line that contains the title of the poem we just discussed from his previous collection.[72] When we consider the imagery of "La mesa puesta" ["The Set Table"] alongside the later "Climas interiores" ["Interior Climes"] (a *vaso comunicante* with Bonnard)—we are forced to ask ourselves if the French painter also inspired the earlier poem as well. Like many of Blanco's poems with strong imagery, "La mesa puesta" can both stand alone and in the context of a specific artist.

Synecdoche appears again in "Wyethiana" ["Wyethiana"], this time in a simple meat hook:

"Wyethiana"
Admiraba la alcayata
su sombra
y lo que depende de ella

y el gorrión que pasaba volando
y que nada (tal vez)
tenía que ver con esta escena

Vermont,
2 de julio de 2010[73]

["Wyethiana"
He admired the meat hook
its shadow
and all that depended on it
and the swallow passing by in flight
and that had nothing (perhaps)
to do with anything in this scene.

Vermont,
July 2, 2010]

The complex intertexts and paratexts of "Wyethiana" suggest a backward reading of the poem. In the first, or actually *last*, place, the poetic voice wants us to know that they are in Vermont, in the United States. The second stanza is about making connections or, more precisely, trying to find tenuous connections between parts of a scene. Next, remembering that in Spanish, William Carlos Williams's iconic "The Red Wheelbarrow" begins "cuánto depende / de una / carretilla / roja" ["so much depends / upon / a red wheel / barrow"] Blanco's poem's form, crystal clear language, and especially third verse suggest we read "Wyethiana" in the key of American imagism.

Moving upward from the paratext, we finally arrive to the meat hook, its shadow, and the poem's title. "La alcayata" [The meat hook] provides both clarity and ambiguity to this scene by making us wonder if the poet is looking at a real meat hook in a barn and recalling an image from a Wyeth painting or maybe is visiting a gallery in Vermont and viewing the painting itself. Mitchell notes that "Words can 'cite,' but never 'sight' their objects,"[74] and that is certainly the case here—both Andrew Wyeth and son Jamie Wyeth have paintings that feature meat hooks, though the reference to its shadow in the second verse probably points us to Andrew's striking portrait "Karl HS" from 1954. In the end, "Wyethiana" seems to be as much a case of what we might call *ekphrastic doubt* as of *ekphrastic hope* since the text provides us with more questions than answers. The dated reference to Vermont makes us wonder if the poem retells a scene from a painting, a moment from real life, or if perhaps the speaker got lost in the connections between different twentieth-century American art forms while on a trip. Furthermore, the poem appears in a section called "Tarjetas postales" ["Postcards"] rather than a section of texts inspired by visual artists, so should it be read as a privileging of place? Or, should we merely accept this poem as we might a collage and enjoy the relationships of it, with "no ideas but in things"?

Another similar form of ekphrasis occurs when a poem explicitly names a painter or painting within a poem, something Blanco does at least twice with Francisco de Goya. If we read "Perros" ["Dogs"] before noting the *hacedor* with whom it corresponds, we get one impression:

"Perros"

Ya no es uno
(como en el último cuadro de Goya)
son muchos . . .

Y todos quieren lo mismo.[75]

["Dogs"

Not just one anymore
(as in Goya's last picture)
but many . . .

And they all want the same thing.]

"Perros" is dedicated (in the appendix) to Mexican artist Ricardo Martínez and uses the famous Goya image as a way to emphasize the momentum and fear caused by the dogs of Martínez's *Llorona* series in which the legendary Weeping Woman is being pursued by packs of dogs. The unity of purpose in Blanco's last line leads us to connect his poem with Martínez's dogs as a way highlighting and deepening the sense of despair in the *Llorona* [Weeping Woman] paintings.

In a similar way, "El nacimiento de una idea" ["The Birth of an Idea"] from *La hora y la neblina* [*Time and Mist*] creates a visual simile comparing the birth of an idea to Botticelli's "Birth of Venus." This iconic image is used again in an ekphrastic passage from "Déjà vu" ["Déjà vu"] that compels us to see Eden in one and only one particular way. The allusion to the Birth of Venus effectively closes off this part of the text to all other interpretations . . . and in our minds, we readers *bounce*, as it were, between Blanco's poem and the painting. This is a fine example of what Linda Hutcheon has labeled "postmodern parody"—the ironic revisiting of past literary or artistic models. Hutcheon's conception of the term is not related to mockery. Instead, she relies on the etymology of *parodia* as "counter-song" or "song beside."[76] Just like dedications and epigraphs, parody is one of Blanco's many modes of, to use Hutcheon's term, "coming to terms with the texts of the rich and intimidating legacy of the past."[77]

"Viento del norte" ["Northern Wind"] is a more traditional ekphrasis in that it re-creates the scene of a Winslow Homer painting. This is achieved through just a few specific words connecting the visual to the verbal: *olas, nubes, mástil, ladearse, niños y grandes*, and *contrapeso* [waves, clouds, mast, leaning, children and adults, counterweight]. Homer is acknowledged in the appendix and the poem's visual elements point to his picture "A Fair Wind" (1873–1876), while simultaneously excluding some similar paintings. As in "A Fair Wind," the figures in the text are also enjoying ("*gozando*") their time in the heeling catboat. Furthermore, the sonnet uses an unattributed literary quote to complicate its interartistic intertextuality since "*Olas espumosas / y nubes bordadas . . .*" ["Foamy seas and lacey clouds"] and the sing-song rhythm of a sea shanty both to contribute to the ambience of the text.

"Viento del norte"

"Olas espumosas
y nubes bordadas . . ."
Todas esas cosas
están superadas . . .

Por más que ese mástil
se parezca a un arce,
la barca vibrátil
comienza a ladearse.

Con niños y grandes
en el contrapeso
gozando como antes

Las nubes de yeso,
los barcos mercantes,
las costas de hueso.[78]

["Northern Wind"

"*Foamy seas
and lacey clouds . . .*"
All those things
are overcome . . .

Although that mast
looks like an oak tree,
the tender boat
begins to heel.

Both children and adults
on the high side
once again enjoying

The plaster clouds,
the merchant ships,
the bone coast.]

"Ruptura" ["Rupture"], on the other hand, takes its re-creation of a painting a step farther by interacting with it. This text creates a vignette from the 1955 canvas of the same name by Remedios Varo (1908–1963). Some of the ekphrastic synecdoches in the poem include "*unas cortinas con alas*," "*una escalinata*," and "*la mandorla de tu cuerpo*" [curtains with wings, a flight of stairs, the mandorla of your body]. Blanco's speaker (the *yo*) addresses the mandorla-shaped figure of the painting as if she were Varo herself, and in the last stanza, switches to a present tense and thus mixes his invented ekphrastic narrative with one of the biographical interpretations of the painting and its title: that it represents either Varo's break with the Church or possibly her exile.

¡Me deslumbra tanto la mandorla de tu cuerpo
que se eleva desde la leve punta del zapato
como la luna llena que habrá de columbrarse
sobre el cielo rojo cuando la noche sea la dueña
hasta colmar la esperanza de volver al fin
a reposar tus sueños en su verdadera casa!

Siento que has ido más lejos que nunca
en la comprensión de tus recuerdos
y que ya nada podrá detenerte . . .

O así me lo parece ahora que te escucho
platicar sin disculpas que nadie ha pedido
la admirable y triste historia de tu ruptura.[79]

[I am as dazzled by the mandorla of your body
that rises up on tip-toes
as by the full moon that makes itself seen
in the red skies when the night will rule
until fulfilling the hope of finally returning
to sleep in its own house.

I feel you have gone farther than ever
in understanding your memories
and that nothing can stop you . . .

Or so it seems now that I listen to you
confidently comment that nobody has asked
the admirable and sad story of your rupture.]

Perhaps Blanco's most effective example of ekphrasis is this concrete poem dedicated to Swiss sculptor Alberto Giacometti:

"Hombre"
As
cen
sión
pu
ra
al
ma
de
hue
so
co
lum
na
ver
te
bral
río
de
lu
ces
len
gua
de
fue
go[80]

["Man"
Pu
re
as
ce
nt
so
ul

of
bo
ne
spi
nal
co
lu
mn
ri
ver
of
li
ght
ton
gue
of
fi
re]

Form mirrors content on more than just surface levels here since the verses recall the elongated perspective favored by Giacometti in his long, thin works in bronze. Even more intriguing is how the breakdown of words into sets of two to four letters re-creates the sculptor's impressionistic handling of details of his figures' faces or hands. Just as a faint smudge might form the eye of a Giacometti figure, Blanco's lines are not preformed units or syllables but rather packets of letters and sounds that create a visual and aural rhythm. Any one verse, like a horizontal slice of the statue, would hold little interest or meaning outside of its whole.

When Mitchell writes that ekphrasis is "a curiosity," he puts his finger right on the key emotion that underlies Blanco's use of this kind of poem. The poet's insatiable artistic curiosity is what fuels his obsession to find the kind of connections that haunt the speaker of "Wyethiana." These connections hold great importance for Blanco, be it through artistic references, the marriage of form and content in concrete poems, or the union of individual notes of music into chords. "The central goal of *ekphrastic* hope," Mitchell writes, "might be called 'the overcoming of otherness'" since "*ekphrastic* hope and fear express our anxieties about merging with others."[81] Ekphrasis for Alberto Blanco is a metaphor of the search for communion that runs through all his poetry and collages. Blanco's poems that evoke the visual arts urge us to overcome our fears of otherness and to visualize new possibilities of harmony between both artistic genres and people—a poetics of empathy.

The Constellation of the Rose

Cuenta de los guías [*Account of the Guides*] is a bold prose poem in 260 meticulously crafted stanzas, similar to *cantos*, that Álvaro Mutis has called "una oración" [a prayer] and Carlos Zamora has described as "un viaje que se bifurca en dos direcciones: . . . la ruta iniciática hacia el interior de sí mismo . . . [y] la otra hacia el lenguaje" [a voyage that splits in two directions: . . . an interior route of initiation . . . [and] another toward language].[82] The book, which was recently re-edited and now finds its home in 2018's *A la luz de siempre*, is a high-water mark in Blanco's poetics because of its length, its range of expression, and the breadth of its thematic reach. It is also among Blanco's most challenging and hermetic poetic works due to its complex syntax and fragmented visual and temporal perspectives. In this section we contain our analysis to a few of the key images that help structure the swirl of *Cuenta de los guías*, a poem that could easily be the subject of an entire monograph.

Earlier in this chapter we discussed the technique of poetic collage, of which *Cuenta de los guías* is Blanco's most prominent example. Collage not only brings items from the outside in, it also widens a poem's horizon of signification and exploits gaps in space and distance to open up a text for the reader. *Cuenta de los guías* uses chips of language to create a suggestive or intuitive atmosphere that defies linear or grammatical interpretations. In contrast to the smooth comparisons of similes, many metaphors here are created by force. In the absence of familiar connections between subjects and objects, the reader must find new ways to create meaning, a process that runs parallel to one of the text's main themes—that a difficult meditative journey can lead to spiritual insight. As we touched on in our introduction, Blanco opens *Cuenta de los guías* with a poetic collage of avant-garde metaphors:

> Con la luna entre las cejas, con su paciencia, con las ágatas que guiñan y lo saben: una vez más, río de peces, árbol del cielo, son hojas que nunca volverán . . . criaturillas que encuentran su destino en el borde anaranjado del mantel.[83]
>
> [With the moon between eyebrows, with its patience, with quartz that winks and knows: one more time, river of fish, tree of sky, are leaves that won't return . . . little creatures meeting their destinies at the orange border of the tablecloth].

Just as the cubists achieved in their synthetic pieces, the images of the first verse intentionally defy conventional associations of syntax, temporality, and cause and effect by dissociating figures from their familiar grounds. The expectation caused in the reader's mind by conjunctions like "*con*" [with] and the unmodified pronoun "*lo*" [it] creates a space for us to draw our own conclusions about which clauses might modify which subjects and where we readers are grounded in the text.

Poem 25,[84] like many others in the book, also plays with figure and ground in a way reminiscent of collage:

> La mañana brota lentamente de las puntas adormecidas de un durazno, de la vara prodigiosa envuelta en humo. Es necesaria una salida cautelosa: no hay más estrategia que la de un bombín.
>
> Es un pago muy alto el que han pedido por esta curación: ser otros. ¡Qué fácil es cambiar un pedazo de papel por un objeto, pero qué difícil es cambiar uno mismo! Con razón ya quieren pasar de año, de dimensión.
>
> De frente, en el espejo, un desayuno memorable, inmemorial, con los ojos de rendija y las montañas de dos horas de sueño, con los signos de interrogación sobre la cama.
>
> Ya la luz dora los cascos y llegamos al escudo del mar. Unos desgraciados cantan para deleitar el oído del burro, y entre tantos gritos es difícil escuchar el propio ritmo.
>
> Un mar interior arremete contra el muelle más viejo, contra el malecón de la especie . . . retrocede, y las palabras se diluyen en la superficie dorada del pescado.
>
> Es inmensa nuestra fortuna.[85]

> [Morning breaks slowly from the sleepy points of a peach, from the enormous stick bundled in smoke. We have to be careful going out: no more strategy than a bowler hat.
>
> This cure comes at a steep price: being someone else. It's so easy to exchange a piece of paper for an object, but it's hard to change oneself! Rightly they want to move on to the next grade, the next dimension.
>
> Face-on, in the mirror, a memorable breakfast, immemorial, with cracked eyes and bags from two hours of sleep, with question marks over the bed.
>
> Light already shines on the helmets and we arrive to the shield of the sea. A few unlucky ones sing to please a donkey, and between so many cries it is hard to hear the rhythm.
>
> An interior sea beats against the oldest docks, against the breakwater of the species . . . it recedes and the words get diluted in the golden surface of fish.
>
> Our fortune is great.]

Regardless of whether this poem is read in series or not, the first thing we are struck with is the random nature of its images (*mañana, durazno, vara, humo, bombín*, etc. [morning, peach tree, bar, smoke, bowler]). In the next lines the poet zooms out and comments on the story line of the spiritual journey ("esta curación" [this path to recovery]) in double-voiced terms that speak of consumer culture as bits of paper (money) that are easily exchanged for objects. As in collage, exchange and overlay are key strategies here. In the vein of Picasso and Braque's early work, the only unity is the unexpected and forced juxtaposition of images (the hat, time travel, the image in the mirror, the words that dissolve on the outside of the fish, etc.) and their context, all framed, as in collage, in a rather traditional rectangle.

In a discussion of cognitive poetics and literary foregrounding, Peter Stockwell notes that "certain aspects of literary texts are commonly seen as being more important or salient than others."[86] This technique is especially important for texts like *Cuenta de los guías* that feature "a rich complex of potentially interesting objects vying for attention."[87] In texts like these, the reader is forced to pay special attention to images the poet "spotlights" or "throws into relief" through practices that confer them prominence. *Cuenta de los guías* employs privileged positioning (i.e., important ideas in the first or last verse), metapoetic directives (directly addressing the reader in the second person), and the repetition of certain rhythms and motifs to structure the poetic swirl of the book. Jacobo Sefamí notes, "la continuidad está dada, como en todo libro de poesía, por ciertas imágenes que se interconectan" [continuity is achieved, as in all books of poems, by certain images that interconnect].[88] What we see in the poem are shards of larger ordering elements and traces of geometric, numerological, geographic, or narrative structures such as the I Ching, the four elements, the search for *satori* (Buddhist enlightenment), games of chess, Jack Kerouac's *On the Road*, the constellations, popular songs, Dante's rose, alchemy, and other metaphors of spiritual pilgrimages. The fragments of these familiar patterns don't create a *camino* for us; instead, they are like signs posted too far apart that indicate trails already well worn away. In a sense, they hint to us that there is a way, a system at work here, but do not reveal much about it.

An oft-cited verse of *Cuenta de los guías*, probably because of its metapoetic clarity, is ". . . la prosa encadena. / La poesía desencadena" [. . . prose chains things up. / Poetry breaks chains . . .]—one of the cornerstones of Blanco's poetics.[89] When writing prose, authors know where they are going to send their readers . . . maybe not always *before* writing, but certainly *after* a narrative is crafted. Poetry, in contrast, is about not knowing because poets by definition have a different relationship with language and different end goals than fiction writers. In essays and interviews Blanco defines poetry as simply a different relationship with language: ". . . una forma distinta de emplear el lenguaje de como se hace normalmente. Casi podríamos decir que al revés. La poesía es el otro lado del lenguaje" [. . . a different way of using language than we normally do. We could almost say it is the opposite. Poetry is the other side of language].[90]

In *El llamado y el don*, Blanco posits that rather than crafting emotions into images, chips of poetic language present themselves to receptive poets, whose job it is to pass along these mysterious fragments to their readers. In this model, poetry is the fruit of a gifted artist (one that has the "*don*" of the book's title) who is called by language to write. Quoting José Martí, Guillermo Sucre, and others, the poet stresses a perhaps unexpected relationship of cause and effect here—that language is the "*jinete*" [rider] and not the "*caballo*" [horse] of the poetic act.[91] Young poets, he writes, may begin by using language to express emotions and ideas, but later they need to transition to making new ideas and emotions from words themselves: "El poeta no utiliza las palabras para decir, sino para ser dicho" [Poets do not use words to say things, but rather to be said].[92] This belief helps us understand the intentionality of the literally hundreds of avant-garde metaphors of *Cuenta de los guías* that suggest or create associations in very intuitive ways: "la poesía habla de lo que nunca nos había dolido antes, de lo que no habíamos recordado nunca, de lo que ni siquiera sabíamos que queríamos, sentíamos o pensábamos" [Poetry talks about pain we had never felt before, about things we had never remembered, about what we never even knew we were wanting, feeling or thinking].[93]

Still, no matter how dedicated a reader we are of poems, we cannot be expected to work through a 260-page prose poem without some clues along the way about where we are going. In *Cuenta de los guías*, the speaker's spiritual path toward understanding parallels the reader's desire for meaning. One of the main ways Blanco establishes this parallel journey is through the strategic repetition of two main images: stars and roses.

A star is born in the last verse, a privileged position, of the first poem: "Hay una estrella que se enciende porque el Padre lo quiere" [There is a star shining because the Father wills it][94] and then reappears in the third, fifth, and eleventh poems as well as in nine more of the fifty-two texts of "El largo camino hacia Ti" [*The Long Road to You*], the first section of *Cuenta de los guías*.

One function of these stars is to set in motion the archetype of the "estrella señal" [signaling star] that guided the three biblical *Reyes Magos* [Three Wise Men]. In another sense, though, stars are also metaphors of poetic language itself. This verse from poem 91, for example, draws parallels between celestial bodies and metaphors that hold together their associated elements through semantic and syntactic friction: "Una estrella es una enorme explosión que permanece unida en virtud de la gravitación. El tamaño de la estrella es un continuo regateo entre la gravedad que busca comprimirla y el calor que quiere hacerla crecer" [A star is an enormous explosion that stays together because of gravity. The size of the star is a constant negotiation between gravity, that tries to compress it, and heat, that forces it to grow].[95]

Like gravity, the drive to create meaning in the text and life is an unquenchable thirst: "Y estoy—de pronto—a la orilla del mar: las olas rompen malecones y los pensamientos deshechos se extienden a nuestros pies. / Puntos luminosos . . . ¿Por qué siento una insaciable sed de certidumbres hasta el final?"[I am—suddenly—at the edge of the sea: the waves break on the jetties and broken thoughts spread at our feet. / Luminous points . . . Why do I feel an insatiable thirst for certainty up to the end?].[96] In the context of stars, the speaker's thirst for connection is what led ancient peoples to create the first constellations—as poem 123 notes: “Las formas llaman a las formas: no se te da lo que te mereces sino lo que se te asemeja” [Forms call out to other forms: you are not given what you deserve but rather what takes after you].[97] Mallarmé’s constellations are a clear point of reference here, even if our vision of these celestial drawings is obscured by clouds: “Listas de estrellas con sus nombres, sus propiedades, trayectorias y colores . . . hay un laberinto transparente donde nuestra atención se centra. Sus ramificaciones carecen—en apariencia—de orden, pero nada aquí es gratuito” [Lists of stars with their names, their properties, trajectories and colors . . . there is a transparent labyrinth that draws our attention. Its divisions lack—by all appearances—order, but nothing here is gratuitous].[98] The intentional alignment of Blanco’s stars gives the poetic universe of *Cuenta de los guías* its own music of the spheres through “estrellas pautadas . . . acordes en el cielo” [patterned stars . . . chords in the sky].[99]

As we see in the title “La constelación de la rosa” [“The Constellation of the Rose”], the second section of *Cuenta de los guías* begins by combining astral images with other important ones from the text: “el ajedrez de estrellas” [the chess match of the stars], “la constelación del Espíritu” [the constellation of the Spirit], “La constelación de la mesa es una rosa mental” [The constellation of the table is a mental rose], etc.[100] Blanco’s emphasis on the rose and his rose constellation were inspired, like many of the vignettes in the book, by an extratextual event at poet Juan Martínez’s house in Tijuana but also have clear literary precursors in Dante’s mystic vision in the *Paradise*. The word “rosa” is an interesting case of heteroglossia in the poem since it alternately refers to the literal flower, the compass rose, the Aztec tradition of “flor y canto” [flower songs], the number five, and also, interestingly, a cluster of stars . . . all of this in addition to the new meanings Blanco assigns through his creative metaphors: “la rosa brilla por su ausencia” [the rose that shines through its absence], “estas rosas potables de San Francisco” [these potable San Francisco roses], “magnífica rosa de movimientos submarinos” [magnificent rose of submarine movements], etc.[101]

Stars and roses draw our attention in the first 130 stanzas (the first half) of *Cuenta de los guías*, through intentional placement and repetition. There are fourteen mentions of stars as “estrellas” or “astros” in the book’s first fifty-two poems, eleven in part 2, and twenty in part 3, accompanied by some fifty references to roses, often in clusters of three. Together, these images set the rhythm of quests in motion in the book’s first half.

Cuenta de los guías is a hard poem to read. Like other forms of avant-garde art, its freedoms can be overwhelming. The text dazzles us with a kaleidoscope of images, but, through repetition and a few strategically placed road signs, the reader open to discovery can connect with the book’s difficult mental and spiritual journeys. Blanco’s roses and stars make us look for patterns in the wilderness of the poem and thus change our perception of all of the poem’s images.

CHAPTER 2

Space

Many of the chapters of *A la luz de siempre* [*In Constant Light*] frame their poems as coming from or existing between two or more times and places. Titles like *Poemas traídos del sueño* [*Poems from Dreams*], *Poemas vistos* [*Seen Poems*], *Tarjetas postales* [*Postcards*], *Romances de ultramar* [*Ballads from Overseas*], and *Tiempo extra* [*Overtime*] tap into the same empathetic desire for connection that similarly inspires Blanco's ekphrastic poems. While the *poesía visual* [visual poetry] and poetry influenced by collage we studied in chapter 1 certainly have their spatial dimensions, this chapter centers on texts that are dependent on multiple contexts of space or push the limitations of two- and three-dimensional representation. Primarily, we see such spatial play in poems that intentionally create and document links to other artists, genres, times, and places. Maps, film, and borders are also especially remarkable intersections of spatial representation, and the poet uses all three to consider the relationships and energy of liminal spaces. We conclude with a look at the role of travel, borders, and form in *Cuenta de los guías* [*Account of the Guides*].

The Exergue Effect

Along with their visual pyrotechnics and division into sets or families, one of the most distinctive characteristics of Blanco's poetry is its pervasive use of epigraphs, dedications, exergues, and other kinds of marginalia or "paratexts." One might remember the "Referencias" ["References"] from the catalogue essay for the collage exhibit mentioned in chapter 1, for example, or think of the list of 234 "hacedores" in the appendix of *La hora y la neblina* [*Time and Mist*]. Blanco addresses these lists in that book's "Nota preliminar" [Prefatory Note]:

> Por lo que toca a los poemas que tienen que ver tanto con las artes visuales, como con la música, el cine, y la obra de muchos poetas—vasos comunicantes . . . verdaderos *relámpagos paralelos*—hago constar en un índice de artistas—o *hacedores*—las relaciones que en muchas formas, y también de muchas formas, se han entretejido entre poemas y obras.
>
> Y por lo que hace a los versos que aparecen de vez en cuando en letra cursiva, los he tomado prestados de otros poetas. De sus orígenes doy fe en las notas al final del libro.[1]
>
> [In terms of the poems that have to do with the visual arts, as well as with music, filmmaking, and the work of many poets—communicating vessels . . . true *parallel lightning strikes*—I document in an index of artists—or inspirational creators—the relationships that in many ways, and also by many ways, have been woven between my poems and the work of others.
>
> With regard to the lines that occasionally appear in italics, I have borrowed them from other poets. I reveal their sources in the notes at the end of the book.]

As we saw with collage, the metaphors the poet uses to describe the relationship between his original poems and the names of artists that inspire them are spatial—one comes from the chemistry labs of his youth (communicating vessels), while others ("parallel lightning strikes" and "forms that intertwine poems and the works [that inspired them]") also present abstract ideas in terms of form, proximity, distance, and contact.

In *Paratexts*, Gérard Genette examines the relationship of literature to its physical contexts, that is, to the binding, publishing house, prologue and epilogue, epigraphs, dedications, and cover art that are its necessary complements. For Genette, epigraphs make apparent a relationship, either public or private, between a text and person.[2] This relationship is similar to a frame since it creates a new space that directs our reading by forcing us to question the connection between what we are about to read and the person quoted or referenced. Unlike classical literature, in which poets wrote dedications in order to seek patronage for their work, the relationships contemporary writers create through their quotations are usually aesthetic—the dedicatee has inspired, in some way or another, the poem she or he presides over. Or, as Genette mentions, "the dedicatee is always in some way responsible for the work that is dedicated to him [or her] and to which he brings a little of his support and therefore participation."[3] Stendhal wrote that the function of an epigraph is to "heighten the reader's feeling,"[4] while Michel Charles notes that the function of an exergue ("A small space usually on the reverse of a coin or medal, below the principal device, for any minor inscription, the date, engraver's initials, etc. Also, the inscription there inserted")[5] "is easily to give food for thought without one's knowing what the thought is."[6] In terms of poems based on music, Eric Prieto notes: "Writers who invoke music as a model for their work are telling readers to read backward, so to speak, that is, to decode the work by seeking out the type of representation exemplified in the text . . . a reader's task is to read up from the representation, to ask what type(s) of representation are being exemplified (there may be many), which type of these are pertinent in the present context, and what their significance is."[7] This kind of reading is inevitable in all of Blanco's *hacedor* poems since the reader finds themself suspended between text and appendix (for the name of the artist). The contemporary reader undoubtedly then triangulates this connection by reaching out to the internet to research different works that may be referenced by the poem on the page. This method of reading is at once innovative and very old, based, as E. H. Gombrich reminds us, in the tradition of glossing ancient manuscripts or providing captions, context, and code to pieces on gallery walls.[8]

With these ideas in mind, Blanco's decision to place the names of his *hacedores* in appendices, rather than beside the poems they correspond to, becomes an even more interesting one. Genette signals the importance of the placement of epigraphs in his study of paratexts and notes that when they precede a text they are taken as prescriptive, but while when they follow a text they can appear more "authoritatively conclusive."[9] Strictly speaking, Blanco's *hacedores* are not quite epigraphs, but rather "exergues" since they are placed "*en exergue*" or "off the work" and are usually not quotes of particular texts but rather, for the most part, names of artists, a fact that opens up vast fields of suggestion for the reader.[10]

The physical distance between poem and dedicatee widens a text's referential frame beyond our view and holds the promise of at least two possible readings for these texts: one of the poem itself standing alone and a second by the light of the artist referenced. Taken this way, the dedicatees or *hacedores* truly participate in rewriting Blanco's poems. This is the case with "Dedicatoria" [Dedication], whose title calls immediate attention to the game at hand:

"Dedicatoria"

El aire de la primavera
que en la sangre se agita
celebra los misterios del arte
mientras ladran los perros.

Y yo estoy convencido
de que el trabajo bien hecho
me hace—más allá del dolor
de las traiciones pasadas—
indiferente a dónde habrá
de caer el próximo rayo.[11]

["Dedication"
The spring air
that awakens our blood
celebrates the mysteries of art
while dogs bark outside.

And I am convinced
that work well done
makes me—beyond the pain
of old betrayals—
indifferent to where lightning
will strike next.]

Genette notes that proclaiming the relationship of one piece of art to another through a dedication has a strong performative element and "Dedicatoria" concerns the mysterious contact between art and viewer.[12] It's about the feeling of arousal we get from appreciating things well made and how they can drive us to distraction and change the way we see the world. As mentioned in Blanco's *Zeta Tijuana* interview, the idea here is that art will make us focus more on life's positives than on its monsters. "Dedicatoria" is, explicitly, a dedication to viewing, to the viewer, to a way of reading that presents texts in the frame of others, in this case, in the context of the American abstract expressionist painter Franz Klein.

What kind of reading does this particular *hacedor* open up for us? The bold black marks of Klein's work recall those of Jackson Pollock and other abstract expressionists who distributed paint through a combination of bodily movements and the power of gravity to place their drips. Klein's marks, like Robert Motherwell's, often obliquely recall letters or other familiar forms. This fact contains echoes of the form and function of ideograms and the avant-garde's play with unfamiliar characters of other alphabets. A seemingly familiar form seduces our eye with the possibility of meaning and then denies that same connection as abstraction triumphs over representation. As in much modern art, these kinds of texts are more about the interplay of positive and negative space than about imitating and conveying an artist's emotional state or signifying meanings in the traditional sense.

Blanco's use of marginalia creates a special and spatial sensation for the reader, what Genette has called "the epigraph effect" in which the mere presence of a foreign fragment sets the tone, tenor, and genre of the text it accompanies. Epigraphs and dedications bring together the reader, poem, and dedicatee by inviting a special guest to the seat of honor at the table of the text. Exergues tempt us into looking for direct connections and quickly send us to the slippery slope of a poet's intentions, which are ultimately unknowable. As Genette notes, "the use of an epigraph is always a mute gesture whose interpretation is left up to the reader."[13] Blanco's paratexts, like his use of collage, show us how art transcends genre, is intertextual, and, as he writes of inspiration, is equally about being inspired as it is about inspiring others. The sheer abundance of Blanco's *vasos comunicantes* [communicating vessels] tells us that the poet cannot write without reading, seeing, or remembering the work of other artists and that we too should read the same way.

"Poética del espacio" ["A Poetics of Space"] tackles these ideas head-on through many of the techniques favored by our poet: negation, the interplay of positive and negative space, and the exergue effect:

Veo la puerta
pero no hay muro
es decir
no hay puerta

Oigo la flauta
pero no hay nada
dentro de la flauta

Siento que puedo pasar
pero no hay a dónde pasar

Veo
    Oigo
        Siento
Pero no el ojo con que veo
Pero no el oído con que escucho
Pero no el cuerpo con que siento[14]

[I see the door
but there is no wall
which is to say
there is no door

I hear the flute
but there is nothing
inside the flute

I feel I can get through
but there is nowhere to go

I see
    Hear
        Feel
But not with my eyes do I see
But not with my ears do I listen
But not with the body do I feel]

"Poética del espacio" is a poem about sight and a "poema visual" due to its innovative stanza structure. The text explores the nature of verbal images and features a strong tension between two- and three-dimensional spaces. Finally, the counterpoint of the "yo" ["I"] of the first four stanzas and the negations in the final stanza creates even more friction.

Though this is not often the case, the poem's *hacedor* may help us understand its shifting perspectives, negations, and play with dimensions and senses in the text. Argentine artist Lucio Fontana (1899–1968) was best known for creating new spatial dimensions in his canvases through strategically placed slits and holes. Influenced by new technologies after World War II, in 1947 Fontana single-handedly founded the avant-garde movement *spatzialismo* [spatialism] that sought to bring new multidimensional depth to easel painting. While Fontana's sculptures and installations moved easily into a third dimension, painting "demanded radical surgery: the rupturing of the picture's flatness."[15]

When viewed by the light of *spatzialismo*, "Poética del espacio" both opens and closes. The third stanza, for example, appears to describe the sensation of wanting to pass through a slit canvas to the image of depth behind it. In this way, the poem touches multiple dimensions by means of the exergue effect.

Time and Place Stamps

As we saw in "Wyethiana" ["Wyethiana"] in chapter 1, many of Blanco's poems have what might be termed "time and place" stamps. *La hora y la neblina*, for example, contains collections named *Poemas vistos* [*Seen Poems*], *Poemas traídos del sueño* [*Poems from Dreams*], and *Cuarenta romances de ultramar* [*Forty Ballads from Overseas*], which indicate that their poems are the result of a search for inspiration beyond the world of the arts. The poems of these sections incorporate explicitly external images and ideas in order to craft distinctive poetic spaces on the page. In addition, these texts contain a sustained and multifaceted inquiry into the difference and distance between space and place that informs the work of philosophers and theorists such as Michel de Certeau, Michel Foucault, Gaston Bachelard, Henri Lefebvre, and Marc Augé.

To overtly label a poem as coming from "things seen," from dreams, or from distinct places or times highlights the spatial and temporal tensions at the heart of the making of collages. As an example, *Tarjetas postales* from *A la luz de siempre* creates an aural collage from the music of unfamiliar Icelandic and Estonian languages:

"Íslensku Steinarnir"
Islandia
donde los borregos son piedras
y las piedras son borregos:
kindurnar.[16]

"Tintinnabuli"
Una raya de gis
en la planicie de Paide
—de Tallinn a Tartu
de Tartu a Tallinn—[17]

["Íslensku Steinarnir"

Iceland
where the lambs are stone
and the stones lambs:
kindurnar.

"Tintinnabuli"
A line of chalk
on the plains of Paide
—from Tallinn to Tartu
from Tartu to Tallinn—]

Like all Blanco's *Tarjetas postales*, these two poems bear chronologically ordered time and place exergues ("Islandia, 8 de septiembre de 2011"[18] [Iceland, September 8, 2011] and "Estonia, 13 de septiembre de 2011"[19] [Estonia, September 13, 2011]) that introduce an innovative narrative element from both inside and outside the individual texts. While postcards tend to be first person micro-epistles, Blanco instead uses the section's title and exergues to craft an open-ended story for readers to piece together from individual poems that, like the oranges in the Krishnamurti grove of the section's final poem, both stand alone and contribute to a greater picture.

Although its title hints at another travel narrative, in reality *Cuarenta romances de ultramar* treat distance in metaphorical and abstract ways through three sets of love poems about overcoming emotional, physical, and poetic distances. The first section, "Tú" ["You"], begins with very short poems of four verses that grow incrementally to five, six, seven, and all the way up to twenty-eight verses in the final text. This incremental progression reflects the growth of a relationship between the speaker and his lover through well-seasoned yet nonetheless clear echoes of Neruda's early work. Images of individuals closing emotional distances through dialogues, touches, and physical descriptions evolve into more fully developed and more refined descriptions of communion. The second section is more abstract and interior with faint references to the Odyssey, while the third movement, consisting of seven actual *romances* [ballads], features many moments of synthesis, such as "La estrella" ["The Star"]:

Un Ecuador y dos Polos,
dos voces y una verdad

a la mitad del camino
y el camino a la mitad.

No te entiendo—dijo ella;
no te entiendo—dijo él.
Y encendieron una estrella
para poderse entender.[20]

[One Equator and two Poles,
two voices and one truth
in the middle of the road
and halfway down the road.

I don't understand you—said she;
I don't understand you—said he.
And they lit a star
to understand each other.

One Equator and two Poles,
two voices and one truth
in the middle of the road
and halfway down the road.]

The image of the globe in "La Estrella" balances togetherness and distance, difference and similarity. Visually, this globe is reminiscent of the yin/yang symbol, a preferred trope of this poet we will explore in greater depth in chapter 4. The globe is also a symbol for a literal journey come full circle, as well as for a loving relationship that nonetheless allows its partners to maintain their individuality as complements.

"*Poemas traídos del sueño*," also from *La hora y la neblina*, contains more than forty texts, each anchored to an exergue with a corresponding day, month, and year as well as place in which, presumably, the speaker dreamed the poem. Despite the title's possible implication, these are not particularly surrealistic or impressionistic texts, though many deal with sleep or dreaming and the last word of the section's last poem is "despertar" ["awaken"]. As in *Tarjetas postales*, the chain of chronologically ordered dates and places suggests a narrative about the actual poet since there are no indications of other personae or dates earlier than Blanco's date of birth or later than the book's date of publication (2017 for this second edition).

The exergue from "Emblema" contributes to the implied narrative structure of the section:

"Emblema"
Y yo que todavía creo en la posibilidad
de aparecer en el horizonte

de todos los momentos
en que has estado
sola

(Primer fragmento traído del sueño
a fines de mayo de 1971, México)[21]

["Emblem"
And I who still believe in the possibility
of appearing on the horizon
of every moment
you have been
alone.

(First fragment from a dream
end of May 1971, Mexico).]

The poem's title "Emblema" reinforces the prominence of the date and time stamp since exergues can literally be glosses or labels for images while books of emblems, by definition, contain "drawings with accompanying interpretations of their allegorical meaning."[22] Literal definitions are useful for understanding other aspects of the poem, as well. If an emblem is "a picture of an object (or the object itself) serving as a symbolical representation of an abstract quality, an action, state of things, class of persons, etc."[23] it helps dispel the idea that "Emblema" was dreamed as a *poema visual*. Instead, the poem's title directs us to read it and the texts that follow it as emblematic representations of dreams.

From the outside, it's hard to connect the real places named in these texts with their content. As an example, two poems from the border city of El Paso, Texas, invite us to speculate on such connections since "Sí y no" ["Yes and no"] is about contradictions (like those found in border towns) and "El paso del tiempo" ["El Paso Time"] plays with the city's name. Still, neither poem gives us more than a hint of the relationship between the poem and the place where the dream occurred. The places associated with these dream poems are thus rewritten as spaces of representation, rather than places in the conventional, humanistic sense. So our traditional understanding of a *place* such as "Santa Fe, New Mexico" is reconfigured in these poems to the very small "lived space," to use Lefebvre's term, of being the setting for a particular dream. As Eric Prieto writes, the goal of this kind of text plus *exergue* is to cobble together a representation that will make sense to the poet—"not to provide universally valid explanations or definitions."[24] We will return to these considerations in this chapter's next section.

"Sueño en una estación de trenes al amanecer" ["Dream of a Train Station at Dawn"] examines the paradoxes of space and place through the image of a speaker walking through a train that has yet to leave its station. All of this occurs here in a poem dreamed in Valle de Bravo, Mexico, a town that, incidentally, has no train station.

Estoy en una estación
a bordo de un tren

Camino de carro en carro
de puerta en puerta

Paso gabinetes y fuelles
ventanas encendidas

Pero al poco tiempo
ya no hay ventanas

No hay fuelles ni carros
no hay tren ni estación

Sólo la luna dormida
sólo el cielo y la tierra

Y las blancas estrellas
que iluminan este poema

(18 de febrero de 1988, Valle de Bravo)[25]

[I am in a station
aboard a train

I walk from car to car
from door to door

I pass cabins and compartments
lit up windows

But soon
there are no windows

No compartments or cars
no train or station

Only the sleeping moon
only the sky and earth

And the white stars
that light this poem.

(February 18, 1988, Valle de Bravo)]

Blanco's dream poems feature an interesting balance of precision and abstraction. Even when a setting is vague, it is described in great detail, whether it be a train station, highway, room, road, or other place or experience. "El sueño" [The Dream], for example, creates an elaborate structure of *cajas chinas* without employing a single preposition of location:

El sueño
es un sueño
que sueña alguien
que sueña
que está soñando
un sueño

(18 de abril de 1992, México)[26]

[The dream
is a dream
that someone dreams
who dreams
she's dreaming
a dream

(April 18, 1992, Mexico)]

Poemas traídos del sueño features a number of metapoems based on spatial metaphors. "La poesía" [Poetry] depicts poetry as a road and "Un poema" ["A poem"] is a key made of words that allows us to unlock a door separating the known from the unknown. Fittingly, "El umbral" ["Threshold"] is another variation on the metapoetic question of interior and exterior space:

El misterio
de la puerta
no está adentro
ni está afuera

Solamente
puede estar
un momento
en el umbral

El misterio
del poema
no está dentro
ni está fuera

Fugazmente
viene a estar
un instante
en este umbral

(18 de diciembre de 2002, México)[27]

[The mystery
of the door

is neither inside
nor outside

We are only
on this
threshold
for a moment

The mystery
of the poem
is neither inside
nor outside

Fleetingly
it exists
for an instant
on this threshold

(December 18, 2002, Mexico)]

"El umbral" defines the mysterious experience of the poem as a dynamic process, characterized by the movement of reading and interpreting, that actualizes or energizes the text. Notice that by placing the phrase "este umbral" ["this threshold"] at the end of the last verse, we are left hanging, visually, thematically, and literally on the threshold, ready to leave the poem behind (inside, as it were) and to start firming up our preliminary (and exterior) conclusions about it. The "aesthetic of process"[28] we see in "En el umbral" appears as well across the work of the French poststructuralists—Foucault envisioned power as an activated network of relationships and Michel de Certeau defined space as a place put into practice.[29] For de Certeau, as for Blanco, a poem is a dynamic act in which a reader cocreates meanings with the poet, his words, and, often, the words of others introduced through paratexts. Paz, of course, exploited this idea of active space in "Blanco" and elsewhere.

Travel

As we saw in the poems dreamed in El Paso, Texas, Blanco conjugates many theories of place in his travel poems, from existential versions of the Heraclitan idea of never wading into the same river twice in "Napa River Dream"[30] to the ways in which art inscribes a place for us in "Encuentro" ["Meeting"]:

Hoy vi a Paul Celan:
Era una hoja seca
flotando sobre el Sena . . .

(París 11 de noviembre de 1997)[31]

[Today I saw Paul Celan:
He was a wrinkled leaf
floating on the Seine . . .

(Paris, November 11, 1997)]

The "exergue effect" can be especially strong in poems about travel. "Las hormigas de la Villa Grimaldi" ["The Ants at the Villa Grimaldi"] for example, bears the paratext "Santiago de Chile 21 de marzo de 2001" ["Santiago, Chile, March 21, 2001] and begins with a few simple declarative verses about the place that any visitor might make:

Aquí están,
aquí han estado siempre . . .
las hormigas de la Villa Grimaldi.

¿Hasta dónde—siempre—estarán?

Quién sabe . . .
Lo cierto es que hoy están aquí,
trabajando infatigables—como siempre—
sin esperar nada a cambio:
ni reconocimiento en este mundo
ni trascendencia en el otro.

Y simplemente siguen haciendo
lo que las hormigas hacen . . .
sin rencor, sin olvido, sin perdón.[32]

[They are here,
they have always been here . . .
the ants at the Villa Grimaldi.

But who knows?—Will they always be?

Who knows . . .
What is certain is that they are here today,
working away—like always—
without expecting anything in exchange:
neither recognition in this world
nor transcendence in the next.

And they simply keep doing
what ants do . . .
without resentment, without forgetting, without mercy.]

Without being grounded in a specific place and time, there would be no social message to this powerful text, but once we consider the history of Villa Grimaldi, the already symbolic ants take on a new metaphorical level. Between 1973 and 1978 the villa was transformed into the Cuartel Terranova, one of the most notorious secret prisons and torture chambers of Augusto Pinochet's Dirección de Inteligencia Nacional (DINA). In the late 1970s it was dismantled and throughout the 1980s abandoned. Today it is home to a Parque de la Paz [Peace Park], one of many extraordinary sites of memory in a country that has tried valiantly to uncover and shed light upon its past in order to create a more just future.

Returning to the poem, we note that it takes place in 2001, safely insulated from danger by a distance of more than two decades, so clearly the speaker is there as a visitor or tourist. This safety is also reflected in the poem's tone, which is light and conversational. The speaker has the luxury of being able to examine the place, down to the level of its ants, at his leisure. Although he mentions nothing about the villa's history at all, he does focus on the permanence of the ants by repeating, three times, that they will always be here. The tone and the absence of a historical reference are in tension here and reflect the uneasiness any visitor to the Villa Grimaldi would feel of being there and knowing what used to happen in that space. The place, with its stones and trees and insects, endures but its function as a space has been radically changed. Although the absence is what reverberates, the ants present an element of doubt. Do they symbolize a connection with the violent past? Are they an indication that violence will always be there? Or do they simply signify and illustrate the fact that only humankind, and not nature, can transform a park into a space of horror?

The tension one feels reading "Las hormigas de la Villa Grimaldi" ["The Ants at the Villa Grimaldi"] is the kind of situation critics of travel writing are drawn to. Can such locations (what Paul Fussell calls "pseudo-places") truly be tourist destinations? Fussell makes a distinction between travelers (culturally humble students exploring new places) and tourists (superficial consumers purchasing prepackaged comfort and familiarity). He notes that "places are odd and call for interpretation. They are the venues of the traveler. Pseudo-places entice by their familiarity and call for instant recognition: 'We have arrived.'" . . . "The Costa del Sol," he adds as an example, "is a pseudo-place, or Tourist Bubble."[33] While we may experience these uncomfortable feelings upon reading the poem, Blanco's allegorical ants are deaf to such interpretations and instead see all of us as simple visitors to their workplace. Another poem from this section, "The Merwin Plaza," explores time, place, space, and otherness in a less intense, though equally layered context.

> "The Merwin Plaza"
> La plaza pública
> que lleva el nombre
> de Merwin en Kohunlich
>
> (del inglés *cohoon*
> que quiere decir "corozo,"

el fruto de la palma,
y *ridge*, "lomerío")

es el lugar común
donde las palabras
cambian de vestido,
cambian de idioma
como los árboles
cambian de follaje
con cada estación.

(Kohunlich, Febrero del 2000)[34]

[The public plaza
that bears Merwin's
name in Kohunlich
(from the English *cohoon*
that means "corozo,"
or fruit of the palm,
and *ridge*)

is the meeting place
where words
change clothes,
change language
like the trees
change leaves
with each season.

(Kohunlich, February 2000)]

Blanco's poem makes no mention of the original function of the plaza to the Mayas but instead focuses on its symbolic value as a space. As Michel de Certeau has noted, spaces do not appear on maps, places do. Furthermore, de Certeau reminds us that a place such as a street "geographically designed by urban planning is transformed into a space by walkers,"[35] and thus this Mayan plaza in Quintana Roo is the ultimate "lugar común" (pun intended) since it was a pre-Hispanic meeting place that now bears the name of an American archaeologist in a town whose name also evolved from English. In this light, the Merwin Plaza could be one of many places where cultures and languages meet. It is also a site of "transculturation" in the sense Mary Louise Pratt defines as a cultural "contact zone," where imperial modes of representation are assumed by the periphery.[36]

Travel is about displacement, and even when it is voluntary or recreational, finding oneself in a new place causes us to consider ourselves in different ways, especially when jetlag figures into the equation. "Los paisajes de mi mente"

["Landscapes in my Mind"] does an excellent job of re-creating that disoriented feeling we get as we land in a foreign airport after a long, overnight flight. The poem's first two stanzas create confusion through the interplay of inside and out: "El techo de nubes es mi mente y se mueve; / la tierra negra, salpicada de luces de oro, soy yo, y también cambia" [That ceiling of clouds is my mind and it's moving; / that dark earth, splashed with golden lights, is me, and is also changing].[37] The rest of the text features a list of sensorial images, in the cadence of a prayer, that the speaker identifies as himself:

ese café fortísimo en una taza pequeñita y blanca, soy yo,
esa máquina tragamonedas, sola en la primera hora, soy yo,
ese hombre que carga una maleta pesada y se despeina en el
—esfuerzo, soy yo;
esas dos mujeres que pasan del brazo protegiéndose del frío,
—soy yo;[38]

[that robust coffee in the small white cup, is me,
that poker machine, abandoned in the early morning, is me,
that man struggling with a heavy suitcase whose hair is in his eyes, is me;
those two women that pass by arm in arm against the cold, are me;]

Despite his attempts to identify with all the new things around him, in the end, the speaker loses his own identity: "Solamente yo no soy yo" ["Only I am not me"][39]—an apt description of the immersion and transformation that occurs through travel. A particularly interesting aspect of this poem is found in the push/pull relationship between its title ("Los paisajes de mi mente") and its exergue (Aeropuerto de Milán, Otoño de 1997 [Milan Airport, Fall 1997]). In one sense, the paratext both contextualizes and contradicts the title while, perhaps, also helping ground us in the idea that physical travel also implies changes in perspective that have effects on our subjectivity.

Travel is a main motif of the section "La hora y la neblina" since each of the sixty-four poems collected within it contain intentional time and place stamps. Blanco addresses the inevitable question of why in the final poem of the book, "El viaje" ["The Voyage"]—the only one that does not link to a specific date and place.

Por más que he viajado
nunca me he movido de mi lugar.

Yo siempre he estado aquí:
sobre la faz de la tierra,
a la sombra de la luna,
bajo la luz del sol.[40]

[For all I have traveled
I have never moved from this place.

I have always been here:
on the face of the earth,
in the shadow of the moon,
beneath the light of the sun.]

The absence of a reference to a specific trip reinforces the idea that the poems we have just read have taken us everywhere and, in another sense, nowhere. We both traveled to Ireland, to Chartres, to Milan, and didn't. The poems we created as readers shared their journeys with us, moved us through time and space, and caused us to transform, even if only in very small ways. When we take these ideas on travel and Blanco's *poética transformalista* [transformalist poetics] into account, a seemingly simple text such as "Lombardía" ["Lombardy"] takes on greater resonance and depth:

La naturaleza
cumple con su parte:
inspira.

Cumplamos nosotros
con la nuestra:
inspiremos.

Lombardía, Otoño de 1997[41]

[Nature
does its part:
it inspires.

Let's do
ours
and inspire others.

Lombardy, Fall 1997]

"Mapas"

In his wide-ranging study "The Visual Image: Its Place in Communication," E. H. Gombrich notes that Leonardo da Vinci's famous drawings of water and whirlpools are not so much mimetic representations but rather "visualizations of the forces at work" or "diagrammatic mapping" since they suppress certain features "for the sake of conceptual clarity."[42] Gombrich then goes on to show how suppression, normalization, and transformation also control the images we see on maps. Blanco takes up these same ideas in the series of eight poems titled "Mapas" ["Maps"] from *La raíz cuadrada del cielo* [*The Square Root of Heaven*].[43] The individual texts that compose "Mapas" are meditative and light of tone, with each poem providing new perspectives on the representational possibilities of their subject. Together, they are a radically innovative way of poeticizing space through a complementary blend of poetic and prosaic language.

In its form and content, "Mapas" recalls Wallace Stevens's "Thirteen Ways of Looking at a Blackbird" since both poems share a strong spatial and visual bent, have a mysterious tone, and feature an extended play between numbered fragments and a whole. Both texts also include the repetition of the central image from the title in each of their sections (maps and blackbirds) and yet, at the same time, redefine this object at every turn. This is to say that both texts are ontological inquiries—Blanco, for example, uses forms of the verb *ser* [to be] and *no ser* [to not be] eleven times in the first fifteen lines of his text. More than a simple synthesis or unresolved combination of thesis and antithesis, "Mapas" provides a collage of complementary definitions of what maps are and are not.

Gombrich's main point about maps is that, despite their apparent claims, maps lack the quality of genuine representation or "iconicity."[44] From the beginning, Blanco's poems examine such aspects of visual representation in overt ways through concrete, prosaic verses:

> Comencemos por el principio:
> *La Tierra* no es La Tierra.
> *El mapa no es el territorio.*
> El territorio no es el mapa.
>
> Un mapa es una imagen.
> Un mapa es un modo de hablar.
> Un mapa es un conjunto de recuerdos.
> Un mapa es una representación proporcional.[45]
>
> [Let's begin at the beginning:
> *The Earth* is not The Earth.
> *The map is not the territory.*
> The territory is not the map.
>
> A map is an image.
> A map is a way of speaking.
> A map is a collection of memories.
> A map is a proportional representation.][46]

Along with the use of the first-person singular and a quotation from Alfred Korzybski in verse 2, the declarative nature of the second stanza is an example of the critical voice that balances the more abstract and mysterious notes of Blanco's poems. This complementary blend of poetic and prosaic language is reflected as well in the stanza's visual form and the dual nature of maps themselves.

Adding a philosophical layer to its critical approach, the final verses of poem I feature the kind of logic and tone inspired by Zen koans:

> Todo mapa es una imagen, un cuadro, una metáfora,
> una descripción . . .
> Pero no toda descripción, metáfora, imagen o, para el caso,
> todo cuadro es—por necesidad—un mapa.
> Pero puede llegar a serlo.[47]
>
> [Every map is an image, a painting, a metaphor,
> a description . . .
> But not every description, metaphor, image, or, for that matter, not every
> painting
> is—necessarily—a map.
> Although it could become one.]

When the poet writes that "*El mapa no es el territorio*" [*The map is not the territory*] or "No crecen árboles en un mapa" [Trees do not grow on maps] or "Los mapas de la tierra no son la tierra" [Maps of the earth are not the earth],[48] he is tapping into the same obsessive questions about the distance between physical objects and their representation that drove the linguistic studies of Ferdinand de Saussure and Alfred Korzybski, the philosophies of Ludwig Wittgenstein, Walter Benjamin, and Jean Baudrillard, and the visual avant-gardes of the early twentieth century.

As we move through the series of texts, questions of dimensionality begin to unfold. In poem II we read that maps are simply another example of Nabi painter Maurice Denis's definition of a painting as "un arreglo de formas y colores sobre una superficie bidimensional" ["an arrangement of forms and colors on a two dimensional surface"][49] and that "Si todo el territorio fuera homogéneo, sólo se acotaría en un mapa el perfil de los límites del territorio" [If all territory were homogeneous, only a profile of the boundaries of the territory would show up on a map].[50] While our imaginations may be three dimensional, "Un mapa del mundo real no es menos imaginario que un mapa de un mundo imaginario" [A map of the real world is no less imaginary than a map of the imaginary world][51]—an interesting overlap with what Baudrillard called "representational imaginary" or "simulacra."[52]

Poem III, however, complicates spatial representation through the addition of another dimension—time: "Un mapa no es más que una representación bidimensional de un mundo tridimensional que recorre un fantasma: el tiempo" [A map is nothing more than a two-dimensional representation of a three-dimensional world that is traveled by the ghost of time].[53] Here, we are introduced to the complex notion of the spacetime continuum, a lifelong fascination for the poet that will resurface in his science poems (see chapter 5). In another correspondence with the science poems (specifically, "Primera teoría termodinámica" [First Theory of Thermodynamics]), poem IV explores fundamental aspects of sequence in the context of spatial representation. Must travel precede the creation of maps? Do maps follow the same natural laws as myths? Since each of these poems must have, by definition, an element of the unknown, poem IV concludes as follows:

> Los mapas, al principio, fueron relatos de viajes.
> Después los mapas fueron paisajes al ras del horizonte:
> narraciones visuales.
> Finalmente, vistas a vuelo de pájaro: poemas geográficos.
>
> Un mapa es una manifestación artística del miedo a lo desconocido.[54]
>
> [Maps, in the beginning, were chronicles of trips taken.
> Later, maps were landscapes viewed from ground level:
> visual narratives.
> Finally, seen from a bird's eye view: geographic poems.
>
> A map is an artistic manifestation of our fear of the unknown.]

Poem V tells us that in the past, maps of the earth also contained maps of the skies and that the separation of those two parts reflects how science has overtaken mythological explanations of creation. Despite this change, if the environment continues to be treated unsustainably there may not even be land to show on the maps of the future. Another duality with implications for the polarities of poetic and prosaic language in this poem is introduced by an embedded quotation from the Tao Te Ching: "*La verdad que se puede decir no es la verdad*" [*A truth that can be spoken is not the truth*].

Blanco puts poem V into dialogue with paratexts in one more way, as well. Gombrich notes that some of the main characteristics of maps are contour lines, political boundaries, population density, and "the addition of a key to the standardized code."[55] A map's key functions as a paratext or exergue that, like the names of *hacedores*, informs and frames our interpretations of its features. Stanza 4 states that on a map: "Un punto es un pueblo. / Una línea es una carretera" [A point is a town. / A line is a highway].[56] Clearly, what we see when we read a map or consult its key is metaphors and these metaphors are what make this text a poem.

The ecological message of poem V is expanded upon in poem's VI's critique of maps as ways to contain and control territory: "Un mapa a la medida de la ambición de un hombre" [A map the size of humanity's ambition].[57] Poem VI considers the power dynamics of representing space by contrasting inside and out, domination and conservation. Even though maps can be used to contain, "Todos los puntos de referencia en un mapa ven hacia afuera" [All points of reference on a map look outward].[58]

In an interesting variation on the flip/flop of literal and figurative language that powers these texts, poem VII takes the final verse of poem VI at its word and gives maps another new dimension—subjectivity: "Los mapas nos miran de frente cuando dan cuenta de las superficies. / Cuando quieren dar cuenta de las profundidades, nos miran de lado" [Maps look us in the face when they speak of surfaces. / They look at us sideways when they wish to speak of depth].[59] This idea ties into Blanco's theories of visual poetry ("usar las palabras para ver") [using words to see] and prefigures the final, perhaps inevitable, mystery of poem VIII. The penultimate verse uses that prosaic, declarative voice for a clever, yet understandable statement, while the last line, in contrast, leaves us with a little mystery to think about: "En mapas no se ha andado nada. / En poesía no hay nada escrito" [There are no footprints on maps. / There is no writing in poetry].[60]

Blanco's "mapas" are like Harold Bloom's maps of misreading since all readings are misreadings and all reproductions are flawed. When the poet arranges his texts in sets like *Norte, Sur, Este,* and *Oeste* [North, South, East, West] he is giving a consciously limited structure to an already imperfect text. "Los cuarto vientos, los cuatro ríos, las cuarto puertas," he writes in "Mapas," "los cuatro pilares de la tierra de los que hablan los mitos / no son más que las cuarto esquinas de un mapa" [The four pillars of earth spoken of in myths are nothing more than the four corners of a map].[61] The four corners of the map are the four corners of the paper we read, of course, but despite the appearance of structure, Blanco's poetic maps are invitations to leave the grid.

The line in poem VII, "¿Qué son los colores en un mapa sino un sueño?" [Are the colors on a map anything more than a dream?], focuses on the gap between signifier and signified that is just as present in a photograph of any changing coastline or the shrinking perimeter of any rainforest in the world as it is in a map.[62] Landforms change and even satellite images of them, like photographs of people, are always immediately outdated. Of this kind of hyperreal relationship Baudrillard writes: "The territory no longer precedes the map, nor survives it. Henceforth, it is the map that precedes the territory—precession of simulacra—it is the map that engenders the territory."[63]

Maps similarly lead us to Walter Benjamin's notion of *aura* by provoking the question of what gets lost in duplication and what special qualities an original holds, while reproductions lead us to consider plurality and the nature of fractals.[64] In a sense, "Mapas" is an early fractal of Blanco's poetics since it contains so many of the main concerns of his later work: the nature of mimesis and spatial representation, the interplay of positive and negative spaces, the relationships between quotes and paratexts, questions over the limits of dimensionality, ecology, Eastern religion, quantum mechanics, the use of poetry to see, and a conclusion featuring the poetic energy provided by mystery.

Montage and Movie Stars

Whereas the notion of *aura* from "The Work of Art in the Age of Mechanical Reproduction" helps expand our understanding of "Mapas," the form of Walter Benjamin's *Passagenwerk*, more than any specific idea within, provides an intriguing lens through which to view some of Blanco's more recent poetry.[65] Benjamin's *The Arcades Project*, as it is known in English, contains over nine hundred pages of quotations, notes, sketches, essays, letters, epigraphs, and innumerable prose fragments whose structure is patterned on the street passages or arcades of Paris. Two salient characteristics of *The Arcades Project* are, first, its preponderance of quotations—so many that its editor writes that the quotes "eventually far outnumber the commentaries"—and, second, its form as a literary montage.[66] Howard Eiland and Kevin McLaughlin, *The Arcades Project*'s principal translators, describe the montages of Benjamin's later works as masses of thought fragments structured and characterized by the "philosophic play of distances, transitions, and intersections" as well as "shifting contexts and ironic juxtapositions."[67] In a move that began with the influence of the surrealists, Benjamin saw in his new genre the ability to engage the present moment more fully than the traditional essay could while simultaneously, through a patchwork text, providing a critique of encroaching consumer culture. Interestingly, the later technique was already being employed by the Latin American *modernistas* in their poems and stories overrun with what Roberto González Echevarría and Cathy Jrade have called the "overwhelming proliferation of imported manufactured items" resulting from late nineteenth-century economic imperialism.[68]

The privileging of the fragment, especially the imported or foreign cultural object, and rejection of authoritarian unity should come as no surprise given Benjamin's historical moment. The 1920s and 1930s featured the rise of European fascism but were also the time of Max Ernst and other members of the avant-garde's experimentations with DADA and surrealist collage. In chapter 1 we explored Blanco's use of poetic collage in a two-dimensional setting, but here we will look at variations on his poetry as three-dimensional montage.

"Siete imágenes y un collage" ["Seven Images and a Collage"], from *A la luz de siempre*, for example, presents a series of dramatic and seemingly unrelated vignettes from the lives of seven artists in succession.

> "Siete imágenes y un collage"
>
> La pequeña cacatúa rosa de Max Ernst muere justo cuando nace Luni, su hermanita. Ernst, al recibir ambas noticias al mismo tiempo, se desvanece de la impresión.
>
> Max Jacob, incapaz de pagar el alquiler del frac y también del taxi, llega a pie al estreno de "Tricorne" y es arrollado por un auto frente al teatro.

Salva la vida milagrosamente y decide enclaustrarse en el monasterio de Saint-Benoit.

Frida Kahlo, desnuda y bañada de sangre y polvo de oro, es retirada del camión hecho chatarra después del accidente mientras la gente grita: ¡la bailarina, la bailarina!

El célebre *marchand* de obras de arte, Ambroise Vollard, muere desnucado por una estatua en bronce de Maillol al frenar abruptamente el coche en el que viajaba.

El velo de una viuda llevado por el viento se estampa en el rostro de Picasso anunciándole la muerte de Apollinaire.

Al sacar del agua a la madre de Magritte, que ha cometido suicidio, surge su cabeza envuelta en su propia ropa como si fuera una mortaja. De aquí surge la pintura "El beso." A punto de morir, Henry Moore, ya muy viejo, recibe a una ancianita que había sido el amor platónico de su primera juventud. Como despedida, le pide un beso en la boca.[69]

["Seven Images and a Collage"

Max Ernst's small pink cockatiel dies just when Loni, his sister, is born. Ernst, upon receiving both pieces of news at the same time, faints from the impact.

Max Jacob, incapable of paying for both his rented tuxedo and his taxi, arrives on foot to the premiere of "Tricorne" and is run down by a car in front of the theater. Miraculously his life is saved and he decides to cloister himself in the monastery of Saint-Benoit.

Frida Kahlo, naked and bathed in blood and gold leaf, is pulled from the bus in ruins after the accident while people yelled: the ballerina! The ballerina!

The famous art merchant Ambroise Vollard, has his neck broken by a bronze statue by Maillol and dies after the car he was traveling in brakes too abruptly.

The veil of a widow carried by the wind drapes across Picasso's face announcing to him the death of Apollinaire.

When removing Magritte's mother from the water after her suicide, her head became wrapped in her own clothing as if it were a shroud. This is what inspired the painting "The Kiss."

About to die, Henry Moore, already quite old, gets visited by an old lady that was the Platonic love of his early childhood. In parting, she asks for a kiss on the mouth.]

Each prosaic "imagen" describes a different intersection of art and violence or death. The seven stanzas are more than just images, though, since each vignette has a narrative element and a strong dose of irony. Like metaphor, irony is a trope of incongruence. In its most basic form, it can be about expressing something by means of its opposite, but here, it is about unexpected cause and effect: Max Jacob cannot afford a taxi and is then, ironically, run down by a car. The injured and immobile Frida Kahlo is called a ballerina by witnesses to her accident and Vollard is decapitated by a statue. By bringing two or more unanticipated elements together, each scene holds more narrative punch than even the people involved in it suspects, and thus, each individual frame of this poem reflects the technique that gathered them together to form one eclectic whole.

Another dimension to this poem is provided by its *hacedor*, or source of inspiration noted in the appendix, Jiří Kolář, the Czech poet and visual artist. Kolář's collages often present two or more well-known works of art simultaneously, in intermittent parallel strips in order to present two stories or experiences (as well as a third, of course) at the same time. They are inclusive in the way Linda Hutcheon and others find as essential to irony by presenting multiple concepts at the same time. And so, despite the poem's title, the dynamic action of each of its juxtaposed stanzas, when taken together with the spatial implications of the exergue effect, make it more akin to a series of spliced scenes in a film than a traditional two-dimensional collage.

Blanco's 2014 collection *Medio Cine* treats narrative in an overt and intentional way through its connections with the work of forty famous film directors.[70] Many of these poems seem to be closer to their sources than the poet's other *vasos comunicantes* and some, such as "Metrópolis," have very concrete referents:

> Dan vueltas inexorables
> las manecillas en su laberinto
> como si en verdad quisieran
> contarnos toda la vida.[71]
>
> [The ticking hands run
> unrelentingly around their labyrinth
> as if wanting nothing more
> than to count down all our lives.][72]

Blanco's choice of words reflects the visuals of the clock scene of Fritz Lang's 1927 silent-film classic in direct ways—the first verse highlights the crushing misery of the workers' ten-hour shifts through a circular image that implies a lack of escape. This is expanded upon in the second verse where the clock is developed into a metaphorical labyrinth and its hands personified and given the evil intent that Lang proposed in the third and four verses. This personification and the "nos" of "contarnos" breaks the poem's "fourth wall" and essentially drops the reader into the poem's labyrinth as an engaged participant.

"Viva México" [Viva Mexico] contains not one, but multiple cinematic references:

"Viva México"

¿A dónde se van las calles
de este pueblo somnoliento,
las montañas y los valles,
cuando se los lleva el viento?[73]

[Where do the streets,
the mountains, and valleys
of this sleepy town go
when the wind sweeps them away?]

While the *hacedor* is Sergei Eisenstein, director of the influential but incomplete project *¡Qué viva México!*, the poem's last line is a clear nod to Victor Fleming's classic *Gone with the Wind*. Both movies are attempts to forge cinematic epics of nation building after civil war, revolution, and World War I. In addition, the presence of two juxtaposed cinematic references through poetic montage recalls techniques that Eisenstein theorized about in his essays on film editing: "Montage is an idea that arises from the collision of independent shots—shots even opposite to one another."[74] As in collage or literary montage, the relationship of proximity between unlikely narrative texts is the key.

The long poem "Cine Álamos" ["Cine Álamos"] connects cinematic techniques to the Mexican countryside through a quite literal and deliberate pun. When the speaker notes that the infamous Mexico City movie theater of his youth was named after the silver mining town in Sonora whose land gave birth to his mother, his grandmother, and one of the biggest stars of the Mexican silver screen, he writes: "Así, el nitrato de plata dejó grabado para la posteridad / el rostro perfecto de María Félix, / hija predilecta de Álamos" [And thus the local silver nitrate immortalized for posterity / the perfect profile of María Félix, / favorite daughter of Álamos].[75] As Peter Stockwell notes in *Cognitive Poetics*, both punning and repetition are key techniques writers use to pull certain images into the foreground and draw our attention to them.[76] In a similar way to *Cuenta de los guías*, an analysis of the dominant images in *Medio Cine* reveals an interesting lexical motif—nine of the forty poems make some reference to stars (*estrellas, astros, desastres,* etc.) [stars, celestial bodies, disasters, etc.]. This pattern, in the context of cinema, establishes an allegorical relationship between literal celestial bodies and, of course, movie stars such as María Félix in "Cine Alamos"

["Cine Álamos"]. The result is a collection that creates a new kind of poetic space or screen upon which to stargaze.

As with his "Mapas" Blanco's many poems about the heavens also tend to comment metapoetically on poetic form, whether it be on the level of the individual text itself or the book as a whole. "La eternidad y un día" ["Eternity and a Day"] (inspired by Greek director Theo Angelopoulos and his film of the same name), for example, could just as easily be about a book of poems as the night sky:

> Una ristra de estrellas unidas
> por el cielo que las separa
>
> Una galaxia de constelaciones
> unidas por el espacio vacío
>
> Un espacio unificado al fin
> por el poder de la palabra[77]
>
> [A string of stars threaded together
> by the same sky that divides them
>
> A galaxy of constellations
> united by hollow space
>
> And space finally unified
> by the power of words]

Furthermore, the poem uses "galaxias" [galaxies] and "constelaciones" [constellations], two heavily charged words from poets that Blanco clearly admires: Haroldo de Campos, Eugen Gomringer, and Stéphane Mallarmé. As we saw in our discussion of *Cuenta de los guías* in chapter 1, "CONSTELLATION" is one of the most important words at the end of "Un coup de dés" ["A Roll of the Dice"] and the process of creating constellations by connecting stars is a frequent metaphor for the Mexican poet as well.[78]

Medio Cine's constellation of movie stars, cinematic subject matter, and "play of distances, transitions, and intersections" invites the reader to consider the book as a *montage* since film is such a dynamic medium and, unlike in collage, the individual shots of a movie have multiple and complex temporal and spatial qualities. Gilles Deleuze notes that Eisenstein saw montage as "the whole of the film, the Idea."[79] And Eisenstein himself writes that in the editing room, "the differentiation in montage-pieces lies in their lack of existence as single units. Each piece can evoke no more than a certain association."[80] "Emotional effect . . . ," he continues, "begins only with the reconstruction of [an] event in montage fragments, each of which will summon a certain association—the sum of which will be an all-embracing complex of emotional feeling."[81] From this point of view, "Pájaros de alambre," the poem dedicated to Alfred Hitchcock, is a montage:

El sol ya recoge todas sus sombras
y el aire contiene su aliento

Esta es la noche: los pájaros de alambre
tocan las estrellas con su pico

Su forma se confunde lentamente
con el rumor de las hojas

Y el sueño les enciende las pupilas
con el sol de otro mundo[82]

["The Birds on a Wire"

The sun sweeps up its shadows
and the air holds its breath

This is night: the birds on the wire
lift their beaks to the stars

Their melody slowly intermingles
with the rustling of the leaves

And sleep lights up their eyes
with the sun of another world]

Eisenstein notes that directors should not be slaves to plot and the Blanco poem is clearly not. We do not learn much about what happens in the Hitchcock film in "Pájaros de alambre," but we do participate in its suspense by holding our breath and glimpsing something vague and sinister in the eyes of the birds. Interestingly, the text's individual camera shots employ visual and auditory cues and indulge in figurative language like personification in stanza 1 and synesthesia in stanza 3 to achieve effects that realistic film simply cannot.

The poems of *Medio Cine* are chronologically ordered by the birthdate of their directors, and the book's powerful first and last poems, "Luz silenciosa" [Silent Light] and "¿Luz silenciosa?" [Silent Light?] (analyzed in chapter 3), are paired in a relationship of circularity that opens and then gives closure to the collection. Blanco's decades of work with collage and studies of Max Ernst, Walter Benjamin, and Sergei Eisenstein transform the distinct voices and images of *Medio Cine* into one poetic montage of film, literature, visual arts, and music.

Three Spatial Strategies for *Cuenta de los guías*

1992's *Cuenta de los guías* is a bold prose poem in 260 sections of fragmented images that narrates, as Carlos Zamora has written, "la aventura y el tránsito de la voz poética por la línea fronteriza entre México y los Estados Unidos, teniendo como eje central la frontera entre las dos Californias."[83] Ulalume González de León notes that the book's first movement, "El largo camino hacia Ti" [*The Long Road to You*], is both the reflection of a real voyage as well an interior voyage or "Pilgrim's Progress,"[84] while Julio Ortega writes that "viajar quiere decir explorar, reconocer, reconstruir la casa de la palabra en la intemperie" [traveling here implies exploring, recognizing, reconstructing a house of words out in the open].[85] As these critics observe, Blanco's text privileges movement and the journey over the destinations or places visited, so despite the use of names such as San Francisco, Napa, Tijuana, or Las Cruces, readers spend most of their time detached from those, or any other, familiar *places* and, instead, grasping for meaning in the dynamic textual *spaces* of the poem.[86] In this sense, the book is what Michel de Certeau terms a "travel story" around the Mexico/U.S. border since it recounts stories and actions "marked out by the 'citation' of the places that result from them or authorize them."[87] *Cuenta de los guías* is a broad, deep, and mysterious poem that teases readers with incomplete itineraries of meaning and setting rather than providing us with a totalizing map. In this section, we suggest three spatial points of reference to help the reader navigate the poem: travel, borders, and empirical (rather than human-made) units of time.[88]

The book's opening poems convey a sense of motion through images of transition such as a staircase, a highway, a train, an airport, a tunnel, or a letter slipped mysteriously under a closed door. Symbols and signs of movement help give narrative momentum to fragmented and hermetic lines that, otherwise, would result in a choppy or static reading experience:

> Una carta pasa, delgada, por debajo de la puerta: en un lugar desconocido nos esperan, con esa paciencia confundida con la roca, que el lagarto lleva sobre sus lomos como una bendición.[89]
>
> [A letter slides, thin, from underneath the door: they await us in an unknown place, with that patience confused with stone, that the lizard bears on its loins like a blessing.]
>
> A la mañana siguiente, como cirqueros trashumantes acostumbrados a su viaje, ponemos en juego los nombres sobre el mar picado de botellas.[90]
>
> [The next morning, like traveling circus performers in the rhythm of their lives, we set out names onto an ocean strewn with bottles.]

Both in first verses and elsewhere, *Cuenta de los guías* teases the reader over and over about its settings. There are a lot of places mentioned but most are merely parts of images, or elements of the larger symbolic space. In poem 22, for example, we find a road, an ocean, and beaches but they all appear to be part of an "arquitectura interior" [interior architecture], the journey into the subconscious that parallels the book's travels along the Mexico/U.S. border. We are reminded of the line from "Mapas": "Mapas exteriores: geografía. / Mapas interiores: psicografía" ["Exterior maps: geography. / Interior maps: psychography"]:[91]

> El largo camino hacia ti mismo, entre ferias patibularias y el anuncio de tu ausencia. El dolor sigue a la duda como la carreta sigue al buey ensimismado. Aquí estuvo el diablo, con la uña negra describió su caída.
>
> Pero el mar lava por igual espíritus y playas, la noche concede el perdón del sueño: por más oscuridad hay una cama. En sus sábanas blancas el cuerpo se protege de las palabras.
>
> Una vez más la arquitectura interior nos dicta este espacio: playas abandonadas que el borracho del lunes recorre como un cómico ahíto ya de su rutina. Detrás pueden verse las olas punteadas por aves, que recuerdan la danza, la doncella, y el ojo del hombre que la observa.[92]

> [That long path to you yourself, with gallows humor and the announcement of your absence. Pain follows doubt like the wagon tails the daydreaming ox. The devil was here, and with his black fingernail spoke of the fall.
>
> But the sea cleans both spirits and beaches, and night pardons sleep: as dark as it is, there is a bed. In its white sheets a body protects itself from words.
>
> Once again the interior architecture designs this space for us: abandoned beaches that Monday's drunkard prowls like a comedian tired of his own jokes. In the distance we can see the waves punctuated with birds that remember dances, young women, and the eye of the man that watches her.]

In the final lines of *El arco y la lira* [*The Bow and the Lyre*] Octavio Paz notes that "Nuestra poesía es conciencia de la separación y tentativa por reunir lo que fue separado" [Our poetry is knowledge of separation and the attempt to unite what was separated].[93] Travel motifs are especially suited to this kind of critical poetry, and as its title implies, the long road to Tijuana parallels the long road to *satori* and the other metaphors of communion the text suggests. The privileging of movement over place is similar to what happens in meditation or talk therapy in which the process is the destination.

But travel, especially in the 1970s, is not solely about communion. Fussell writes that "an insistent leitmotif of writing between the [world] wars, for both successful and would-be escapees, is *I Hate It Here*," or what might be called a general dissatisfaction with conditions at home.[94] He also notes the influence of "pernicious fathers," weather, pollution, legal problems, and lack of food, as other reasons that incite people to leave their houses. *Cuenta de los guías* was written after repeated bohemian trips *on the road* from Mexico DF to the rough margins of Tijuana. In part, the book retells a young poet's physical and spiritual journeys and his immersion in the thought and zeitgeist of 1960s and 1970s counterculture. Clearly, and interestingly, the flight to the liminal spaces of the desert and border is also the swerve of a young poet trying to make his mark in a country dominated by one urban literary center and figures such as Paz.

In addition to the geographical reality of the Sonoran border desert, as we will examine in greater detail in chapter 3, deserts are also symbolic spaces in Blanco's work. They are spaces of displacement and nomadism; deserts are lawless, with no visible signs of history or nation. The desert is Blanco's antidote to Mexico City, with no protests, no smog, no VW Beetles, no constant reminders of civilization gone wrong. The freedoms of the desert as a space without signs influenced many artists in the 1970s, from Carlos Castaneda to the Doors. In the desert, movement is harder to map and borders are usually invisible so the traveler's focus changes and becomes more interior.

In his introduction to *Dawn of the Senses*, José Emilio Pacheco notes, "Blanco eligió desde muy joven ser un hombre de fronteras, pero no en el sentido de puertas cerradas o muros de metal sino de vasos comunicantes" [Since his earliest work Blanco chose to be a man of the borders, not in the sense of closed doors or metal walls but rather of communicating vessels].[95] The concept of the permeable borderline is indeed central to Blanco's poetry and is the second vector of attention that helps the reader position herself in the text. Some of Blanco's most interesting work on frontiers is found in his poems about geometry and quantum mechanics that zoom in on a line so aggressively they reveal the space between the individual dots that compose it. This perspective parallels that wave/particle duality since it indicates that lines are both permeable and impermeable.

The same can be said for borders, both national and otherwise. Michel de Certeau writes that borders are what define a space ("it is the partition of space that structures it"), while Marc Augé notes that borders or "frontiers" are not walls but, conversely, "thresholds" . . . and focuses of "intense ritual activity."[96] In *Cuenta de los guías*, borders are portrayed as relative and porous, like just one more of so many other human constructs. Poem 217, about the United States, displays many examples: "Un país sin nombre propio no tiene forma propia. / Un horizonte sin principio ni fin. / ¿O es que estamos unidos más allá del nombre y de la forma?" [A country without a proper name has no proper form. / A horizon without beginning or end. / Or are we perhaps united in ways beyond name or form?].[97] The final verse of this poem also comments metapoetically on borders of similarity and difference through words with strong rhymes, the conjunction "and," and the use of slashes (resembling borders) instead of line breaks: "pozos y pasos / días y guías / fechas y flechas" [wells and steps / days and guides / dates and arrows].[98] Rhyme here works visually, audibly, and lexically, a technique important enough to the poet that he chooses to both begin and end the poem with it.

Blanco's borders are often presented under erasure, as the "product of social translations, transformations, and experience" that Edward Soja calls "spatiality."[99] Fussell's understanding of the dynamics of borderlands also helps us untangle the abstract political boundaries of *Cuenta de los guías* and recall the influence of collage in Blanco's work: "Fragmenting and dividing anew and parceling-out and shifting around and repositioning—these are the actions implicit in the redrafting of frontiers. All these actions betray a concern with current space instead of time or tradition. All imply an awareness of reality as disjointed, dissociated, fractured. These actions of dividing anew and shifting provide the method of collage in painting, and in writing they provide the method we recognize as conspicuously 'modern': the method of anomalous juxtaposition."[100] Unmistakably, Blanco's critique of the appropriation of the name America "como si todo fuera suyo" [as if everything were theirs] reflects the United States' traditionally aggressive foreign policy, not just in cases such as the Mexican-American War but also in more subtle ways as well.[101] The quote from the Supertramp song "Desayuno en América" ["Breakfast in America"] furthers Blanco's commentary on the kind of cultural contact we find on borders and the cultural imperialism that will eventually bring about globalization or the victory of similarity over difference, that is, the further erosion of borders themselves. To this point, Augé notes, "The ideal, egalitarian world may come not through the abolition of frontiers, but through their recognition."[102]

Poem 246 fills out another border description in a way familiar to Blanco's readers: "Y en un abrir de ojos estoy otra vez en la línea: con un pie en un mundo y otro en otro: ¡calendarios! / La pluma en la diestra, el corazón al lado izquierdo y el centro en todas partes . . ." [In a blink of the eye I am back on that line: with one foot in this world and one in another: calendars! / My pen to the right and my heart to the left side and the center everywhere . . .].[103] In these lines, the speaker straddles a border between sleep and wakefulness and his right and left sides that create hemispheres punctuated by his heart and hand. These kinds of borders are essential to one of the central tropes of Blanco's poetry: the Taoist *tai chi* or *taijitu* symbol. The yin/yang image allows the poet to represent both contained and free space through the presence of its internal division. As we explore in chapter 4, *Cuenta de los guías*, like all the poet's work, is replete with images that encompass opposites or polarities like the horizon line between sky and water, a tree and its mirrored root systems, or empty bottles that juxtapose inside and out:

. . . Hay tantas formas de armar este rompecabezas, que cada solución inventa un problema distinto . . . y lo resuelve.

Ajedrez de la vida: blanco, negro; masculino, femenino; derecho, izquierdo. Se trata, desde luego, de toda la balanza, del juego completo . . . pero en el lado izquierdo palpita el corazón.[104]

[. . . There are so many ways to solve this puzzle that each solution creates new and different problems . . . and then solves them.

Chessboard of life: white, black; masculine, feminine; right, left. In the end, it's all about balance, the whole set . . . but on the left side beats the heart.]

Poem 250 sums up this complementary vision of borders and how they set opposites alongside each other while at the same time creating a liminal experience that would be unattainable deeper "in-country," as it were:

. . . A lo largo del alambre de púas
a la sombra del camión oxidado
al amparo de los anuncios de neón.

Hay que cruzar la línea cuantas veces sea necesario.
Observar lo que allí es verdad y lo que no.

Pasar por el intersticio entre ambos mundos:

El masculino / la femenina
el pensamiento / la sentimienta
el siempre uno / las diferencias.

La realidad es hija de los dos
y se parece mucho a los dos
pero no es ninguno de los dos.[105]

[. . . Along the barbed wire fence
in the shadow of the rusty truck
shielded by the neon signs.

You have to cross the line as many times as necessary.
Observe what is true there and what is not.

Pass through the interstice between two worlds:

Masculine / feminine
thought / emotion
oneness / difference.

Reality is the child of both
and appears similar to both
but is neither one of the two.]

Animus and anima, similarity and difference, the combination of oppositions coming together to create something dynamically interdependent is the essence of the *taijitu* or yin/yang symbol. Below are just three of the many poetic *taijitus* in *Cuenta de los guías*:

> Atanores del cuerpo, unión de obrero y obra, de aire y fuego, de agua y fuego, tierra y fuego. ¡Sopladores de vidrio, quiero un nuevo corazón![106]
>
> [Athanors of the body, the union of worker and work, of air and fire, of water and fire, earth and fire. Glass blowers, I want a new heart!]
>
> No hay diferencia entre el mar y el cielo, sólo un imán perpetuo que jala las olas, mueve las nubes, hace girar los pensamientos y rima la sangre con los huesos.[107]
>
> [There is no difference between the sea and the sky, only a perpetual magnet that pulls the waves, moves the clouds, swirls the thoughts and rhymes blood and bone.]
>
> La vida es una: en el jardín florido, en la pendiente, en el sueño tremendo, en el ruidoso restorán.
> Pero hay día y hay noche.
> Y ambos polos polemizan, y de su amor surge un sonido trascendente:
> Más allá de la batalla de los sexos; más allá de la llama purificadora;
> más allá de la tregua que pactan los contrarios; más allá de los
> procesos curativos; . . .
> Un beso entre la química orgánica y la química inorgánica.
> Un sonido que es en sí mismo mar y cielo en un sólo refrán: la vida es otra.[108]
>
> [Life is one: in the garden in flower, in things to come, in deep sleep, in a noisy restaurant.
> But there is day and night.
> And both poles cause polemics, and from their love comes a transcendent sound:
> Beyond the battle of the sexes; beyond the purifying flame; beyond the truce
> signed by rivals; beyond the curative processes; . . .
> A kiss between organic and inorganic chemistry.
> A sound that is this same sea and sky in one refrain: life is something else.]

The use of the yin/yang symbol and rhyme we see in these verses reaches its climax in the last poem of the book, which we will examine in chapters 3 and 4. As a sign in rotation, the *taijitu* embodies motion and the present moment and its desire to capture the form of time takes another expression in *Cuenta de los guías* as well.

There is an important syntactical and metaphorical crystallization beginning midway through part 2 of the book that solidifies in parts 4 and 5. We see this stylistic change in poetic utterances that are longer and include more traditional syntax rather than just sprayed bursts of partial images. Notice how *el amor* [love] and *el viento* [wind], the subjects of these first lines of poem 209, the first of part 5, continue through the commas and into subsequent clauses:

> Sólo el amor hace tierra, sólo el amor camina sobre el agua, sólo el amor se oculta en el fuego.
>
> Y un viento redondea la tierra, curva el agua y aviva el fuego. Y algo innombrable mueve al viento. Y esto innombrable cambia lo que nosotros llamamos "las condiciones."[109]

> [Only love makes the earth, only love walks on water, only love hides in the fire.
>
> And a wind encircles the earth, curves along the water and kindles the fire. And something unnamable moves the wind. And this unnamable force changes what we call "conditions."]

"Quinto Viento" [Fifth Wind], the fifth section, is particularly self-referential and also characterized by increased experimentation with spatial arrangement of verses such those of poem 239:

> Hay que ponerle sitio a la ciudad viendo de frente.
> Pues en verdad el cantar es algo distinto:
>
> Un espacio virginal en la palabra.
>   Una nota intacta en cada instante.
>   Un paisaje nuevo en cada pupila.
>
> Un vuelo por nada
>   un encaje en Dios
>   un desatino controlado.[110]

> [We must take control of the city head-on.
> But in truth the song is something different:
>
> A virginial space in the word.
>   An intact note in each instant.
>   A new landscape in every eye.
>
> An aimless flight
>   a God's design
>   a controlled frenzy.]

After reading four sections of paragraph-style prose poems, the change in verse form in "Quinto Viento" piques our awareness to visual forms. Carlos Zamora has called this a triumph of poetry over prose.[111] As we see in poem 211, the change in form helps set up the revelation of the metastructure or "metaperspectiva" of *Cuenta de los guías* in poem 230:

> Todo confluye: los hechos se ordenan según las leyes de la metaperspectiva. Encuentros fortuitos que señalan la dirección de la promesa.
> Un viento de pinos se aleja, y el viento seco de los desiertos me llama.
> Pregunto la hora una y otra vez . . . una estrategia absurda para abreviar el tiempo.
> Confío en mi destino personal tanto como en mi estrella gemela.[112]

> [Everything comes together: the facts are ordered according to the laws of metaperspective. Chance encounters signal the direction of promise.
> A pine wind blows away, and the dry desert wind calls me.
> I ask what time it is over and over again . . . an absurd strategy to kill time.
> I confide in my personal destiny as much as in my twin star.]

The third and final spatial strategy we will highlight from *Cuenta de los guías*, one that is organic to life in the desert, is the representation of units of time with empirical images like days rather than hours, or years rather than months. Natural phenomena such as sunset, dawn, or the return of budding leaves tell us when a day or a year has come and gone, but hours and weeks are more abstract since they are subunits, simply fractions of something larger and more empirical.[113] Verses like the following achieve this effect as nature and time are in perfect, circular harmony: "Se cierra el círculo de la noche sobre el pozo ingente. La luciérnaga gira, la palomilla gira, las estrellas giran en sus cápsulas de hielo y fuego. Al sol nadie le gana" [The circle of the night closes above the huge well. The firefly spins, the moth spins, the stars in their capsules of ice and fire spin. But nobody beats the sun].[114]

Remembering Augé's point that thresholds are focuses of "intense ritual activity,"[115] we discover in poem 230 that the metaforms of *Cuenta de los guías* are the Aztec and Mayan calendars (embedded in the title as "cuenta de los guías/días" [*Account of the guides/days*]). As in Paz's *Piedra de sol* [*Sunstone*], we see the numbers that structure the book's five sections:

> Estoy viendo los números: 5 ciclos de 52 unidades. Estoy viendo cómo estos números se multiplican, se dividen, se suman y se restan: 5×4×13=260. El período de gestación de un ser humano.

> Al mismo tiempo estoy viendo el deseo de un mándala expresarse en un tablero de ajedrez: 4×4×4=64.

> Ajedrez y Tzolkin, I Ching y Tonalamatl, cuadrivio de cuadrantes más una flecha cardinal: $(64+1)\times4=260$.
>
> Estoy viendo lo mismo en las pinturas de arena de los Navajos que en La constelación de la rosa: $260/5=52$.
>
> 4 pilares y 4 soles, 4 direcciones y 4 partidas de ajedrez, más la unidad del Quinto Viento: $4\times4\times4\times4+4=260$.[116]
>
> [I see the numbers: 5 cycles of 52 units. I see how these numbers are multiplied, divided, added up, and subtracted: $5\times4\times13=260$. The period of gestation for a human being.
>
> At the same time I see the desire of a mandala to express itself in a chessboard: $4\times4\times4=64$.
>
> Chess and *Tzolkin*, I Ching and *Tonalamatl*, quadrivium of quadrants and a guiding arrow: $(64+1)\times4=260$.
>
> I see the same in the sand paintings of the Navajos as in the constellation of the rose: $260/5=52$.
>
> 4 pillars and 4 suns, 4 directions and 4 chess matches, plus the unity of the Fifth Wind: $4\times4\times4\times4+4=260$.]

Thus we see how the 260-day Mayan *tzolkin* and Aztec *tonalpohualli* underlie the form of *Cuenta de los guías* with its five sections of fifty-two poems, each containing four subcycles of thirteen poems, for a total of 260 entries. Despite the strength of this metastructure, the book embraces rather than rejects interpretation from a multitude of traditions. The pre-Columbian ritual calendars are here and acknowledged but do not dominate. Instead the book invites us to meditate on the shared symmetries and harmonies between patterns from Christian, Vedic, Buddhist, Native American, and other religious traditions.

The irony that the reader of *Cuenta de los guías* needs the help of a guide is not lost on any that attempt to enter it. Rather than abandoning all hope, if we turn our attention to expressions of movement, travel, borders, and natural manifestations of time, it is possible to find footholds, as it were, in the slippery spaces and places of the text.

CHAPTER 3

Sound

Pink Floyd's progressive rock concept album *The Dark Side of the Moon* begins with "Speak to Me," a minute-long sonic buildup in which a faint heartbeat grows in volume, swirls together with sampled motifs and voices from other songs, and then climaxes in the slow, airy groove of the next track, "Breathe." Similarly, Alberto Blanco's essay "La música" from *La poesía y el presente* [*Poetry and the Present*] also relies on a heartbeat in its introduction: "recordando que viajé durante dos corazones por su vientre" [remembering I traveled during two hearts through her womb].[1] The image is not Blanco's but rather a quote from César Vallejo's poem "El buen sentido" ["Good Sense"]. The fact that a Peruvian poet, an English rock band, and a Mexican writer all see the womb as the place where art begins is no coincidence since the muffled thump of a mother's heart is everyone's very first contact with music. In his essay, Blanco expresses his admiration for how Vallejo writes "*durante* dos corazones," ("during" or "throughout two hearts") using a preposition of time rather than space to characterize the heart's song. In describing this earliest music, Blanco employs a small alliteration that pays tribute to Vallejo: "el son del corazón" [the song of the heart].[2]

Just as all of us are aware of music from our earliest moments, Alberto Blanco's artistic project began in the revolutionary Mexican countercultural movement known as La Onda.[3] The axis of this cultural moment for Blanco, as for many across the world, was the Beatles' 1966 album *Revolver*; "todo gira alrededor de ese disco," he says of its international importance.[4] As in France, Chile, the United States, and elsewhere, music was a key element to the youth movements of the 1960s that came to a head in the streets of Paris, Prague, and Mexico's *Plaza de las Tres Culturas*.[5] At the time of the massacre of student protesters in 1968, Blanco was seventeen years old. The next year, as Mexico's *xipiteca* culture became more visible, he became the singer in the psychedelic rock band La Comuna. The band's live shows from 1970 to 1975 mixed spoken word poetry with music and performance art in the style of the "happenings" of the late 1950s and 1960s. In 1971, La Comuna recorded an album with Mexico's Peerless Records label, one the company eventually destroyed after a fierce battle of artistic and ideological differences. Only a few copies of the four songs of a 45 survive.

After La Comuna's eventual breakup, Blanco learned to play piano and formed the more jazz-focused band Las Plumas Atómicas, who started playing gigs in Mexico City in the mid-1980s. The semiautobiographical prose poem "Había una vez . . ." ["Once upon a time . . ."] discusses this transition from rock lyricist and singer to self-taught rock/jazz pianist during a time when "por increíble que parezca, el rock estaba prohibido en el país" [as hard as it seems to believe, rock music was prohibited in the country].[6] Through the 1970s and 1980s, Blanco played publicly with different iterations of his bands and his innate knowledge of music infuses every aspect of his poetry. As Paz notes in *El arco y la lira* [*The Bow and the Lyre*], the origins of poetry and song are deeply intertwined in the Western tradition and "el son del corazón" is just one of the countless etymological connections between the songs, verses, and ballads of music and poetry.

Music in its most basic form is a "sequence of sounds ordered in time" with rhythm (what Sergei Eisenstein called "phases of tension"), repetition, harmony, and, in the case of lyrics, meaning.[7] Like the visual images in a collage, sounds and songs are defined by the silences that surround them. Since music, especially jazz, is governed by mathematics, it should come as no surprise that three of the musicians in La Comuna and Las Plumas Atómicas were scientists (Blanco, chemistry; Gustavo Martínez-Mekler, physics; Alberto Darszon, biochemistry). Part of Blanco's attraction to music is found in its movement, its abstraction, the unique quality of its sensorial dimension, and as is true in all of his poetic world, music is part of a polarity, here balanced by silence. This passage from the very end of the essay *El canto y el vuelo* [*Song and Flight*] clearly shows that it is hard to overstate the importance of music for understanding Blanco's poetics:[8]

> Escribir buenos versos con un cierto sentido musical no basta. Porque la música es estructura, patrones rítmicos, arquitectura. Es eso y mucho más. Y sin un profundo sentido de la música es punto menos que imposible darle forma, estructura y arquitectura a un poema; sobre todo si el poema es largo. Pero, todavía más importante: sin la música resulta imposible estructurar una serie de poemas; mucho menos aún un libro de poemas . . . y de la posibilidad de construir una arquitectura que contemple una serie de libros—o todos los libros que ha escrito un poeta–, es decir, *una obra*, mejor ni hablar. La música es, en este sentido, y en tanto forma, número, geometría y matemáticas sensibles al oído, la mejor herramienta para emprender estas tareas. Arte de esculpir tiempo, como la poesía (o como Tarkovsky entendió siempre el cine), la música es, sin lugar a dudas, la mejor aliada de la poesía.[9]

> [Writing good verses with a certain musical sense is not enough. Because music is structure, rhythmic patterns, architecture. It's that and much more. And without a deep musical sensibility it's basically impossible to give form, structure and architecture to a poem; especially a long poem. But, even more importantly: without music it's impossible to structure a series of poems, much less a book of poems . . . as for constructing the architecture for a series of books—or all the books a poet has written—that is to say, *an oeuvre*? No way! Music is, in this sense, like form, number, geometry and math, the best tool to undertake these tasks. The art of sculpting time, like poetry (or as Tarkovsky believed of film), music is, without a doubt, poetry's strongest ally.]

Interestingly, the enigmatic form of the prose poem is the vehicle for "Había una vez" the text about Blanco's bands. Besides being narrative, this poem also stands out by being autobiographical in a way Blanco's work rarely is. Even though it is a prose poem, "Había una vez . . ." contains elements of music, rhythm, meter, cadence, tone, all the elements of what was once termed lyric poetry:

> Al paso del tiempo [el poeta] decidió formar un nuevo grupo. Los años no habían pasado en vano, así que todos eran mejores músicos, y ya no tocaban sólo rock, sino que osaban incursionar en el jazz y aun en la música contemporánea. Sin embargo, el poeta, sólo escuchaba rock y música clásica, música clásica y rock.[10]

> [As time went by [the poet] decided to form a new group. The years had not passed in vain, and they had all become better musicians, and now not only played rock, but also made brief incursions into jazz and even contemporary music. Nonetheless, the poet only listened to rock and classical music, classical music and rock.]

This stanza is characterized by its short, highly punctuated utterances that move the narrative along, its use of the third person instead of the first for the autobiographical poetic voice, and the repetition in its last verse. Its change in rhythm helps break the cadence of the lines and call attention to the subject's true musical obsession: listening.

This chapter focuses on different aspects and variations of *melopeia* in Blanco's work, that is, the different ways in which the poet "charges" his verses "over and above their plain meaning, with some musical property, which directs the bearing or trend of that meaning."[11] Following Eric Prieto's warning, we do not engage in extended, direct comparison of poems with specific musical forms but rather examine the ways in which Blanco portrays music's affinities to poetry, the different types of musicality in his verses, and, finally, how sound and silence function as a main polarity in his work.[12]

Sister Arts and Synesthesia

In response to Benoît Santini's interview question "¿le parece que poesía, música y también arte visual se complementan?" [do you think that poetry, music and also visual arts complement each other?], Chilean poet Raúl Zurita notes, "Las barreras que separan la creación son barreras en un 90% artificiales. Ahora, tal vez finalmente, la materia de la poesía sea la palabra y el silencio. Música y poema no son la misma cosa, pero el impulso que los genera, el vértigo que hace que alguien componga y que alguien escriba es el mismo" [the barriers that separate creation are 90 percent artificial. Now, perhaps finally, the raw material of poetry is words and silence. Music and poem are not the same thing, but the impulse that creates then, the vertigo that makes someone compose and someone write is the same].[13] More than a century earlier, Mallarmé thought along these lines in *La musique et les lettres* [*Music and Literature*] with his concept of "l'Idée"—"the internalized metaphorical voice" that music and poetry share as a similar type of thought rather than performance.[14] Eric Prieto writes that "the modern Western distinction between music and poetic language is not universally recognized."[15] The ancient Greeks, for example, grouped music, poetry, and dance together as "*mousike*."[16] Furthermore, George Steiner notes that "the interpenetration of poetry and music is so close that their origin is indivisible and usually rooted in a common myth."[17] Even though La Comuna's idealistic "happenings" eventually faded away, interartistic expression remains fundamental to Alberto Blanco's artistic project, with music being a main thread in the synesthetic weave of his collages, drawings, paintings, poems, and essays.

Returning for a moment to "Había una vez" we see one way in which jazz and poetry are similar modes of inquiry for the young musician:

> Poco a poco comprendió que el jazz no era otra modalidad de la música que conocía, sino que se trataba de algo más radical. Descubrió que el jazz (y sus antecedentes: el *blues*, el *gospel*, el *ragtime*, el *Dixieland*), era, ni más ni menos, la otra forma de hacer música. Una música que nada—o casi nada—tenía que ver con la tradición de la música europea, desde Bach hasta los Beatles, desde Pergolesi hasta Pink Floyd.[18]
>
> [Slowly he came to understand that jazz was not simply just another modality of music that he knew, but rather something more radical. He discovered that jazz (and its antecedents: blues, gospel, ragtime, Dixieland), was, nothing less than other ways of making music. Music that had nothing—or almost nothing—to do with the tradition of European music, from Bach to the Beatles, from Pergolesi to Pink Floyd.]

In interviews and essays, Blanco often claims that poetry might not really even be a "literary" genre, but rather "el otro lado del lenguaje" [language's other side].[19] These lines from the last essay of the trilogy of poetics *El canto y el vuelo* flesh out a definition of what happens on the dark side of language:

> *El canto y el vuelo*, más que una reflexión sobre la poesía tal cual (sea lo que sea que esto signifique) es un estudio serio y apasionado en torno a *las relaciones* entre la poesía y muchas otras artes, actividades y tópicos de nuestra vida. Se trata, pues, más que de plantear una reflexión sobre la poesía como una "esencia," de observar la poesía como *una red de relaciones*; más que pensar en la poesía como si ésta fuera un objeto dado, de comprenderla como un proceso. La poesía como verbo, no como un sustantivo.[20]

> [*Song and Flight*, more than just being a reflection on poetry itself (whatever that may mean) is a serious and impassioned study about *the relationships* between poetry and many other arts, activities and topics in our lives. More than proposing a reflection about poetry as an "essence," it is about observing poetry as a *network of relationships*; more than thinking about poetry as if it were an object, it is about understanding poetry as a process. Poetry as a verb, not as a noun.]

We see this attitude toward poetry explicitly at work in a text like "Phil Bragar pinta un retrato" ["Phil Bragar Paints a Portrait"]. This prose poem about the American/Mexican sculptor and painter (1925–2017) concludes: "Es muy simple: se trata de escuchar con las manos, de escuchar con los ojos, de escuchar atentamente la voz del maestro que todos llevamos dentro" [It's quite simple: it's about listening with your hands, listening with your eyes, listening to the voice of the teacher we all carry within].[21] Here we see many important aspects of Blanco's poetics. First is the conversational tone of "Es muy simple" to ironically introduce a very complex subject. That inviting tone is reflected as well in the *nosotros* that includes the readers in this creative world since it is not just the painter who hears and speaks with the voice of the teacher—it is all of us. Art will inspire us if we are willing to let it in.

Poetry encourages and embraces synesthetic leaps—this is how Vallejo could travel "during" two hearts, or how senses such as seeing or touching can be called listening when experienced through "el otro lado del lenguaje" [the other side of language]. Inspiration, we read in "Phil Bragar pinta un retrato" ["Phil Bragar Paints a Portrait"], comes from both inside and out: "[Phil] Mira, observa, acecha . . . deja que el cuadro le hable. Respeta sus ideas (las de la pintura, no las suyas). Sabe" [[Phil] Watches, observes, lies in wait . . . lets the picture talk to him.[22] He respects its ideas (the picture's, not his own). He knows]. Art does not happen without the appreciating, watching, reading, or listening that corresponds to the painting, sculpting, writing, or singing. This web of complementary interartistic connections is similar to ideas in Baudelaire's synesthetic "Correspondances." As in the classic poem from *Les Fleurs du mal* [*The Flowers of Evil*], in poetry, subjectivity is inverted for Blanco (the art object speaks to the artist) and the edges between the senses blur away. Only in poetry can there be "parfums frais comme de chairs d'enfants" [perfumes as cool as the skin of infants] or hands that can listen to an image.

In another nod to a masterpiece of French poetry, Rimbaud's "Voyelles" ["Vowels"], Blanco acknowledges once again the subjective nature of intuitive connections:

> "Vocales"
> A roja, E negra, I amarilla, U azul, O blanca.
> ¿Por qué no he de hacer mis propias asociaciones
> si la clave de las correspondencias se ha perdido
> (si es que alguna vez de veras existió semejante clave)
> y no queda sino la superstición de un simbolismo hueco?[23]
>
> ["Vowels"
> Red A, black E, yellow I, blue U, white O.
> Why shouldn't I create my own associations
> if the key to these correspondences has been lost
> (assuming there ever was such a key in the first place)
> and nothing is left but the superstition of a hollow symbolism?]

"Vocales" ["Vowels"] touches on the same literary question that concerns Marjorie Perloff in this passage about John Cage: "When, in other words, the poetry of indeterminacy, of anti-symbolism, has reached its outer limit, it comes back once more to such 'basic' literary elements as the hypnotic sound pattern, the chant, the narrative account, the conceptual scheme."[24] As we shall see, many of Blanco's music poems experiment with postsymbolic techniques through prose poetry and rhythmic patterns of sound.

"Cuando la tierra sueña" ["When Earth Dreams"], the prose poem we touched on in chapter 1, features a tight weave of music, poetry, sculpture, and essay that reminds us of Zurita's observation that the differences between artistic genres are 90 percent arbitrary. This long, powerful text about Mexican sculptor Gustavo Pérez (1950–) polishes and condenses its economy of expression as it unfolds in eighteen stanzas that slowly whittle down from thirteen long lines to one single word.

We will examine more of "Cuando la tierra sueña" later in this chapter, as part of our discussion of silence, but for now let's notice the fluidity with which Blanco's speaker moves between art forms:

> *"Cuando la tierra sueña"*
>
> Mallarmé le confesó en una caminata nocturna al joven Valéry que quería escribir un poema con la potencia del cielo estrellado. Gustavo Pérez quiere

construir con las manos una constelación de tierra con la potencia de un poema. ¿Una coincidencia? Yo creo que se trata más bien de desmesuradas ambiciones artísticas que pueden llegar a convertirse en un anhelo. Una aspiración sin ambición. Una inspiración. Como un punto que, aun estando fuera de la hoja de papel, dicta la perspectiva de un dibujo. O como la serie de puntos que gobiernan, desde más allá de los límites de una superficie blanca, la forma de un paisaje. Una verdadera constelación. Como dice Octavio Paz en el capítulo titulado "El revés del dibujo," de su bello ensayo *Los hijos del limo*: "La palabra constelación evoca inmediatamente la idea de música y la de música con sus múltiples asociaciones, del acorde erótico de los cuerpos al acuerdo político entre los hombres, suscita el nombre de Mallarmé. Estamos en el centro de la analogía." Estamos en la semilla de la visión.

En una caminata nocturna al borde de la prolija selva que rodea su taller en Zoncuantla, Gustavo Pérez me confesó que, así como nunca ha tenido ambiciones políticas, ni de poder o de dinero, se halla poseído por una desmesurada ambición artística. Yo le respondí que, tal vez, más que de una ambición se trataba de un anhelo. De una aspiración sin ambición. Una verdadera inspiración. Como ese punto que, aun estando fuera de su cuaderno, gobierna la perspectiva de algunos de sus dibujos (o como una serie de puntos, si es que la perspectiva admite distintos puntos de fuga). Un paisaje que es, a la vez, una constelación de notas. Como si pudiéramos escuchar el otro lado de la noche. O mejor aún: como si lográramos ver el revés del dibujo. Al ritmo de la música de jazz que inunda esta tierra y la penetra con los acordes eróticos y sostenidos de la lluvia, vamos hacia el centro de la analogía en busca de la semilla de la visión.[25]

["When Earth Dreams"

Mallarmé confessed, on a night walk with a young Valery, that he wanted to write a poem with the power of the starry sky. Gustavo Pérez wants to construct with his hands a constellation of earth with the power of a poem. Coincidence? I think it's more about boundless artistic ambition that can become a longing. An aspiration without ambition. An inspiration. Like that point that, even though it lies beyond the sheet of paper, dictates the perspective of a drawing. Or like the series of points that govern, from beyond the limits of a white surface, the form of a landscape. A true constellation. Like Octavio Paz says in the chapter called "The Pattern Reversed," from his beautiful essay *Children of the Mire:* "The word constellation immediately evokes the idea of music and music with its multiple associations, from the erotic chord of bodies, to political accords between people, as well as the name of Mallarmé. We are in the center of the analogy." We are in the seed of vision.

On a night walk beside the thick jungle that surrounds his studio in Zoncuantla, Gustavo Pérez confessed to me that although he has never had political ambitions, power or money, he has found himself possessed by an boundless artistic ambition. I answered that, perhaps, more than ambition it could be called a longing. An aspiration without ambition. A true inspiration. Like that point that, even though it lies beyond his notebook, governs the perspective of many of his drawings (or like a series of points, if the perspective admits different vanishing points). A landscape that is, at the same time, a constellation of notes. As if we could listen to the other side of the night. Or, better yet, as if we could see the other side of the drawing. By the jazz rhythms that flood this land and penetrate it with erotic and sustained chords of the rain, we are going toward the center of the analogy in search of the seed of vision.]

Not only does the poem begin with a rhythm (a nocturnal walk), it relies on the repetition of a series of jazz strategies to build and sustain its pace and tempo. Some of these images transform throughout the poem: the "caminata" [walk] that appears in the first few verses of each strophe becomes a "camino" [path] and eventually falls away much like the vanishing points and other constellations that guide a drawing from outside the edges of the canvas or page. The "yo" [I] from the first stanza reappears like a jazz motif in the second strophe just as the words *aspiración*, *ambición*, and *inspiración* [aspiration, ambition, inspiration] play off each other's sound as part of a progression. Such word play continues with *punto de fuga* [vanishing point or fugue] and the retooling of Paz's words from *Los hijos del limo*: "'Estamos en el centro de la analogía.' Estamos en la semilla de la visión" ["We are in the center of the analogy." We are in the seed of vision], which becomes "vamos hacia el centro de la analogía en busca de la semilla de la visión" [we are heading toward the center of the analogy in search of the seed of vision]. It's a riff and variation, both on Paz and on poems like "Phil Bragar pinta un retrato" and its voice of the teacher we all carry within.

The interplay of part and whole is also key to these two stanzas. In visual terms, Blanco reminds us how lines are made of individual points in the same way waves of light are also composed of individual particles. Other variations on this idea in the poem are its constellations (figures made of stars) and "*acordes*" or musical chords. A major chord, such as a C major, is composed of a triad of individual notes: C, E, and G (the root, third, and fifth notes of the C major scale). As in collage or Baudelaire's "Correspondances," "Cuando la tierra sueña" focuses on the "red de relaciones" [web of relationships] between part and whole, between note and chord or text and context. It finds synesthetic, interartistic kinship in poetry, music, and sculpture and calls our attention to the space between and behind works of art ("el otro lado de la noche" [the other side of the night], "el revés del dibujo" [the back side of the drawing]) in ways that only poetry or jazz can.[26]

Not just white light but all forms of waves fascinate Blanco and "Otro mar más negro" ["Another Blacker Sea"] is one of four poems that consider the ocean from different perspectives and colors (black, red, blue, and green). While all four of the texts emphasize different senses, this one focuses on waves, not only in the water but also waves of sound and light, in a kind of "scientific synesthesia":

"Otro mar más negro"

¿Qué sería la tierra sin el mar?
¿Qué sería la tierra sin la muerte?
Los cables de la luz están cantando
y la línea de espuma es sólo un eco.

¿Qué sería la noche sin el día?
¿Qué sería la noche sin el sueño?
Nada más un oleaje sin sonido,
nada más el vacío de una sombra.

Así aparece lo que recordamos
y así se pierde lo que conocemos:
con los ojos abiertos, el espacio;
con los ojos cerrados, la canción.[27]

[What would the earth be without the sea?
What would the earth be without death?
The fiber optic cables are singing
and the line of foam is only an echo.

What would night be without day?
What would night be without sleep?
Nothing but a silent storm surge,
nothing but the hollow of a shadow.

This is how our memories appear
and this is how we lose what we know:
with eyes opened, space;
with eyes closed, song.]

The first stanza's questions—What is the relationship of an image to its surface? What contains an image? What are our limits?—are similar to those found in the previous poem or in collage. The next two verses are also about connections—high-tension wires sing with waves of electricity and patterns of movement while the ever-shifting trails of foam on a shoreline form echoes of an ocean's waves. The second stanza focuses on negative questions and answers——night without day or dreams is silent, empty, dark. By the third stanza, even though we are in the pattern of the poem's logic, the interplay of positive and negative, of sight and sound is dizzying. Sound and light are poles in the poem that spin in harmony with their complements (silence, darkness) to create our experience in a kaleidoscopic fashion. A large part of the poem's difficulty is related to the breaking of waves, whether they are waves of light through shadow or soundwaves broken by silence. As Leonard Shlain notes, "Although radio waves are at the far end of the electromagnetic spectrum and are invisible, they are a form of light."[28]

Like the performance art happenings that sparked his imagination as a teenager, Blanco's synesthetic poetry crosses artistic borders without hesitation and invites his readers to also look for the depth and unique dimensions of fullness that can come about only through relationships of complementarity.

Tempo, Rhythm, and Rhyme

One of Blanco's many strengths as a poet is the broad range of meters and rhythms in his verses. In fact, the breadth of different sounds in his work nearly equals the diversity of subjects and visual forms he explores. Blanco is just as comfortable with stanzas of two to five syllables as he is with verses of medium length or the kind of long, prosaic lines we saw earlier in this chapter. This experimentation is so successful because the poet listens to his work with a musician's ear and is sensitive to factors like compression, speed, and momentum. His background as a visual artist makes him especially observant of spacing and how line breaks affect the visual impact of a text while a life spent studying and translating poetry has taught him countless traditional forms and meters, dozens of which he practices in each volume of the trilogy. As we will see, the poet is especially skilled at crafting melodious lines with complex tropes and innovative rhyme schemes. In addition, Blanco dedicates many more poems to music and musicians than we are able to explore here.

A common temporal association in Blanco's poems about music is how songs can trigger memories. "Dura como el agua" ["Hard Like Water"], from the early book *Giros de faros* [*Circling Beacons*], uses wordplay, synesthesia ("la escala de sombras" [a scale of shadows]), and a visual form to explore how a sad song cuts dynamically through time. Even though it evaporates like water or incense, music drags the past into the present and even the future: "¿Cómo podré olvidarte si la música persiste?" [How will I be able to forget you if the music still lingers?].[29]

Music in the more recent "Pieza de la segunda visión" ["Second Sight Song"] has a similar function: "Todo ha sucedido ya / esta pieza la conozco / pues la he escuchado en otro sueño" [Everything has happened already / I know this tune / I've heard it in another dream].[30] Here, the price of entering this world is steep: "'La entrada cuesta la razón' / dicen—/ pero el precio es más alto / El precio de entrada es la segunda visión" [Reason is the price of entry / they say / but the real price is even higher / The price of entry is second sight].[31] Just as with music, the gift of supernatural sight is a double edged sword that causes the return of the painful past.

Not all music is painful, of course, as in "Otra canción" [Another Song]:

Mientras
oigo una
canción

el reloj
al oído
me dice

(tic tac)
medita
(tic tac)

me dicta

(tic tac)

otra canción[32]

[While
I listen to
a song

the clock
I hear
tells me

(tick tock)

meditates

(tick tock)

dictates

(tick tock)

another song]

Like a small house that relies on an unseen yet complex foundation and frame, "Otra canción," like many Blanco poems, is deceptively simple. In part, the guise of simplicity is created by the short lines and familiar first-person speaker. As in many of his narrative music poems, this one has characters (a speaker and a watch) and at least three simultaneous timeframes: the speaker's time, the song he is listening to, and the other song, created by the watch. Visually, the use of vertical rather than horizonal interruptions is intriguing and makes us ask ourselves if perhaps horizontal breaks would have been too aggressive and less musical here. The poem's music relies on a rhythm built of repetition of the sounds "me di . . ." and "(tic tac)" and variation ("me dice / medita / me dicta" [tells me / meditates / dictates to me]). These variants reveal an unfolding drama of subjectivity in which the watch changes from merely speaking, to reflecting, to asserting its music. Finally, there is yet one more character in this text, an *hacedor* listed in the appendix, the American rock band Chicago, well known for their top-ten hit song from 1970 "Does Anybody Really Know What Time It Is?"

In the poems about Phil Bragar and Gustavo Pérez we saw how a work of art becomes activated as it is being made and, as part of this process, begins to communicate with its supposed creator. This technique is clearly a central part of Blanco's poetics, so a statement about language and rhythm such as the following should come as no surprise: "el poeta encanta al lenguaje por medio del ritmo; pero, con la misma justicia poética se podría decir que el lenguaje encanta al poeta por medio del ritmo" [the poet charms language through rhythm; but, by the same poetic justice we could say that language charms the poet through rhythm].[33] This quote appears in the essay "La música" to describe the effects of puns ("calambures") in poetry. The conversational tone of Blanco's poems lends itself to wordplay, and his texts are replete with combinations of similar sounding words and phrases that use their rhythm to cast a spell, as it were, over the reader. A basic example that echoes both the sound and sense of the Buddhist koans is "La poesía" ["Poetry"] from *Poemas traídos del sueño* [*Poems from Dreams*]:

La poesía es un camino
que tiene corazón
porque el corazón
es un camino
que tiene poesía

(28 de mayo de 1996, El Paso, Texas)[34]

[Poetry is a path
with heart
because the heart
is a path
with poetry]

(May 28, 1996, El Paso, Texas)

"Flor y fruto" ["Flower and Fruit"], another of the *Poemas traídos del sueño,* takes the familiar cadence and logic of "La poesía" ["Poetry"] (A = B + C because C = B + A) a few steps farther by using a number of different rhythmic combinations:

"Flor y fruto"

El deseo
es la flor del aburrimiento

El aburrimiento
es el fruto del deseo

A más juego
más fuego

A menos otros
menos nosotros

(Mayo de 1993, Cuernavaca)[35]

["Flower and Fruit"

Desire
is the flower of boredom

Boredom
is the fruit of desire

The more there is
the hotter it gets

At least for others
other than us

(May 1993, Cuernavaca)]

The phrasing of the first and third verses creates the expectation that the fourth line might tell us that boredom is the flower of desire, but instead of repeating the pattern of the first stanza, the second stanza circles back to the poem's title. That surprise, combined with the visual difference in line length, contributes to the change of pace (and two sonic puns) with which the poem concludes. The comparison of desire and boredom is more than just for auditory effect, it is part of the poet's constant mathematical play with polarities. A is to B, as B is to A; A is to B and C, as C is to D and A, etc. Thus, "Flor y fruto" is what T. S. Eliot called a "musical poem" since it "uses pattern to superimpose a supplementary layer of meaning over whatever direct, literal meanings the words may have."[36]

So what can we make of this kind of musically informed writing? Clearly it is part of the magical correspondences of language, the kind of experience we can only have through the “red de relaciones” [web of relationships] of true poetry. From the start, Blanco knew that music was fundamental to his way of writing poems, of listening to his language. George Steiner notes that poets, “‘masters of language,’ acknowledge that music *is* the deeper, more numinous code, that language, when truly apprehended, aspires to the condition of music and is brought, by the genius of the poet, to the threshold of that condition.”[37] Sometimes, such musical word play is both playful as well as meaningful:

“Teoría del eco”

¿Qué quedaría de este río sin el agua?
Sólo el lecho.

¿Qué quedaría de esta cama sin amantes?
Sólo el lecho.

¿Qué quedaría de la historia sin el arte?
Sólo el hecho.

¿Qué quedaría del helecho sin las haches?
Sólo el eco . . .[38]

[“Echo Theory”

What is left of this river without its water?
Only its bed.

What would be left of this bed without lovers?
Only the bed.

What would be left of history without art?
Only facts.

What would be left of *helecho* without *hel*?
Only *echo* . . .]

In poetry, the sound of words reveal important thematic moments. Blanco values poetic music so highly that he uses it to punctuate the ending of *Cuenta de los guías*, a landmark moment in his career. Wordplay and rhyme have the final word in this, the last of the book’s 260 stanzas:

Sentí dos destinos   Sentidos distintos
Uno que va más allá del patrimonio y el matrimonio de los opuestos
uno que va del sueño al cuerpo, de la revelación a la revolución
uno que se puede cifrar y transmitir, medir y descifrar
uno que va de la pura diversión a la convergencia
uno que cuenta y uno que canta.
El sueño es uno.[39]

[I felt two destinies   Two distinct feelings
  One that goes beyond the patrimony and matrimony of opposites
    one that goes from sleep to the body, from revelation to revolution
      one that can be encoded and transmited, measured and deciphered
        one that goes from pure diversion to convergence
          one that tells and one that sings
            The dream is one.]

The final stanza of *Cuenta de los guías* is worthy of the dramatic position it holds in this poetic world. Here we see many familiar aspects of Alberto Blanco's poetics: puns, the rhythm made by repeating "uno que" [one that], the division and union of polarities in long, hinged lines, a visual pattern to add momentum to the finale, and the final rhyme that describes two of the main properties of poems: revealing both what is known with *contar* [telling] and what is not, with *cantar* [singing].

Blanco's experimentation with the sonic and musical possibilities of words does not stop in the 1990s with *Cuenta de los guías*. On the contrary, it remains a constant through his most recent work. Of this kind of poetry, Haroldo de Campos reminds us that words are always in charge and that the syllables of the words are what suggest ideas to a poet (283).[40] We find this technique in Blanco in texts like "La vincapervinca" ["The Periwinkle"]. Here, the unusual flow of the flower's name dictates the length of the lines:

"La vincapervinca"

Hierba doncella,
lazo de vida,
dame la mano
para seguir

Dando la pauta,
vincapervinca:
dos corazones
para un latir.

Vínculo y eco
de otro poema:
enredadera
del buen morir.

Corriente alterna,
sístole y diástole,
ahora o nunca
hay que vivir.[41]

["The Periwinkle"

Maiden grass,
bonds of life,
give me a hand
to carry on

Following your pattern,
periwinkle:
two hearts
in one beat.

Bond and echo
of another poem:
creeping vine
of the good death.

Alternating current,
systole and diastole,
now or never
we must live]

Clearly, these experiments with the musical word "vincapervinca" unearth more than just an ode expressed in five syllable verses. Studying the visual pattern ("la pauta") of the word gave the poet the image of two hearts (*vinca* + *per* + *vinca*) tied together (with a rhyming "vínculo") that create one heartbeat. A heartbeat, of course, is really the combination of the systole and diastole, fired by the electricity that keeps us all alive. The heartbeat, the rhythm of life, is a common metaphor for poetry in Blanco's world, as are the other poles in the poem like life and death, and now and never. None of this would have been uncovered without the poet's attention to the rhythmic possibilities of a simple flower's name.

"Cuaderno de viaje" ["Travel Notebook"] provides us one final example of a poem that uses puns, internal rhyme, repetition, and tropes such as *antimetabole* to paint a "paisaje en el oído" [soundscape]:[42]

Viajan los rostros
y viajan los gestos
sin más equipaje
que sus inclinaciones

Quedan los rastros
y tañen las cuerdas
sobre ese paisaje
que las notas dibujan

Con su aliento
reaniman el fuego
para que llegue
encendido
hasta ti
*
Dime dónde
puedo esconderme
definitivamente del ruido

Quiero llegar hasta allí
donde el sonido
ya no es yo
*
Si cada nota
que se devela
es un viaje

Cada viaje
que se revela
es una vida

Un acorde
que no es
sino otro viaje

Otro viaje
que no es
sino otra vida
*
Hay un río
y su nombre
es la música

Hay un hombre
y su río
es la música

Hay un río
sin nombre
es la música[43]

[Faces travel
and gestures travel

without any baggage
but their inclinations

Stains remain
and strings ring
over this landscape
the notes draw

With their breath
they rekindle the fire
so it arrives
alive
to you
*
Tell me
where I can
hide from the noise

I want to go where
the sound is no
longer me
*
If every note
we awaken
is a life

A chord
that is nothing
but another trip

Another trip
that is nothing
but another life
*
There is a river
and its name
is music

There is a man
and his river
is music

There is a river
with no name
that is music]

The poem's rhythms are convincing, persuasive. Rhyme and repetition create the sensation that the connections the writer sees are organic and irrefutably proven through language. As he writes in "Música" ["Music"]:

La
palabra
siempre engaña

La
imagen
siempre miente

Pero
la música
en la oreja ni duda deja[44]

[Words
will always
deceive

Images
will always
betray

But music
in our ears
leaves no room for doubt]

The music of "Cuaderno de viaje" casts a spell over the reader as its individual notes come together to form harmonies, mystical "acordes" [chords] in which disparate elements blend in unexpected and pleasing ways. In "Cuando la tierra sueña" we read of "el acorde erótico de los cuerpos" [the erotic chord of lovers] and "los acordes eróticos y sostenidos de la lluvia" [the erotic and sustained chords of the rain].[45] Blanco's "acordes," similar in some ways to Paz's notion of the "instante," are epiphanies, moments of coincidence that transcend and transform.

The idea of the "acuerdo" also adds a serious counterpoint to the lighthearted "El Grito en Helsinki" [*El Grito* in Helsinki], a poem that dances to its own drummer. In it, the poet describes celebrating *el Grito de Dolores* [The Cry of Dolores] by watching the Finnish rock band the Leningrad Cowboys perform in the crypt of the cathedral in Helsinki. Part of the poem retells a scene from the film *Leningrad Cowboys Go America!* in which the bass player is brought back to life, in Ciudad Acuña, with a shot of liquor:

Y quede constancia
que la rima Coahuila—tequila

está aquí perfectamente justificada,
porque hay veces en la vida
que las cosas riman por su cuenta
y nos ofrecen en el momento menos esperado
un maravilloso *acuerdo.*

La vida (la rima) es como el clima . . .
hay que aceptarla como viene.[46]

[And for the record,
the pairing Coahuila—tequila
is perfectly justified here,
the proof is in the rhyme,
since there are times in life
when things come together all by themselves
and the most unexpected moment
offers us marvelous harmonies.

Life, like rhyme, depends on the clime. . . .
you have to take it as it comes.][47]

As in jazz, Blanco's poems create innovative overlaps of sound and substance that surprise the reader's senses with original harmonies and rhymes that shine.

Musical Paratexts

Earlier we read about Gustavo Pérez's artistic project in terms of "Una verdadera inspiración. Como ese punto que, aun estando fuera de su cuaderno, gobierna la perspectiva de algunos de sus dibujos" [A true inspiration. Like that point that, even though it lies beyond his notebook, governs the perspective of his drawings].[48] Inspiration viewed this way is also an apt metaphor for Blanco's poems paired with *hacedores*. In our examination of the exergue effect in chapter 2 we explored Gérard Genette's notion that dedications make apparent a relationship, either public or private, between a text and person.[49] This relationship is similar to a frame since it creates a new space that directs our reading by forcing us to ask the question, *what is the connection between what we are about to read and the person quoted between title and text*? Much like a case of musical ekphrasis, there are a handful of *hacedor* poems that do acknowledge specific musical lyrics or sources, but in most of these poems, the connections between text and paratext are much less apparent. "Tiempo de verano" ["Summertime"], for example, is a creative variation on the lyrics of Gershwin's famous song "Summertime." After a simple repetition of the first two verses of the song (in Spanish), verses 3 and 4 extract Gershwin's images of a fish and cotton ("catfish are jumpin' / and the cotton is high") and creates new meanings from them:

Tiempo de verano
La vida es tan fácil
Los peces no sueñan
La red de algodón[50]

Summer time
And the livin' is easy
The fish aren't dreaming
Of cotton nets

The same occurs with "alas" [wings] in the next stanza ("One of these mornings you're gonna rise up singing / And you'll spread your wings and you'll take to the sky") and the final refrain which is once again, simply the original lyrics but in Spanish:

El mar los conduce
Más allá del cielo
Abriendo las alas
A un mundo mejor

Escucha en silencio
Las nubes azules

Duérmete tranquila
No llores mi amor[51]

[The sea sends them
beyond the sky
Opening their wings
To a better world

Listen in silence
The blue clouds

Hush little baby
Don't you cry]

Blanco's relationship to the texts he invokes is usually not self-evident, though, and there are many reasons to avoid overanalysis of the role the *hacedores* play in the poems they inspire. A good example is the publication history of "Después de beber un poco de oscuridad" ["After Drinking a Little Darkness"] dedicated in the first edition of *La hora y la neblina* to Bob Dylan:[52]

Dios mío—me dije—
quítame este peso infernal de las espaldas
Déjame entrar. Abre la puerta.

¿Qué no ves que te estoy llamando
directamente al cielo?[53]

[My God—I said to myself—
take this infernal weight off my back
Let me in. Open the door.
Can't you see I'm knocking
on heaven's door?]

In the latest edition of the poem, however, the *hacedor* has been changed to Fleetwood Mac's guitarist Peter Green, even though the text (with its strong allusions to "Knockin' on Heaven's Door") remains the same.

In the same way that the connection between Blanco's poems and *hacedores* is not causal, even if it is not revealed, his work participates in the debate that perplexes musico-literary critics such as Eric Prieto, Monroe Beardsley, Suzanne Langer, and Nelson Goodman: what does instrumental music *mean*, independent of its lyrics and paratexts? Prieto argues that both Monroe Beardsley's expression theory and Suzanne Langer's vision of music's suggestive "unconsummated symbols" fail to find meaningful connections between musical keys or styles and specific, human emotions. In other words, how do we explain that not all songs in major keys are "happy," and how does music refer to specific emotions outside the "nonmusical world"? Is music "symbolic" or merely a process or way of thinking?[54] Like Nelson Goodman's theory of denotation, the fact that Blanco explicitly tells us that his poems are influenced by music, is perhaps the most important "musical" quality they contain by creating a "vector of attention" for the reader. As Prieto and Goodman explain, audiences are in a better position to judge a piece when they know "what to expect."[55] Considered in this light, Blanco's *hacedores* are framing devices or labels that create "conditioned expectations" for his readers. Prieto notes that "writers who invoke music as a model for their work are telling readers to read backward, so to speak, that is, to decode the work by seeking out the type of representation exemplified in the text."[56]

By way of example, this poem creates one experience when read without its *hacedor* . . .

La luna
llena con su luz
cada breve resquicio
mientras los ángeles
tocan a la puerta
del sueño[57]

The moon
shines its light

into every last opening
while the angels knock
on the door of
dreams

. . . and another when considered in the context of its series ("Piedras rodantes" [Rolling Stones]) and connection to Bob Dylan.

As we studied in chapter 2, dedications or epigraphs are often acknowledgments of a Muse or inspiration for a work at hand, but, as Genette points out, the connection between a poem and its epigraph can often be "puzzling" and put the reader's "hermeneutic capacity . . . to the test."[58] "The function of the *exergue*," writes Michel Charles, "is easily to give food for thought without one's knowing what the thought is."[59] Blanco's poetry clearly supports Genette's contention that the exergue effect shapes our understanding of poems whether we can see a connection between an *hacedor* and text or not.

One of the main functions of Blanco's poetic grafts, epigraphs, dedications, intertexts, and collages is what Adolfo Castañón has characterized as the poet using his words to listen: "el poeta utiliza las palabras para escuchar" [the poet using words to listen].[60] Blanco's poems are the explicit product of his reading of other poets, listening to other musicians, viewing works of art, and looking for poetry in the objects and situations of everyday life. "Tiempo de verano" and "Después de beber un poco de oscuridad" both literally incorporate a fragment of an inspirational song but then *transform it* into something different and new—a dynamic and open-ended poetic space defined by the compound interpretative intersection of poet, reader, and epigraph. Since this is not prose, there is no one answer to explain the connection between *hacedores* and their poems.

The poet's awareness of the power of music moves him to address it directly as such in the many poems dedicated to songs. As we saw in "Había una vez," "Phil Bragar pinta un retrato," and "Cuando la tierra sueña" many of Blanco's poems that explore or reference music are also more narrative than his other work. "El humo de la música" ["Music Smoke"], for example, employs two musical quotes (in English) to help create vignettes for us of the before and after of a one-night stand. The first movement focuses solely on a woman, the second on a man:

"El humo de la música"

I
Allí estaba ella, sola,
tratando de descifrar
los mapas del salitre
en la pared del baño,
la trama descolorida

de las viejas cortinas
y los días que faltaban
para volver a casa.

Allí estaba ella,
con la cabeza llena
de vapores de sándalo
los ojos entreabiertos
los párpados pesados
de sombras más que azules,
casi violetas, invitando
a los pliegues de la noche
a consumar las nupcias
de la llama del espíritu
y el humo de la música.

Una almendra dorada
que en medio de la oscuridad
dejó manar de su centro
una canción inolvidable
de notas altísimas
junto al tocador:

It's a little bit funny
This feeling inside . . .

II
Aquella primera y última noche
zarparon barcos de plata oscura,
desfilaron los animales del mundo
azorados delante de nuestros ojos
y con la luna fría y el corazón caliente
se hicieron muy pronto un humo de amor.

"Suelta las amarras"—me dijo ella—
"que vienen tiempos mejores
para tu pobre corazón."

Pero era necesario ir todavía más lejos . . .
buscarle ese filo amable a la vida
que pudiese ofrecer al fin
un halo de bondad.

Ella me llevó entonces de la mano al mar
que palpita en el interior de una nuez

hasta la casa de espejos de la infancia
para dejarme de pie delante de mí mismo,
y algo me murmuró dulcemente al oído
que provocó en mí una epifanía:

And in the end the love you make
Is equal to the love you take.[61]

["Music Smoke"

I
[There she was, alone,
trying to decipher
limescale maps
on the bathroom wall,
the worn out weave
of the old curtains
and the days left
before going back home.

There she was,
her head full of
sandalwood steam
her eyes half opened
her eyelids heavy
with shadows deeper than blue,
almost violet, inviting
the folds of the night
to consume the nuptials
of the flame of spirit
and the smoke of music.

A golden almond
that in the middle of the darkness
let flow from its core
an unforgettable song
of the highest notes
as it played:

It's a little bit funny
This feeling inside . . .

II
That first and last night
two dark silver ships set sail,

all the animals of the world lined up
stunned before our eyes
and with the cold moon and hot hearts
they soon made love smoke.

"Cast off the lines"—she told me—
"better times are coming
for that poor heart of yours."

But it was necessary to go even farther . . .
find that kind thread of life
that can offer in the end
a halo of goodness.

She then led me by the hand to the sea
that beats in the interior of a nut
to the house of mirrors of childhood
to have me stand in front of myself,
and something murmured sweetly in my ear
that caused an epiphany:

And in the end the love you make
Is equal to the love you take.

The first section of the poem uses anaphora (*Allí estaba ella*), alliteration (*párpados pesados*), assonance (*descolorida / cortinas, faltaban / casa*), and *esdrújula* words (*párpados, sándalo, espíritu, música*, etc.) to create rhythms that pair with the title and song quotations. With the exception of three quotes (one from the woman and two from songs) most of the text takes place in the past so we are led to meditate on what remains now, in the present: fragments of songs, memories of love, and an epiphany, all of which remain like smoke after a fire. Music, as we have seen, is really is about time, and Blanco frequently uses songs to explore our place in the present, past, and future.

"El humo de la música" appears in the section *Paisajes en el oído* [*Soundscapes*], which dedicates texts to different bands. This particular poem is paired with the San Francisco psychedelic group It's a Beautiful Day, best known for 1969's "White Bird." The two quotes in English are from Elton John's "Your Song" and the Beatles' "The End." What to make of these references? Perhaps the woman in the first section is like the white bird, alone and dreaming in her golden cage? The first section centers on her (maybe it's "her song"?), and the poem ends with Paul McCartney's couplet that wraps up the frenetic, three-way duel of guitar solos on *Abbey Road*. "The End" is the last studio song recorded by all four Beatles, and despite the sweetness of the quote, the song is what more than one critic has called an epitaph for the band. Does this imply that the night of love described in the poem ended badly? Or are these interpretations too anecdotal to be critically valid? Just because "White Bird" is It's a Beautiful Day's most well-known song, for example, does not mean that this poem necessarily has a connection to it. Since Elton John, the Beatles, and It's a Beautiful Day's songs were all released within a year of each other in 1969–1970, maybe the bands are here simply to set a scene. Looking for connections is part of the inspirational quality of poems Blanco wants to share with his readers, though the perils of drawing those connections too tightly are also apparent.

Songs and bands can have powerful connections to times and places for us. The intriguing "El autobus descompuesto" ["The Broken-Down Bus"], for example, is a seemingly autobiographical poem about a trip in 1965 in which a bus breaks down, temporarily stranding its passengers in the desert. Since *Cuenta de los guías*, deserts have been important places in Blanco's world, and this poem is no exception since it ends with the lines "Todo esto fue lo que sentí / el día que supe que iba a ser padre" [All of this is what I felt / the day I found out I was going to be a father].[62] Blanco treats the desert like a blank sonic canvas and then populates it with a series of sounds that intensify the experience. There are the complaints of the elderly passengers, the crying of a young child, and the "ronroneo del motor" [purring of the motor] of another bus that stops to offer help and then fades off into the chirping of crickets. There is also an accordion, played by a blind woman, and another very important moment for the young musician: "Quizá fue la primera vez en mi vida / que escuché a alguien cantar / una canción de los Beatles" [It was maybe the first time in my life / that I heard someone sing / a song by the Beatles].[63] The poem ends with all the passengers deciding to help fix the bus, "como respondiendo a una misma voz" [as if responding to the same voice].[64] For this reader, the Beatles song both tunes our ear to the other sounds in the poem and, primarily, situates the scene in the mid-1960s.

"Viaje de retorno al desierto de Altar" ["Return Trip to the Altar Desert"] revisits the desert from a more psychedelic perspective, that of the late 60s' Procol Harum tune "In the Autumn of my Madness" and Jim Morrison. Four of the song's constellations are images associated with the Doors: "La constelación del Soldado Desconocido; / la constelación del Barco de Cristal; / la constelación de los Jinetes en la Tormenta; / la constelación del Rey Lagarto" [The Constellation of the Unknown Soldier; / the constellation of the Crystal Ship; / the constellation of the Riders on the Storm; / the constellation of the Lizard King].[65] It's a psychedelic scene in which the flora and fauna (coyotes, snakes) connect with a man, clearly Morrison ("he wants the world and he wants it now"), who appears to be having a psychotropic or shamanistic experience: "La luna y el sol forman un solo rostro; / el hombre y los dos coyotes, un solo ser" ["the moon and the sun form one profile; / the man and the two coyotes, one being].[66]

Many of Blanco's musical referents are from the United States and he has a particular affinity for the jazz, rock, and blues that inspired and was then created by the Beat poets of the 1950s.[67] Blanco's experiences in the 1960s, especially those that led to *Cuenta de los guías*, share the Beats' passion for freedom, transnational travel, Eastern spirituality, the limits of psychedelic drugs, jazz, philosophy, indigenous cultures, and the desert. A poem like "Tenía que estar relampagueando" ["There Must Have Been Lightning"] mimics the rambling bebop rhythms of Allen Ginsberg ("Sin tiempo para la yoga de la mente, el yugo de la lente, la plata en la pantalla y la pareja de siempre" [Without time for the yoga of the mind, the yoke of the lens, the silver in the silver screen and the perfect partner]),[68] and "La desolación de los ángeles en el espejo" ["The Desolation of the Angels in the Mirror"] pays homage to Jack Kerouac's spoken-word phrasing (complete with unanswered questions and sudden exclamations) in the poems he performed live accompanied by pianists like Steve Allen.[69]

La tierra gira
¿a cuántas revoluciones
por minuto?

El jazz borra
los rostros encendidos
por la noche

Y en lo más alto
un momento de blues
ultramarino

¡Furia del rock!
los sonidos nos liberan
de las palabras

¿Cómo escuchar
el disco de la luna
sin su color?

Día nublado
el tigre no se oculta
en la montaña

El hombre corre
ciervo de paradojas
pero no su conciencia

Para el enfermo
entre la tierra y el cielo
¡la hierbabuena!

Los patos grandes
les comen el mandado
a los patitos

Los puros huesos
para las tristes moscas
son suficientes

Y mientras dura
¡sonrían por favor
caricaturas![70]

[The earth turns
But how many times
per minute?

Jazz erases
the lit up faces
at night

And at its heights
a moment of
ultramarine blues

Fury of rock!
the sound frees us
from the lyrics

How can we listen
to the moon's
white album?

Cloudy day
the tiger's not hiding
on the mountain

The man runs
paradoxical deer
but not his consciousness

For the sick one
between the earth and sky
Mint!

The big ducks
eat the ducklings's
share

For the sad flies
pure bones
are enough

And while it lasts
Smile, you
caricatures!]

Silence

The verses of "La desolación de los ángeles en el espejo" be-bop across the page to show us how poetry can make music and making music is about rhythmically manipulating silence. The relationship between silence and poetry is ancient, essential, and multifaceted. Octavio Paz notes that "La poesía nace en el silencio . . . en el no poder decir" [Poetry is born in silence . . . in not being able to speak].[71] For Blanco, silence is what exists *Antes De Nacer* [*before birth / D.N.A.*], as both the alpha and the omega, the goal of a spiritual life, the state of oneness and knowing: "Volver al silencio a través de las palabras" [Returning to silence through words].[72] Life is a process of listening, of straining to make out the message of the other side of language, of poetry. In the important essay "El silencio" ["Silence"] in *El canto y el vuelo*, Blanco notes: "la poesía es un intento por decir lo que no se puede decir. . . . Del silencio viene la palabra imantada y al silencio mismo la palabra imantada ha de volver" [poetry is an attempt to say what cannot be said. . . . From silence comes the magnetized word and to that same silence the magnetized word will return].[73]

We come across references to the importance of silence as an origin in all of Blanco's longer and more important pieces. Life before the word is like the canvas or surface upon which the poet constructs some of his most powerful poems. In an interview, he describes the structure of *Antes De Nacer* as "la estructura de un zíper: se abre y se cierra. Dos largas ristras de versos que se hablan y callan; se contradicen y se apoyan; se abren y se cierran" [the structure of a zipper: it opens and closes. Two long wreathes of verse that talk with each other and fall silent; that contradict and support each other; that open each other up and close each other down].[74] The reader needs the silence in a long poem like *ADN* to find a place to rest and reflect.[75] The same could be said of the short lines and stanzas of the eleven-page-long "Duermevela" ["Halfsleep"], which concludes by pointing our awareness to the centrality of silence as an underlying strength and source of potential:

> Hay una estación de trenes
> al final del sueño
>
> No estoy solo
> en el inmenso andén
> pero como si lo estuviera
>
> El silencio es impresionante
>
> Sin más equipaje
> que mis recuerdos
> abordo el tren
> que me corresponde
> y viendo por la ventanilla
> espero pacientemente la salida
>
> Una densa neblina
> invade la estación

cuando suena un silbato penetrante
en el interior de mis oídos

A la hora de la hora
la máquina no se mueve

Todo cambia en un instante
¡Estoy despierto!
¡Pero yo ya no quiero más poemas!

Yo sólo quiero
el silencio que viene
después de los poemas
y que estaba allí
desde el principio

El silencio de la duermevela
más hondo que el peso
de los objetos dormidos
en la penumbra

El silencio más largo
que las sombras del amanecer

El silencio vivo
antes de que imaginara siquiera
el primer poema[76]

[There is a train station
at the end of the dream

I am not alone
on the huge platform
but as if I were all alone

The silence is impressive

Without any other baggage
than my memories
I board the train
that I'm supposed to
and look through the window
as I patiently await our departure

A dense fog
invades the station
when a violent whistle
cuts into my ears

When it's time
the machine does not move

Everything changes in an instant

I'm awake!
But I don't want any more poems now!

I only want
the silence that comes
after the poems
and that was there
from the beginning

The silence of halfsleep
deeper than the weight
of the sleeping objects
in the twilight

A longer silence
than the silence of dawn

The living silence
before the faintest inkling
of the first poem]

The silence of "Duermevela" ["Halfsleep"] connects with the poet's meditative state, a calm, Zen experience of semiawareness. This silence is often double voiced, as it were, "a living silence" in which the absence of language is also the absence of signs on the page and is thus both auditory and spatial. On the page, living silence can play out in both subtle and, as in the case below, more obvious ways:

"Poema visual para 18 instrumentos"

violín violoncelo piano maracas marimba
violín violoncelo piano maracas marimba
violín violoncelo piano maracas marimba
violín violoncelo piano maracas marimba
violín violoncelo piano maracas marimba
violín violoncelo maracas marimba
violoncelo bajo maracas marimba
voz violoncelo bajo
voz violoncelo bajo piano xilófono
voz violoncelo bajo piano xilófono
piano xilófono
marimba xilófono piano xilófono

marimba xilófono piano xilófono
marimba xilófono xilófono
marimba xilófono metalófono xilófono
marimba xilófono metalófono xilófono
marimba xilófono metalófono
marimba xilófono matalófono marimba
xilófono metalófono marimba
piano metalófono marimba
piano clarinete bajo metalófono marimba
piano clarinete bajo metalófono marimba
piano clariente bajo metalófono marimba
piano clarinete bajo metalófono marimba
clarinete bajo
bajo clarinete bajo voz voz voz bajo voz
bajo clarinete bajo voz voz voz bajo voz
bajo clarinete bajo voz voz voz bajo voz
bajo clarinete bajo voz voz voz bajo voz[77]

[“Visual Poem for 18 Instruments”
violin violoncello piano maracas marimba
violin violoncello piano maracas marimba
violin violoncello piano maracas marimba
violin violoncello piano maracas marimba
violin violoncello piano maracas marimba
violin violoncello maracas marimba
violoncello bass maracas marimba
voice violoncello bass
voice violoncello bass piano xylophone
voice violoncello bass piano xylophone
piano xylophone
marimba xylophone piano xylophone
marimba xylophone piano xylophone
marimba xylophone xylophone
marimba xylophone mellophone xylophone
marimba xylophone mellophone xylophone
marimba xylophone mellophone
marimba xylophone mellophone marimba
xylophone mellophone marimba
piano mellophone marimba
piano bass clarinet mellophone marimba
piano bass clarinet mellophone marimba
piano bass clarinet mellophone marimba

piano bass clarinet mellophone marimba
bass clarinet
bass bass clarinet voice voice voice bass voice
bass bass clarinet voice voice voice bass voice
bass bass clarinet voice voice voice bass voice
bass bass clarinet voice voice voice bass voice]

In a nod to John Cage's "Lecture on Nothing," "Poema visual para 18 instrumentos" deploys a visual pattern to illustrate the role that silence or breath plays in the making of music.[78] The white spaces, what Johanna Drucker terms "not sound," here are essential to balancing the visual form and acoustic qualities of the poem's words. As Drucker notes, "Visual codes of transmission operate on their own terms as instructions during the reading event," so the poem's white spaces are, in effect, "*heard* in silent reading."[79] Part of the text's depth is the temptation we can't help but feel to read it as a musical score by filling it in with our mental memories of the instruments named (i.e., a bass where we read "bajo"). This is even more complex with "voz," which can be a voice (male or female) either as an instrument or as the vehicle for an unwritten lyric. Thus silence is activated in much the way we examined in the negative spaces of Blanco's collages—as the necessary complement in a tension of push and pull that together create the third experience, "una tercera vía" ["a third way"], of the poem. As Orlando White notes, "It's up to us, the poets, to write and unwrite and interpret and re-interpret the page through *space* by making language and silence collaborate."[80]

The intriguing visual poem "K" (connected to American jazz pianist Keith Jarret) uses a negative concrete form mimicking the letter K to interweave silence and sound and create auditory effects. The break that leads to line 2, for example, makes us pause and the right justification adds force to the idea of an echo, as if it were bouncing off an unseen right wall of the text:

"K"
El relámpago y el eco tremendo del trueno
el eco
de una melodía jamás escuchada
contra otra
distinta de la anterior
sobrepuestas
indistinguibles
una de otra
del ritmo
a la luz
del ritmo
de la masacre

del viejo orden

hasta el nacimiento

de los nuevos sentidos

en la conversación

de los tonos mayores y menores

de notas azules

en la eterna búsqueda del silencio perfecto

el silencio[81]

[The lightning strike and tremendous echo of thunder

the echo

of a melody never heard

against another

different from the other

overlapping

indistinguishable

one from the other

of the rhythm

to the light

of the rhythm

of the massacre

of the old order

until the birth

of the new senses

in the conversation

of the major and minor tones

of blue notes

in the eternal search for perfect silence

of silence]

The sound and sense of the poem flows, intentionally interrupted, from the right-justified lines down and to the left, to the next verse, often with surprising effects: "del ritmo / de la masacre / del viejo orden" [from the rhythm / of the massacre / of the old order]. In figurative ways, "K" is about rebirth, which begins in the poem around the repetition of "el ritmo" [the rhythm] near the hinge of the letter's form. As in "Duermevela," silence is the goal of an "eternal search" for an ideal state of mind and being, one that "K" describes as a musical piece in which major, minor, and blue notes come together.

The poem's final line is thus an invitation to silence, a coded silence that results from the product of a combination of sounds. In visual terms, the large swaths of color in Mark Rothko's bold color field paintings provide a similar experience. As in the desert, the absence of detail can cause discomfort in some viewers in a way not unrelated to the stillness of mind that is the ultimate goal of meditation.

White spaces can be used to divide as well as to control tempo. In previous centuries, when poetry's connection to orality was stronger, spaces were sometimes, though not always, used to allow a reader to breathe. As recently as in the 1950s, Charles Olsen's notion of "projective verse" urged poets to transfer that physical energy of breath into their verses. Orlando White calls these pauses the "functional white," that is, "the throat of paper, inhaling language and exhaling sound and silence."[82]

The poem "Silogismos" ["Syllogisms"] from "Metapoemas" ["Metapoems"] in *A la luz de siempre* deals with silence in a nonvisual way by inviting its reader to deduce conclusions about different aspects of poetry based on assumptions. Adding to the complexity of the text is the fact that its three stanzas create a metasyllogism in which the definitions of image and music from the first two riddles are incorporated into the third stanza's characterization of poetry. In addition to its stated content, this poem also suggests a way of thinking, especially with regard to form and content, that is part of the equation of poetry.

"Silogismos"

I
La imagen
es silencio para la mente
y música para los ojos.

II
La música
es imagen para la mente
y silencio para los ojos.

III
La poesía
es imagen para la mente
y música para los ojos.[83]

[I
The image
is silence for the mind
and music for the eyes.

II
Music
is an image for the mind
and silence for the eyes.

III
Poetry
is an image for the mind
and music for the eyes.]

In "Silogismos" silence and sound can be contemporaneous or can "interpenetrate" to use the term from Zen Buddhism that John Cage preferred. When the eyes enjoy an image the mind is silent, and when the mind *views* music (to use Blanco's term) our eyes can rest. The synesthetic metaphors of "Silogismos" thus offer both a definition of poetry and a glimpse of something larger. Cage is an important influence on Blanco. His "4′ 33," the four-minute thirty-three-second composition widely known as "the silent piece," is composed of nothing more than the ambient noise made by a room of musicians *not* playing. Cage insisted that this fertile negative space is open "to the acceptance of anything" as it challenges genre and the Western musical tradition.[84]

In *Where the Heart Beats*, a fascinating study of Cage, art critic Kay Larson describes the musician's reaction after a visit to Harvard's anechoic chamber—a room scientifically designed to block out 99.8 percent of all sound. When Cage enters the chamber he is shocked that instead of nothing, he hears a dull roar and high whining sound. Cage exits the chamber and describes what he heard to an engineer who explains that the high whine was the firing of his neurons, while the dull roar was his blood flowing through his veins.[85] Larson notes that this experience of the lack of silence was an epiphany for Cage, who realized that he had previously been seeing life as a series of separate opposites, such as silence and sound, that, in reality, are intertwined and inseparable. As Larson writes, "In the quietest place on earth he hears *himself.* Seeking silence, looking for the vacuum where *he* is not—Cage hears the ceaseless buzz of *being* . . . everything interpenetrates. . . . Form is emptiness and emptiness is form."[86]

Blanco opens and closes the collection *Medio cine* with a pair of poems that participate in a similar examination of light, space, and sound as Cage in the anechoic chamber. The first recalls those moments when a film begins to roll in a darkened movie theater but with an emphasis on the lack of dialogue, as in silent films:

"Luz silenciosa"

El espacio que se abre
es la noche que comienza:
Un sueño flotando sin sombra de duda.

El compás que se cierra
es la noche que termina:

La luz que las palabras no tocaron jamás.[87]

["Silent Light"

As night-time falls
a space unfolds:

A dream floating free from doubt's shadow.

As night's light pales
a rhythm retreats:

The light untouched by words.]

The last poem in the collection recalls the first in its title, form, and theme. Even though it is inspired by contemporary Mexican film director Carlos Reygadas, it clearly references the scene Larson describes of John Cage at Harvard.

"¿Luz silenciosa?"

Ese zumbido agudo son las estrellas;
ese rumor profundo es la tierra.

No hay silencio allá fuera.

Ese zumbido agudo es el sistema nervioso;
ese rumor profundo es la sangre.

Acá dentro . . . tampoco.[88]

["Silent Light?"

That sharp buzz is the stars;
that deep roar the earth.

Nothing is silent out there.

That sharp buzz is my neurons firing;
that deep roar my blood.

In here? No, not here either.]

Together this pair of poems uncovers the depth of silence and thus, metaphorically in the context of this book, of silent film. Silence here is like the white space found within a poem that itself exists upon the "functional white space" that surrounds and frames it. Existence is coexistence. Sound and silence need each other. Light is both wave and particle.

"Manifestación silenciosa" [Silent Protest] shows us one final face of silence, the one that preoccupied George Steiner in *Language and Silence*—"silencio voluntario" [voluntary silence] or how to wield silence as a political weapon.[89] The poem's present tense drops us into the streets of Mexico City during the September 13, 1968, silent protest where there were "ten thousand people maybe more / people talking without speaking," as the reference to Simon & Garfunkel suggests.

"Manifestación silenciosa"

Tarde o temprano
alguien que escuche estos pasos
en un futuro sentirá de nuevo
aquel calor que animaba el pulso
y subía a golpes por la vida,
aquella sangre que inflamara las antorchas,
los rostros, las vés de la victoria
en una espléndida celebración.

Un triunfo del silencio voluntario
frente al rumor impuesto.

Un triunfo musical
sobre el barullo ensordecedor.

Porque no es lo mismo guardar silencio
que quedarse callado.

Porque no es igual
la acción que la reacción.

Luces en la plaza y estrellas en el cielo,
destellos en los cascos azules y en los lentes
oscuros, transparentes de tanto verano: septiembre
ardiendo en las vitrinas de cada aparador.

Las bocacalles estaban bloqueadas
pero adentro aquello era una fiesta,
un baño público, una limpia: la forja
en ese instante de una ciudad gozosa.

Una inmensa columna de muchachos y muchachas
seguía nutriendo la plaza con su savia
y a punto de desbordarse ese silencio
se encendieron las horas sin reloj.

Si las luces de los semáforos estaban apagadas
las velas interiores—en cambio—estaban listas;

Si el alumbrado público parpadeaba débilmente
la lumbre de la muchedumbre formaba un corazón.

Eran pocas las ventanas iluminadas por el miedo
pero se vislumbraba un fuego nuevo en cada cosa:

Periódicos, bolsas, pañuelos, improvisadas teas,
cualquier combustible era bueno para la ocasión.

La sombra de los muros del Palacio Nacional
nos pareció más ominosa aún que el profundo bramido
que sentimos correr como un escalofrío
bajo el pavimento cuando los tanques rodaron.

Una constelación sin nombre se propagó en la plaza
y a falta de bandera—el asta se erguía desierta—
guardamos entre todos un silencio atronador.
Yo tenía diecisiete años.

Pudo durar aquella noche inolvidable mil años
o pudo ser una sola noche inaugural
o la última de todas las noches
o la única noche concedida.

El caso es que, cuando volvimos a casa
recorriendo a pie la enorme distancia,
llenos de orgullo, resarcidos, animados,
sentimos que algo nuevo, distinto
había surgido en nuestras vidas.

Una solidaridad esclarecida
y puesta en práctica: un gesto
un acuerdo, un viento, una pasión.

Aquel silencio
nos hizo aterrizar—al fin—
en el centro mismo de la tormenta
y nos hizo poner los ojos
en el ojo del huracán.

Unos cuantos días después
llovieron lágrimas de sangre.

Tuvieron que pasar otros diecisiete años
para que un amargo septiembre
viniera a sacudirnos
y nos viera salir
del estupor.[90]

[Sooner or later
someone hearing these steps
in the future will feel once again
that heat that quickened the pulse
and rose up violently within us,
that blood that fueled the torches,
the faces, the Vs for Victory
in a splendid celebration.

A triumph of silence
over the imposed murmur.

A triumph of music
over the deafening din.

Because keeping quiet is not the same thing
as not saying anything.

Because acting is not the same
as reacting.

Lights in the plaza and stars in the sky,
sparkling on the blue helmets and the dark
lenses, transparent from so much summer: September
burning in the glass of every shop window.

The alleys were blocked
but inside there was a party,
a public bath, a cleansing: the forge
in that moment of a joyful city.

An immense column of boys and girls
fed the plaza with their sap
and when that silence was about to overflow
the clock-less hours lit up.

Although the streetlights were out
our internal flames—instead—were lit and ready;

Although the public lighting blinked weakly
the glow of the crowd formed a heart.

Only a few windows were lit up by fear
but a new fire glowed in everything else:

Newspapers, bags, handkerchiefs, improvised torches,
anything flammable was good for the occasion.

The shadow of the walls of the National Palace
seemed more ominous to us than the deep growl
that we felt run like a shiver
below the pavement when the tanks rolled in.

A nameless constellation was formed in the plaza
and without the flag—the flagpole was bare—
we maintained a thunderous silence.
I was seventeen years old.

That unforgettable night could have lasted a thousand years
or it could have been just one inaugural night
or the last night of all
or the only night we had.

The thing is that, when we returned home
covering the enormous distance on foot,
full of pride, proud, lively,
we felt something new, different
had risen up in our lives.

A newly found solidarity
and way of being: a gesture
an agreement, a wind, a passion.

That silence
made us touch down—finally—
in the very heart of the storm
and made us fix our eyes
on the eye of the hurricane.

A few days later
tears of blood rained down.

And another seventeen years had to pass
until one bitter September
shook us up and
out of our
stupor.]

The first stanza describes the silent music of the march in the footfalls of the protestors, the pulse of their anxious heartbeats, the music of silent solidarity that drowned out the background noise of the city. The light of the marchers' torches contrasts with the city's electric lights, and their youth is described in the terms of nature as the lifeblood of a tree or a living constellation. For Javier Galindo Ulloa, in this poem "la imagen del silencio es una respuesta enérgica contra las amenazas de aquel gobierno" [the image of silence is an energetic response to the threats of that government].[91] Silence here is also described as the calm in the eye of the hurricane that would strike at Tlatelolco and then again in the 1985 earthquake. In Mexico's Silent March, a generation known for its music used music's complement to deliver a thunderous yet quiet message of protest, memory, change, and absence.

CHAPTER 4

Texture

In the last paragraph of *El llamado y el don* [*The Calling and the Gift*], Blanco's book about poetry's relationship to the past, we read that "Toda obra poética nace, crece, se desarrolla y muere para volver a nacer en la pupila" [Every poetic work is born, grows, develops and dies only to be reborn in the eye].[1] Poetry, like all information, is communicated through time, originally through the recitation of memorized songs, but then, more recently, through writing and reading. Poems are born with a poet but are then reborn when put into practice by readers.

The inseparable nature of reading and writing has been a constant source of fascination for literary theorists, particularly European poststructuralists, deconstructionists, and practitioners of "*rezeptionsästhetik*" [Reader's Response criticism] that have been so transatlantically influential since the 1970s. Creative writers, visual artists, and poets prefigure the criticism written by their commentators, of course, and the self-referential art created by and since Baudelaire, Rimbaud, and Mallarmé has become one of the most prominent modes of poetic expression of the twentieth and twenty-first centuries. Before, during, and after the avant-garde, poets, linguists, philosophers, and literary theorists have questioned language's ability to bridge the gap from signifier to signified and have developed a myriad of approaches to understanding a reader's response to the open text that she or he helps write.

In the most basic sense, reading is the dynamic process that takes place between an individual and a text, but reading also implies an active unpacking, interpretation, and cocreation of meaning. In the late 1960s Roland Barthes coined the terms *lisible* and *scriptible* to describe "readerly texts" that are more direct or literal in their language and "writerly texts" whose tropes open them to interpretation and propel the reader into a more active role, what Cortázar would later term a *lector cómplice* (reader-accomplice). Michel de Certeau reminds us that a reader "invents in texts something different from what they 'intended.'"[2] De Certeau's reader combines fragments and "creates something un-known in the space organized by their capacity for allowing an indefinite plurality of meanings."[3]

Cognitive poetics, one of the more recent approaches to understanding such processes, was born from the marriage of linguistics, the study of language, and psychology, the study of behavior.[4] Peter Stockwell notes that the experience of reading literature is one of "rational decision-making and creative meaning construction."[5] In its early stages, cognitive psychology used analog technologies such as eye tracking to study how readers select certain tropes and ideas and then construct meaning from them. Critics now employ cognitive poetics to explore how writers capture our attention by creating striking figures through language. In doing so, Stockwell notes that "literature draws attention to its own condition of existence, which is its texture."[6] Texture is thus the conceptual depth created by the figures and grounds cocreated by readers and writers.

Recognizing texture can be especially tricky with highly metaphorical language such as poetry. For Stockwell, "The readerly process of resolving a metaphorical reading . . . is called vehicle-construction."[7] "Vehicle" refers to the target or new element of a metaphor's comparison. Targets, Stockwell notes, are typically featured first, before a source domain. So the lines "La poesía en nuestro tiempo ocupa / en la naturaleza acosada del mundo de los hombres / el lugar de una pequeña reserva" [Poetry in our time occupies / in natural world threatened by the world of men / the place of a small reserve] create the conceptual metaphor that "poetry is a nature reserve."[8] The poem "Reserva" ["Reserve"] then extends that metaphor in the manner of an allegory:

"Reserva"

La poesía en nuestro tiempo ocupa
en la naturaleza acosada del mundo de los hombres
el lugar de una pequeña reserva.

Pero esta zona protegida de las ambiciones del mundo,
aunque cada vez más pequeña, tiene sus encantos.

Resguardada de los vaivenes del mercado,
aún conserva algo de su rara belleza . . .
pero, ¿será así por mucho tiempo?

Las criaturas del lenguaje que la habitan
abren desmesuradamente los ojos
tratando de anticipar el próximo peligro.

Saben que el estrépito de las máquinas
—cada vez más cercanas—no augura nada bueno.
Cada día que pasa en la reserva es un verdadero milagro.[9]

["Reserve"

Poetry in our time occupies
in the natural world threatened by the world of men
the space of a small reserve.

Still, this zone, protected against the world's ambitions,
even though it is growing smaller, has its charms.

Protected from the ups and downs of the market,
it still conserves a rare kind of beauty . . .
but, for how long?

The language creatures that inhabit it
keep their eyes wide open
trying to anticipate the next threat.

They know that the roar of machinery
—closer every day—does not foretell anything good.

Every day in the reserve is a true miracle.]

"Reserva" tells us about poetry's perilous, marginal position in relation to society and the market system. The first stanza loops back to the title and that linguistic repetition locks in our attention to the poem's key metaphor. The nature vocabulary used to describe poetry (*protegida*, [protected], *pequeña* [small], *encanto* [charm], *belleza* [beauty], *milagro* [miracle]) contrasts sharply with the human-made descriptions of the rest of the world (*ambiciones* [ambitions], *vaivenes* [ups and downs], *mercado* [market], *peligro* [threat], *máquinas* [machines], *nada bueno* [nothing good]). As the experienced reader of Blanco's poetry might expect, the poet added a visual element to his verses to create rhythmic tension and reinforce the poem's message. There is also a turning point in the question about poetry's future in verse 8, one of the two shortest lines in the poem and a visual fulcrum of the text's short and long verses.

Like so many of Blanco's poems, "Reserva" is organized around a counterpoint—"poesía" and "el mundo de los hombres." These two concepts coexist as opposite, though connected, poles. The verses, or, more specifically, the process of reading the verses, is what makes poetry happen: "La poesía es ese fluido invisible que corre entre sendos polos unidos por el milagro de la lectura" [Poetry is that invisible fluid that runs between separate though connected poles through the miracle of reading].[10] As in the quote that opens this chapter, reading activates the text, which has no power without it.

As Barthes, Stockwell, and others have noted, reading poetry is different from reading other kinds of texts . . . so different that in his essays Blanco questions whether we should even use the verb "leer" [to read] with regard to poetry:

"Habría que buscar otro verbo. ¿Por qué? Porque la poesía no se escribe para decir lo que sabemos, creemos, sentimos, pensamos, vemos y deseamos . . . sino para que lo desconocido se manifieste y se comunique con nosotros. Para que nos lea" [We really should find another verb. Why? Because poetry is not written to say what we think, believe, feel, think, see and want . . . but rather so that the unknown can become manifest and communicate with us].[11] It should be obvious by now that Blanco's definition of reading poetry also involves a radically different understanding of what poetry is and is not. The process of reading and writing poetry is about delving into the unknown, not re-creating or simply just expressing the known. "Elogio de la luz" ["An Elegy to Light"] shares one element of this idea:

> "Elogio de la luz"
> La poesía
>   es una
>   pregunta
> La prosa
>   es una
>   respuesta
> La prosa
>   es sólo
>   un camino
> La poesía
>   es la luz
>   del camino[12]
>
> ["An Elegy to Light"
>
> Poetry
>   is a
>   question
> Prose
>   is an
>   answer
> Prose
>   is only
>   a path
> Poetry
>   lights
>   that path]

Poetry and prose can appear together since they are literary poles or complements. "Un poema" ["A Poem"] defines poetry in a lightly metaphorical, almost prosaic way:

"Un poema"

Un poema es un objeto mágico:
una llave de palabras que nos permite
abrir las cerraduras y franquear la puerta
entre lo conocido y lo desconocido

(22 de julio de 1998, México)[13]

["A poem"

A poem is a magical object:
a key made of words that allows us
to open the lock and pass through the door
between the known and the unknown

(July 22, 1998, Mexico)]

"Un poema" delivers a specific message, like prose, but does so through two clear metaphors that break the rules that govern literal language. As we mentioned in our introduction, Blanco makes a distinction between "Poesía" [Poetry] and "poesía" [poetry]. "Poesía" is "la esencia misma del arte" [the very essence of art],[14] while "poesía" is "una forma de arte que se vale del lenguaje para expresarse" [an artform that uses languages to express itself][15] or "el otro lado del lenguaje" [the other side of language]. The third section of "Teoría del poema" ["Poem Theory"] explains it in these words:

La poesía es
el camino hacia lo que no conocemos.

La Poesía es
lo que no podemos llegar a conocer . . .

La poesía
  es el camino
    a La Poesía.[16]

[If poetry is
a path to what we do not know,

Poetry is
what we can never come to know . . .

Thus poetry
  is the path
    to Poetry.]

It bears repeating that the title "Un poema," which may at first seem casual, is actually quite important since Blanco does not repeat the titles of any of his poems. He may change or edit or rewrite titles but there is only one "Un poema" in his vast poetic trilogy. When considered in the light of this "rule of the game," the poem's humble title actually bestows much importance to the text. Below, we see another thought experiment on what happens when "Poetry" is accosted by "el mundo de los hombres" ["the world of men"]:

"Un día en la vida
de la lengua"

Sale
al alba
—Poesía—
y se pasa
todo el día
batallando
con el mundo
desconcertado
de los hombres . . .

Regresa al anochecer hecha una prosa.[17]

["A Day in the Life
of Language"

Up
at dawn
—Poetry—
passes
the whole day
fighting with
the bewildered
world of men . . .

And returns home at night worn down to prose.]

Day-to-day life outside the aforementioned "reserve" suppresses and flattens the expressive possibilities of the language of "Poetry," "la cima y la gloria de toda la creación humana" [the height and glory of all human creation].[18] When communication is more direct, more banal, there are less possibilities for transformation (less texture) or transcendence into "el otro lado." Despite these challenges, however, the visual form of "Un día en la vida de la lengua" depicts how poetry can overcome the battles of everyday life and still transform language into art.

The following paragraph from the end of the essay "La escritura" [Writing] discusses how we balance the forces at play in poems like "Un día en la vida de la lengua." In it we see many of the key elements of Blanco's poetic project:

> La experiencia de leer poesía implica una forma distinta de aproximarse a los polos del espacio y el tiempo en la literatura. Implica otro modo de balancearse, otro equilibrio, otra forma de oscilar. El ir y venir entre el ojo y el oído del poema, entre lo que sabemos y lo que no sabemos, entre la palabra y el silencio, entre esos dos polos opuestos y complementarios de siempre, tiene una clara función: sin él no hay oleaje, corriente ni contrapunto. No hay obra que redondear.[19]

> [The experience of reading poetry implies a different way of approaching the poles of space and time in literature. It implies another way of balancing, another equilibrium, another way of oscillating. The interplay between the look and sound of a poem, between what we know and what we don't know, between the word and silence, between these two opposite and always complementary poles, has a clear function: without it there is no surge, current or counterpoint. There is no work to round off.]

Here we find a directive for how to both read and write poems and see clearly the inseparable nature of readers and writers and the vital importance of the unknown. The visual aspect of a poem needs the aural element, just as knowledge needs mystery to create a flow of energy. Active reading is that flow, that process, and reading, the essay tells us, "rounds off" a text. This metaphor is vitally important to Blanco's overall body of work with its divisions into circular cycles. And reading poetry, as we will explore below, can transport us to another dimension.

This chapter explores how Blanco represents reading and writing as interconnected complements or poles in poems based on *hacedores* [inspirational creators], poems about readers, metapoems, and poems that feature the yin/yang symbol, a visual embodiment of his poetics. We focus on how Blanco's poetry and essays suggest we interpret them and conclude with a discussion of poetry's power to break the rules of everyday prose.

Reading and Writing Writers

Julio Ortega once wrote that the work of José Emilio Pacheco is "una poesía distintivamente hecha desde la lectura: lee el mundo y lee los textos como una misma escritura descifrada, y en esa actividad la poesía está hecha de muchas otras lecturas, como un objeto resonante y colectivo" [poetry uniquely made from reading: it reads the world and reads other texts as if they were written in the same code, and in doing so, his poetry is made from other readings, like a collective and resonant object].[20] While the same certainly holds true for Blanco's essays on poetics, reading is also explicitly central to his poems related to literary *hacedores*. Poems framed as *vasos comunicantes* [communicating vessels] urge their readers to search for linguistic winks and nods to the work of their dedicatees. Even if we come up empty-handed in the end, the effort put into the search is one of the main power sources and textures of these poems. As we saw when discussing texts connected to the work of visual artists and musicians, some of these *relámpagos paralelos* [parallel lighting strikes] draw more directly on their sources than others. The more obscure poems (ones in which the connection between text and paratext is less clear) cause the active reader to work hard to craft a new experience, independent from established ideas about specific artists. These more open poems can be said to have more texture and depth than those containing familiar literary landmarks.

A small number of *hacedor* poems, such as the three we examine below, use deliberate points of reference or recognizable forms or citations from writers to make intertextual collages. The paratexts of Blanco's *vasos comunicantes* manipulate a reader's schemata, the contexts upon which we foreground these poems. Both overt and more subtle versions of these texts function like metaphors that create new poems (vehicles) from established source works. A text like the lighthearted "Soneto monomaniaco" ["Monomaniacal Sonnet"], with its reference to Francisco de Quevedo, makes us question the connection between the dedicatee and the text at hand as well as forcing us to wonder if the Blanco's notion of "Quevedo" will match up with "our Quevedo":

"Soneto monomaniaco"
Di:
¿Qué?
¿Fui?
¡Fue!
Y . . .
¿Qué?
¿Sí?
¡Sé!
¡Ah,
la
fe
Del
que
ve![21]

["Monomaniacal Sonnet"
Say:
What?
Was I?
You were
And . . .
What?

Yes?
I know!
Oh
the
faith
Of
the
viewer]

Form reflects content on many levels here. First, the puckish sense of humor that created this sonnet would probably have been pleasing to Quevedo (though Blanco wisely kept his sonnet to the stern Góngora in twelve-syllable lines). Second, the poem echoes the famous rhythm of "Ah de la vida . . ." ["Ah What of Life . . ."]: "Soy un fue, y un será, y un es cansado" ["I am a *was*, a *will be*, and a tired *is*"]. Blanco's cleverly rhymed sonnet is not concrete poetry, per se, though it does lean in the direction of poems whose typographic form reflects their message. In the end, it is an ironic revisiting of one the most revered verse forms and bards of Spain's Siglo de Oro. As Hutcheon notes, parody like this is "an authorized transgression" that is "both "repetition and difference . . . both conservative and transformative."[22]

As a *relámpago paralelo*, "Soneto monomaniaco" is written by a reader whose idealized reader is also . . . a reader. Furthermore, the subject of the poem itself is the faith of the reader: "¡Ah, / la / fe / Del / que / ve!" All the possible pairings of complements here return to the inseparable nature of reading and writing:

real poet	+	real reader
implied poet	+	implied reader
poet/reader	+	reader of Blanco/ reader of other poets
reader/poet	+	creator of meanings
poetic voice	+	reader in the poem, etc.

The permutations of complementarity these poems conjure up are fueled by the energy the reader brings to the text—empathetic energy for connection and communion—and poems feature energy of their own in the metaphors that give them "conceptual depth" or texture. "Más transparente" ["More transparent"] creates a dialogue with Octavio Paz through a cerebral game played through form and, as in music, repetition:

"Más transparente"

NACISTE PARA VIVIR EN UNA ISLA

Más transparente
Que esa gota de agua
Entre los dedos de la enredadera

Mi pensamiento tiende un puente
De ti misma a ti misma
        Mírate
Más real que el cuerpo que habitas
Fija en el centro de mi frente
*

FIJA EN EL CENTRO DE MI FRENTE

Más transparente
Que esa gota de agua
Entre los dedos de la enredadera
Mi pensamiento tiende un puente
De ti misma a ti misma
        Mírate
Más real que el cuerpo que habitas
*

MÁS REAL QUE EL CUERPO QUE HABITAS

Más transparente
Que esa gota de agua
Entre los dedos de la enredadera
Mi pensamiento tiende un puente
De ti misma a ti misma
        Mírate
*

MÍRATE

Más transparente
Que esa gota de agua
Entre los dedos de la enredadera
Mi pensamiento tiende un puente
De ti misma a ti misma
*

DE TI MISMA A TI MISMA
Más transparente
Que esa gota de agua
Entre los dedos de la enredadera
Mi pensamiento tiende un puente
*

MI PENSAMIENTO TIENDE UN PUENTE
Más transparente
Que esa gota de agua
Entre los dedos de la enredadera

*

ENTRE LOS DEDOS DE LA ENREDADERA

Más transparente
Que esa gota de agua[23]

["More Transparent"

YOU WERE BORN TO LIVE ON AN ISLAND

More transparent
than that drop of water
Between the fingers of a vine
My thoughts build a bridge
From you to yourself
            See yourself

More real than the body you inhabit
Fixed in the center of my forehead
*

FIXED IN THE CENTER OF MY FOREHEAD

More transparent
than that drop of water
Between the fingers of a vine
My thoughts build a bridge
From you to yourself
            See yourself
More real than the body you inhabit
*

MORE REAL THAN THE BODY YOU INHABIT

More transparent
than that drop of water
Between the fingers of a vine
My thoughts build a bridge
From you to yourself
            See yourself
*

SEE YOURSELF

More transparent
than that drop of water
Between the fingers of a vine
My thoughts build a bridge
From you to yourself

*

FROM YOU TO YOURSELF

More transparent
than that drop of water
Between the fingers of a vine
My thoughts build a bridge
*

MY THOUGHTS BUILD A BRIDGE

More transparent
than that drop of water
Between the fingers of a vine
*

BETWEEN THE FINGERS OF A VINE

More transparent
than that drop of water]

This visual and aural collage employs repetition and strategic line and stanza breaks to reconfigure our understanding of the intentionally multivoiced adjectives of its source text, Paz's poem "Madrigal." Madrigals, of course, are multivoiced musical compositions, and here the poem's adjectives connect with different nouns: What is "more transparent" in the first section? An island? The speaker's thoughts? One irony of Blanco's version is that his poem opens up the text to being even more transparent than the original since his creative rearrangement highlights the poem's *heteroglossia*.

"Más transparente" contains three dominant voices—Paz, Blanco, and the reader. The use of the second person adds yet another "meta" layer to the text as the reader decides whether to identify with the "tú," or not. The final shorter stanzas open up the text even more. All-in-all, "Más transparente" shows the deft hand of a verbal collagist who is skilled at making us think about the process of reading and the different ways in which we "round off" poems.

"Canto a no yo" ["Song to Not Myself"] displays the multitudes these poems can contain. This pastiche of Walt Whitman's masterpiece mimics the phrasing, scientific vocabulary, and transcendental unity of its original but also takes the poem another step further. Furthermore, it is doubly self-referential since it is explicitly about both writing and reading poetry. In the first stanza, poetry is described as a place to cross over and lose the kind of personal ambitions or cult of authorship Lautréamont critiqued with the statement "poetry must be made by all and not by one." Language, especially the limited subjectivity of the first-person singular, is presented as a flawed medium and impediment to the expression of being:

"Canto a no yo"

Celebro y canto la ausencia de yo.
Y si va implícito un yo en los verbos que utilizo
es porque no hay otra forma de hablar que pudiera resultarnos
-comprensible,
y lo que digo ahora de mí, lo digo de ti y de todos,
pues no hay un átomo en nuestro cuerpo
que no esté en continuo movimiento
transformándose incesantemente en otra cosa.[24]

["Song to Not Myself"

I celebrate and sing the absence of myself.
And if that I is implicit in the Spanish verbs I use
it is because there is no other way to speak that could be understandable
and what I say now of myself, I say of you and of all,
since there is not an atom in our bodies
that is not in constant movement
transforming us incessantly into other things.]

In the second stanza, the poet approaches the idea of oneness through a mixture of scientific discourse and mystery:

¿Cómo podría ser el yo
formado de átomos y de recuerdos,
de nombres y de formas,
de historias personales, inventadas y reales,
de alimentos digeridos con laborioso esfuerzo,
de gases mezclados en sabias proporciones,
de líquidos complejos y maravillosos como la sangre
donde marchan unidas todas las generaciones que de seres humanos
-hemos sido,
mamíferos, invertebrados, insectos y moluscos, criaturas unicelulares,
con todas y cada una de las células llevando el sello de su herencia
en un código de belleza exquisita e inefable,
una inmutable realidad,
si todo lo que nos constituye está cambiando constantemente,
se mueve, se forma y se transforma,
a una velocidad cercana a la de la luz?[25]

[How could I be the I
that is formed by atoms and memories,
names and forms,

personal narratives, invented and real,
foods digested with laborious effort,
gasses mixed in knowing proportions,
complex and marvelous liquids like blood
where all the generations of human beings we have ever been march
together
mammals, invertebrates, insects and mollusks, single cell creatures,
with each and every one of their cells bearing the seal of their legacy
in an exquisitely beautiful and ineffable code,
an immutable reality,
if all that makes us up is constantly changing,
moving, forming and transforming,
at a velocity near that of light?]

A line like "gases mezclados en sabias proporciones" exhibits the kind of tension between the known and unknown that defines Blanco's poetry. It is a statement that forms a question and the energy the reader spends between knowing and not knowing is what powers the text. Just as the poet wrote that "La experiencia de leer poesía implica una forma distinta de aproximarse a los polos del espacio y el tiempo" [The experience of reading poetry implies a distinct form of approaching the poles of space and time],[26] "Canto a no yo" insists that subjectivity is in a state of constant flux at speeds as important yet mysterious as the waves and particles that form light.

If the second stanza dives into the human body like a microscope, the third stanza telescopes out and contextualizes humanity's place in the universe.

¿Si la misma tierra que pisan nuestros pies
flotando en el espacio sideral no se está quieta
ni quieto está el sol en torno al cual nuestro planeta gira,
ni quieta e inmutable está nuestra galaxia,
naciendo y muriendo a cada instante
entre novas, supernovas y hoyos negros, enanas blancas y rojas,
constelaciones escuchadas más que vistas,
y previstas más que escuchadas?[27]

[If the very earth our feet stand upon
floating in outer space is not still
and neither is the sun around which our planet spins,
and our galaxy is neither still not immutable,
being born and dying at each moment
between novas, supernovas and black holes, red and white dwarves,
constellations more often heard than seen
and more often dreamed than heard?]

The next stanza inverts and recalibrates some of Whitman's most famous lines ("Do I contract myself? / Very well then, I contract myself, / (I am large, I contain multitudes)") and then rewrites the allegorical metaphor of "leaves of grass" as "un mar con olas."

Vagamos de forma en forma,
de cuerpo en cuerpo vagamos
y nada de lo que somos es realmente nuestro.
Y nada de lo que somos variada y sorprendentemente somos
pues no somos una multitud a solas sino que somos uno.

Un mar donde la individualidad de cada ola
no es sino el lujo de la forma en un instante
hecho por su propia gracia y para ser
consistente y solidario con el fondo del mar
que en su continuo movimiento necesita de las olas
pero que no es distinto de las olas.
Un mar con olas que no es sino un lujo del lenguaje.[28]

[We wander from form to form,
from body to body we wander,
and no part of what we are is really ours.
No part of what we are, what we eclectically and surprisingly are,
because we are not a multitude alone but rather we are one.

An ocean where the individuality of each wave
is nothing but the luxury of form in a moment
made by its own grace in order to be
consistent and in solidarity with the bottom of the ocean
which, in its continuous movement, needs the waves
but is not separate from the waves.
An ocean with waves that is nothing more than a luxury of language.]

The powerful metaphor of "un mar con olas" is a variation on the wave/particle duality that undergirds Blanco's poetics. Just as Borges noted that "cada escritor crea sus precursores" [all writers create their own precursors] Blanco's metaphor would be impossible without Whitman. The poem ends with a recognition of the "energía original" [original energy] that creates the special space and time of reading and writing poetry that allowed us to have this intense and multivoiced experience:

Los padres que me engendraron están aquí,
y los padres que te engendraron también están aquí,
como están los padres que engendraron a nuestros padres y así
—sucesivamente

hasta ver que todos venimos de la misma madre y del mismo
—padre
más allá del África remota y las primeras migraciones,
más acá de la próxima mutación que habrá de llevarnos
allende las computadoras y la odisea del espacio
sin restricción de la energía original
a dar alma a la naturaleza.[29]

[The parents that conceived me are here,
and the parents that conceived you are also here,
as are the parents that conceived our parents and so on
until we realize that we all come from the same mother and father
farther back than remote Africa and the first migrations,
closer than the next mutation that will have to lead us
away beyond computers and space odysseys
without restricting the original energy
that gives a soul to nature]

Whitman ends his epic with his "yo," but Blanco's poem stays true to its title by avoiding the first-person singular and staying in the *nosotros*. This is not to say that "Canto a no yo" competes with the thematic breadth of Whitman's song, particularly its connections to the process of national grieving after the U.S. Civil War. Instead, it contains a specific variation and clarification of Whitman's message of unity and the place of the individual within society. It also features, by implication, a critique of the American capitalist system.

As this section makes apparent, readers and writers are separate sides of the same coin—a unit we are able to see both sides of simultaneously through the experience of reading poetry.

Writing Readers

Basing an opinion solely on "Reserva" or the *vasos comunicantes*, it might seem easy to rush to judgment about Blanco's hypothetical implied or, to use Stockwell's term, "idealized" reader.[30] "Reserva" describes poetry as a *locus amoenus*, privileged, and apart from everyday life, and the poems based on *hacedores* send even the most knowledgeable readers, listeners of music, or viewers of art scrambling to the internet to learn more about unknown or unfamiliar authors or artists. While there can be no doubt about the actual poet's personal archive of knowledge, it seems disingenuous and unrealistic to assume that his books expect his implied readers to catch all of his allusions. Instead, we need to consider this situation in the context of Blanco's entire body of work and remember the central role the unknown plays in creating the textures of these poems.

In the essays of *El canto y el vuelo*, Blanco mentions over and over that inspiration is something a poet both receives and then gives to readers. His inspired readers then use the empathy, the desire for connection, and the "*ekphrastic* hope" his poems incite to overcome what W. J. T. Mitchell calls "anxieties about merging with others."[31] As "Canto a no yo" shows, part of the fear of otherness is normalized through the poet's insistence that he is a reader writing texts for other readers who then create their own versions of the poems.

Wolfgang Iser's differentiation between implied reader and real reader is a frequent touchstone in Blanco's poems, particularly in *La hora y la neblina*. "Sueño del lenguaje" ["A Dream of Language"], for example, conjugates reader response's notions of real author, implied author, implied reader, and real reader:

Nada de lo que digo
es sólo un sueño
del lenguaje;

También existe
el que sueña
este lenguaje.

Y, por si fuera poco,
el que lo escucha
y lo comprende.

Nada de lo que digo
es sólo un sueño
del lenguaje.

Porque aquí estás tú.[32]

[None of what I say
is only a dream
of language;

There also exists
the one who dreams
this language.

And, for what it's worth,
the one who listens to
and understands it.

None of what I say
is only a dream
of language.

Because you are here.]

Stanza 1 critiques ideas such as the death of the author and Deconstruction's insistence on the indeterminacy of signs. The first-person subject of "digo" would traditionally be assumed to be the implied poet, but the second stanza adds another layer, one that dreams of and prefigures the appearance of language. Stanza 3 refers to a reader or, perhaps, back to the implied poet that listens to and understands inspiration that comes from within. The formal break of the final stanza and position of the conclusive "tú" reinforces the idea that a real poet is speaking to a real reader.

The switch to the second person, when used sparingly, is a forceful and startling way to highlight an actual reader. Blanco uses the second person to address the reader in a few different ways and for different ends. In "Winter Sea," for example, the poet describes following a lover along the beach by walking in her footsteps. The first six stanzas repeat "hasta" [until] and variations of "seguir" [to follow] to highlight the rhythm and separation between the speaker and the one making the original footprints.

Sigo las huellas
de alguien en la playa:

Sigo a la misma mujer
que hace veinte años siguiera
hasta la casa en las montañas,
hasta el origen de los bosques,
hasta el espejo en el volcán.[33]

[I'm following the footprints
of someone on the beach:

I'm following the same woman
that twenty years ago I would follow
up to the house in the mountains,
out to the beginning of the forest,
into the mirror of the volcano.]

Stanzas 7 and 8 employ visual flourishes to launch the poem from a literal to a more figurative level. Notice how "dirección" [direction] in verse 23 causes a change of speed and how verse 24, about mimesis, imitates the length of verse 22 and thus takes the poem in another (visual) direction:

No es fácil andar
por la vida siguiendo
las huellas de alguien más . . .
por más atractivas que parezcan.

Lo único que se consigue
en esta dirección
es una mímesis perfecta[34]

[It's not easy walking
through life following
someone else's footsteps . . .
as attractive as they may be.

The only thing gained
in that direction
is a perfect imitation]

Stanza 9 uses another graphic form to highlight a change in time and rhythm:

—una distancia
  un tiempo
    un ritmo—

que no nos corresponde,
un viaje en otro cuerpo
y un camino diferente.

Mas por otra parte es tan fácil
dejarse llevar por el vaivén . . .
saber que no estoy solo
en esta playa fría.[35]

[–a distance
  a tempo
    a rhythm—

that does not belong to us
a trip in another body
and on a different path.

Yet on the other hand it's so easy
to let yourself be led by the rhythm . . .
knowing that I am not alone
on this cold beach.]

After opening up walking to its many possible levels of allegory (love, education, parenting, perhaps faith), the speaker ends by using that second person to zoom in on the relationship with the reader:

Saber que alguien me antecede
como yo mismo antecedo
tus pasos sigilosos

—sí, estoy hablando de ti,
cómplice lector, lectora—

recorriendo este poema.

North Beach, San Francisco
Noviembre de 1989[36]

[Knowing that someone comes before me
as I myself come before
your discreet steps

—yes, I am talking to you,
my reader accomplice—

that traverse this poem.

North Beach, San Francisco
November 1989]

Part of the novelty of this particular text is how it cleverly intersperses leading and following. The poem's multilayered metaphor, then, is that a person walking in another person's footprints in the sand is like a poet writing a poem and, also, like a reader reading a poem.

Perhaps Blanco's use of the second person in *La hora y la neblina* can be traced back to 1980's *El largo camino hacia Ti* [*The Long Road to You*], the first movement of 1990's epic *Cuenta de los guías* [*Account of the Guides*]. In those dense texts, the poetic voice uses the second person as a bold (though scarce) ordering device in the fragmented poetic wilderness of his longest and most challenging poems. Of *Cuenta de los guías* Marco Antonio Campos notes: "El libro es una suerte de bella narración hecha por un yo (o un nosotros) alucinado(s) que cuentan sus experiencias y reflexiones a alguien (un personaje ideal) que más que leerlo debe oírlo" [The book is a kind of pretty narration told by an amazed I (or a we) that recounts their experiences and reflections to someone (an ideal character) that more than read it should hear it]."[37] Nonetheless, it's easy for the reader to feel overlooked or lost amid a sea of images, so when we *are* addressed directly by Blanco's "directives," it's startling, even if we are, after all, the second party in the collective *nosotros* that sometimes assumes the subject position of this book.[38]

Poem 16 of *Cuenta de los guías* begins with the kind of enumeration that characterizes the larger poem in 260 cantos and then recognizes the physical connection of reader and book:

El canto de las criaturas en el buen camino, las palabras de plata sobre el lienzo azul, la mirada en la frente limpia del firmamento.

Tú la has visto también. Sientes su calor en la palma de tu mano, los hilos paralelos, la serpiente de plumas luminosas.[39]

[The song of the creatures on the good path, the silver words on a blue canvas, the look on the clean forehead of the firmament.

You have also seen it. You feel its warmth in the palm of your hand, the parallel threads, the snake with luminous feathers.]

El largo camino hacia Ti is the first of five sections of *Cuenta de los guías*. Poem 52, its important last poem, drops us into the same room as the speaker and addresses us through the double (or triple) voiced "Ti" of the section's title:

Justo la proporción necesaria para llegar al fin sin que falte, sin que sobre . . . la duda, la pasión, la permanencia. No nos hemos movido de esta habitación y sin embargo el espíritu ve más alto, más seguro.

Es un largo camino, un largo camino hacia Ti, hacia el principio.[40]

[Exactly the necessary proportion to get to the end without anything missing, anything left over . . . doubt, passion, permanence. We haven't moved from this room and nonetheless our spirits are up, feeling safer.

It is a long road, a long road to you, to the beginning.]

Occasionally, as in poem 104, the speaker turns and addresses his readers directly in the second person. These directives help anchor us and help keep our attention as we move through an abstract swirl of language and subjects:

Allí donde fallamos, pido fuerza, no para ser más y más poderoso que mi hermano, sino para entrar a una batalla crucial conmigo mismo, y salir como si nada.

¿Y tú, no quieres entrar?[41]

[There where we fail, I ask for help, not to be more and more powerful than my brother, but rather to enter a crucial battle against myself, and to emerge unscathed.

How about you? Don't you want to come in?]

A little further down the path we come across the especially metapoetic poem 183. Not only does the poetic guide (perhaps the *guía* of the title) call us readers out by name here, it also comments on the momentum of the text, which is about to speed up by relying more heavily on fuller, more traditional verses. The poem also makes a promise. The promise of a birth, even a figurative one, is another of the ways in which Blanco creates tension and anticipation in order to keep us reading and moving forward through this forest of words.

> Aquí te recuerdo a ti, sí, a ti que me lees en este preciso instante:
> Te tengo presente como no podrías—tal vez—imaginarlo . . . con la misma certeza con la que asciende el humo o el agua cae.
> Y poco a poco, gracias a una laboriosa recreación, gracias a la continuidad del día y la noche, vamos adquiriendo cierta velocidad.
> Y lo que está por nacer—o quien está por nacer—comienza a jalar hacia sí todas las estrellas.[42]

> [Here I remember you, yes, you who reads me at this very moment:
> I have you in mind more than you could—perhaps—imagine . . . with the same certainty with which smoke rises or water falls.
> Little by little, thanks to an arduous recreation, thanks to the continuity of the day and night, we are gaining some momentum.
> And what is to be born—or who is to be born—begins to pull close all the stars.]

As the last quote from *Cuenta de los guías* mentions, the process of reading poetry presents new ways of moving through time and space. "Espacio vivo" ["Living Space"] expands upon this process by questioning the dynamic of space and energy exchanged between an actual poet and his poetic voice, between a literal and a figurative blank page, between a reader and her or himself, between poetic voice and implied reader, and between a text and its real reader:

> Aquí vivo.
> Entre estas cuatro orillas vivo.
> Este es mi espacio, mi refugio,
> mi medio, mi herramienta.
>
> ¿A dónde he de ir ahora?
> ¿Acaso hay algo más
> que esta página en blanco
> de mi vida?
>
> Aquí te ves
> y aquí te veo,
> una vez más, lector.
> Aquí se da el encuentro.
>
> ¿Hay algo más para ti
> —por el momento—
> que esta página
> que el destino nos ofrece?

Entre estas cuatro esquinas
hemos de confirmar lo que somos:
¡hilos de luz en la neblina![43]

[I live here.
Between these four shores I live.
This is my space, my refuge,
my medium, my tool.

Where am I supposed to go now?
Perhaps there is something more
than this blank page
in my life?

Here you see yourself
and here I see you,
once again, reader.
The meeting is here.

Is there something more for you
—for the moment—
than this page
that destiny offers us?

Between these four corners
we must confirm what we are:
threads of light in the mist!]

Much as visual artists try out ideas on sketch pads, "Teoría del espacio" expands and reconfigures motives from texts such as "Espacio vivo" to create one of Blanco's culminating poems about reading. Interestingly, the poem also contains echoes of the phrasing and imagery of Mexico's classic pre-Columbian text "Yo lo pregunto" ["I Ask the Question"] by Nezahualcóyotl. "Teoría del espacio" exploits that dynamic between reader and writer through a strong visual form framed, through its title and place in the "Teorías" ["Theories"] series, by the discourse of physics.

"Teoría del espacio"

Vamos a comenzar por el principio:

Estamos aquí.

Ustedes lo saben tan bien como yo.

Unidos por la palabra estamos aquí.
Al servicio de una voz estamos aquí.

Leyendo entre líneas estamos aquí.
Al pie de la letra estamos aquí.

¿Acaso conocemos otro punto
de partida que el estar aquí?

Nunca hemos estado en otro lugar.
Nunca hemos conocido otro tiempo.
Nunca nos hemos visto en el pasado.
Nunca nos encontraremos en el futuro.

Esto es lo que conocemos
y esto lo que compartimos.

No tenemos otro espacio.
No tenemos otro tiempo.
No tenemos otra vida.
No tenemos otro cuerpo.

Estamos aquí.
Sólo aquí.
Aquí.[44]

[Let's start at the beginning:

We are here.

You know it as well as I do.

United by words we are here.
Serving a voice we are here.
Reading between the lines we are here.
Very literally we are here.

Do we even know of another starting
point than being here?

We have never been in another place.
We have never been in another time.
We have never seen each other in the past.
We will never meet in the future.

This is what we know
and what we share.

We don't have another space.
We don't have another time.
We don't have another life.

We don't have another body.
    We are here.
        Only here.
            Here.]

Time's arrow examines space in the poem or, more precisely, poetry's special blend of space-time. The last stanza blends the known and unknown in a particularly intriguing way—first, by combining the two subjects into one verb form (*estamos*) and then repeatedly changing position by dropping the anchor word *aquí* to the next line. The visual progression begs us to question the meanings of the last *aquí*. Is it itself the final step of a dynamic evolution of meaning or does the arrow indicate a space *after* the last verse as the place where the poetic voice and reader cohabitate forever? If so, that space would be the silence of a reader's mind during their first pause after reaching the text's final word. If this is the case, does that last "verse" after "Aquí" exist in the space of the poem? Or is it implied as a present-absence, a negative space created by an arrow of signs? In many ways, "Teoría del espacio" is simply a modernized version of the haunting line "Sólo un poco aquí" [Only here for a short time] attributed to Nezahualcóyotl.

"Teoría del espacio" shows how visual poetry deepens a poem's textures and how our interpretations of texts multiply when viewed as part of broader cycles and informed by the context of a poet's long and winding road of reading. When we read the last line of "Mi tribu" ["My Tribe"] (one of Blanco's most popular early poems dedicated to the Band) as part of what we have just studied, it's hard to not see the poet's tribe as readers:

. . . No hablo de una tribu humana.
No hablo de una tribu planetaria.
No hablo siquiera de una tribu universal.

Hablo de una tribu de la que no se puede hablar.

Una tribu que ha existido siempre
pero cuya existencia está todavía por ser comprobada.

Una tribu que no ha existido nunca
pero cuya existencia
podemos ahora mismo comprobar.[45]

[. . . I'm not talking about a human tribe.
I'm not talking about a planetary tribe.
I'm not even talking about a universal tribe.

I am talking about a tribe that can't be talked about.

A tribe that has always existed
but whose existence has yet to be proven.

A tribe that has not ever existed
but whose existence
we can prove right now.]

"Ahora mismo" is the special time of poetry. Basing himself on the Nobel Prize–winning chemist Ilya Prigogine, in the essay "La ciencia" ["Science"] Blanco affirms "Tiempo inscrito en la materia: esto es el arte. Esto es también la poesía" [Time inscribed in matter: this is art. This is also poetry].[46]

Writing Writing

The early essay "Poesía y poética" [Poetry and Poetics] from *El llamado y el don* discusses how poetics can be termed descriptive (when composed *after* the poetry it studies) or prescriptive (as a guideline to be consulted *before* writing poems). Modern poetics tend toward the more descriptive pole, as does modern poetry.[47] A little later, in the essay "El significado" [Meaning], the poet considers another related phenomenon—poetry written about itself. Blanco attributes this trend, on the one hand, to society's increased "capacidad de autocrítica" [capacity of self-awareness], but he also sees the possibility, drawing on ideas by Emil Cioran, that contemporary forms of art are reducing their audience so quickly that soon, perhaps only artists will be left to read and appreciate the arts.[48]

We have already seen many types of self-referential poetry in this chapter but like so many of the descendants of Baudelaire ("'ese abuelo instantáneo' de la poesía moderna" [that instant grandfather of modern poetry])[49] Blanco's work is replete with references to his "semblante" [reader whom he resembles]. In the last section we discussed how the second person is used to anchor the reader in *Cuenta de los guías* but that "tú" also adds new layers of metapoetic interest. A little past the midway point of the book, the poetic voice calls for our attention and then challenges us: "Si eres un buen jugador puedes ver de antemano los próximos movimientos de esta partida alegórica: jazz-a-brass" [If you are a good player you can foretell the next movements in this allegorical deal: jazz-a-brass].[50] He then notes:

> Hay tantas formas de armar este rompecabezas, que cada solución inventa un problema distinto . . . y lo resuelve.
>
> Ajedrez de la vida: blanco, negro; masculino, femenino; derecho, izquierdo. Se trata, desde luego, de toda la balanza, del juego completo . . . pero en el lado izquierdo palpita el corazón[51]

> [There are so many ways to solve this puzzle, that each solution invents a new and different problem . . . and resolves it.
>
> Chessboard of life: white, black; masculine, feminine; right, left. It's all about, of course, balance, the complete set . . . but on the left side beats the heart]

First we are teased with traces of the incomplete metanarratives that help form the book (literary allegories, long poems, jazz, chess, dialectical puzzles), and then we are locked out "even if we are good players" by a system that solves itself. A problematic poem in which "cada solución inventa un problema distinto . . . y lo resuelve" [every solution invents a distinct problem . . . and resolves it], *Cuenta de los guías* contains two voices, two poles, that mirror the act of reading and writing. As Cioran noted, this particular kind of metapoetry runs the risk of replacing the reader and creating "un universo privado e incomunicable" [a private and incommunicable universe].[52]

While modern writers and readers are more like each other than ever, the simple act of reading itself will not make someone a poet. This is where the mystery of inspiration comes in, what Blanco calls "el llamado" [the call]. In the fascinating creed that concludes the essay "La tradición" ["Tradition"], the writer states his belief that everyone is an artist in some sense of the word and that the way to discover what kind of artist we are is to listen for and follow a call or calling ("ese llamado particular que nos dice que clase de artistas, hacedores, poetas, somos" [that particular call that tells us what kind of artist, creator, poet, we are][53] and to then act: "Primero la visión y después la realización. Inspiración y construcción" [First the vision, and then fulfillment. Inspiration and construction].[54]

"Poema visto en una pluma atómica" ["Poem Seen in a Ballpoint Pen"] is one of many Blanco poems to wonder at the mystery of inspiration. Stanzas 1 through 4 and the final stanza 8 wonder at the subjectivity of an inspired writer, but stanzas 5, 6, and 7 are about the writer as reader and the importance of that blend of complements. Even if the writer is also a reader, his "yo" [I] can live only in the minds of others:

"Poema visto en una pluma atómica"

¡Cómo salen palabras de mi boca!
¡Cómo cantan al tacto del papel!
¡Cómo brotan sin yo mismo
saber qué es lo que digo!

Vienen de dentro
pero no las conozco.

Es como si alguien
las dijera a través de mí.

Como si alguien más
en este momento me pensara.

Yo conozco esa sensación
de ser una presencia en otro cuerpo . . .

Y conozco también el vacío
que sigue a las palabras.

Pero sin el contacto humano
que enciende mi escritura
no tengo explicación
ni sentido alguno.

Sólo soy quien soy
mientras escribo.[55]

[How these words stream from my mouth!
How they sing when they meet the paper!
How they flow without I myself
knowing what I say!

They come from within
but I don't know them.

It's as if someone
spoke them through me.

As if someone else
at this moment were thinking through me.

I know that sensation
of being present in another body.

I also know the emptiness
that follows words.

But without human contact
to light up my writing
I have no explanation
or any meaning at all.

I only am who I am
while I'm writing.]

The dualities of "yo—no yo" [I—not I] that drove the Whitman poem and "poeta—lector" [poet—reader] from the text above also resurface in "Autorretrato" [Self-Portrait]:

"Autorretrato"

Toda la fuerza de un autorretrato
se dirige sin duda a la ilusión

de que no hay más altura que la humana
ni más centro que *yo*.

Así el autorretrato del artista
se encuentra dominado por la inútil
pasión de hacer un Dios de cada *yo*
para retar al tiempo.

Pues *yo* soy el que pinta autorretratos;
también soy el que escribe este poema:
yo soy el que gobierna esta cuarteta . . .
¿o soy un fingidor?

¿O soy un instrumento de fortuna,
un tubo donde soplan otros vientos,
un árbol que del cielo se desplanta
para tocar el suelo?[56]

[The main goal of a self-portrait
is, without a doubt, to promote the illusion
that there is nothing higher than humanity
nor more central than *I*.

And so self-portraits of artists
seem to be dominated by the futile
desire to make a God of every *I*
in order to challenge time.

I am the one that paints self-portraits
I am also the one writing this poem:
I and the one that rules this quatrain . . .
or am I a pretender?

Or am I an instrument of luck
a tube through which other winds blow,
a tree uprooted from the sky
in order to touch the ground?]

One of the cornerstones of Blanco's poetics is that poets need to pass the inspiration they receive on to their readers—"esta 'necesidad interior' en el poeta debe manifestarse como una 'necesidad interior' en la obra" [this "internal need" in the poet should become manifest as an "internal need" in the work].[57] These ideas are similarly found in the poet's interest in other repeating patterns such as fractals.

In every poet's universe there are both indirect and direct metapoetic motifs. As we will examine below, the image of a line that extends from the center of a circle to its edge (a radius or half its diameter) is a one of Blanco's most original metaphors for the process of writing poetry. We see this trope at work in the first poem of "El tacto y la mirada" ["Touch and Sight"] from *A la luz de siempre* in which inspiration is embodied as "Los ángeles geómetras" ["The Geometry of Angels"]:

Dando vueltas y vueltas
en torno a la tierra
tratando de echar luz
entre la forma original
de dibujar un círculo
la línea recta
y la palabra justa
el sueño de los ángeles
que sobrevuela ese territorio
que se extiende
entre el día y la noche
nos redime de la soledad[58]

[Turning round and round
around the earth
trying to shed light
between the original form
of drawing a circle
the straight line
and the right word
the dreams of angels
that fly over the spaces
that extend
between the day and night
redeem us from solitude]

Geometry's connections to measuring the earth, mapping our visual horizon, and calculating our position in relation to the stars are all certainly implied in this metaphor. After an intentionally quick example of the speed of poetry, "Poesía" [Poetry] uses metaphors of geometry to tell us what poetry (though not "Poetry") is.

"Poesía"

¿Qué es la poesía
o—acaso—que era?

La estrella polar del mediodía
y el filo cortante de una esfera.[59]

["Poetry"

What is poetry
or—perhaps—what was it?

The pole star at midday
and the cutting edge of a sphere.]

The center and circle motif also appears in the extremely abstract metapoem: "Círculo del horizonte" ["Circle of the Horizon"], an intense, spiritual voyage from linguistic abstraction into literal life. The poem's first section is about polarities, while its second is about union:

Sueño con la obra redonda
que conserva su filo
a pesar de las contradicciones
y justamente a través de ellas

Las que siempre han sido mi sostén
en horas de amargura precisa
mis mejores amigas
la música y la imagen[60]

[I dream of the rounded work
that maintains its edge
despite the contradictions
and precisely through them

Those that have always sustained me
in hours of bitterness
my best friends
music and images]

In *Cuenta de los guías* we read, "La pluma en la diestra, el corazón del lado izquierdo y el centro en todas partes" [With my pen to the right, my heart to the left and the center everywhere].[61] This center is more than just the "yo" [I] or the source of poetry. Enrico Mario Santí notes that the notion of a center in Tantric Buddhism can allude to "'the Way of the Center,' the name given historically to *Madhyamika*, the middle road of Buddhist relativity that was reconceptualized and refined by Nagarjuna, the master of this 'central' tendency which proclaims an emptiness that neither affirms nor denies the world."[62]

The circle and line metaphor and concept of the center appear in most of Alberto Blanco's poems about poetics—from "Teoría poética" ["Poetic Theory"] to "Poética" ["Poetics"]:

La poesía
es un rayo

Entre el centro
de la atención

Y el círculo
del lenguaje.[63]

[Poetry
is a line

Between the center
of our attention

And the circle
of language]

The powerful "(Centro)" ["(Center)"] from *La hora y la neblina* uses most of the poet's main structuring elements (rhyme, concrete poetry, *litotes,* complements, a division into sections based on the compass rose, etc.) to meditate on the center and describe a deep interior dive. The poem's fifth and last section summarizes the text into one tight visual and verbal rhyme:

V
*
**
entro
centro
adentro
encuentro
el epicentro
•
el epicentro
encuentro
adentro
centro
entro
**
*[64]

[V
*
**
I
enter

center
inside
encounter
the epicenter
•
the epicenter
encounter
inside
center
enter
I
**
*

The center is the core in figures of mandalas and the source of the energy that reaches out to listen to language and transform it into a textured mix of images, sounds, ideas, and mysteries.

Hemispheres

It's not hard to imagine where Blanco's passion for polarities comes from. Two of the final entries of his creed in the essay "La tradición" ["Tradition"] read:

> * Creo que la obra de arte—el poema—al seguir el llamado de esta 'necesidad interior'—eso que mueve a las plantas a buscar la luz—no hace más que poner en juego un modo de operar análogo al de la naturaleza.
> * Creo que este modo de operar implica un conocimiento profundo de la naturaleza, así como del material particular—en nuestro caso: el lenguaje—en el cual, y con el cual, ha de realizarse la obra de arte.[65]
>
> [* I believe that a work of art—a poem—by following the call of an 'internal need'—that which moves the plants toward the light—is not doing anything other than operating in an analogous way to nature.
> * I believe that this way of operating implies a deep knowledge of nature, as well as of matter—in this case: language—in which and with which, a work of art is to be made.]

The first point tells us that there is a biological impulse toward creation, and the second implores us to learn all we can about the source of art: language and, by extension, biology, and neuroscience.

In terms of biology, Leonard Shlain (an important influence on Blanco) notes, "On casual examination, the human brain appears to be a symmetrical, bilobed structure. . . . Yet each hemisphere is in charge of entirely different functions."[66] Language, according to neuroscience, is a function of the brain's left hemisphere, and images are processed by the right lobe. Shlain, like any reasonable student of this incredibly complex and evolving subject, notes that generalizations about the main characteristics of the brain's hemispheres are necessarily imprecise. That being said, research indicates that the two sides of the brain do carry out different tasks: the left side (which controls the right side of the body) appears to be more concerned with making things and, paradoxically, abstract thinking. The left side also is the main processor of language and numbers. The right hemisphere is more concerned with being than with doing, with images rather than words, with metaphor, and with music. Research suggests that the left side thinks more sequentially while the right seems to function in a more "*all-at-once* mode."[67] One of many experiments that have contributed to our understanding of the connections of the lobes involves the French composer Maurice Ravel, "who suffered a stroke in his left hemisphere which left him unable to speak, write, or read musical notation. Yet he could sing and play on the piano from memory any piece he knew before his stroke."[68]

Despite the separation of functions by side, both hemispheres work together, in a mixture of independent and interrelated functioning that is beyond the current grasp of science. Shlain likens this process to weaving on a loom "intertwining the warp and woof of right and left, space and time, art and physics."[69] In the essay "La ciencia" Blanco quotes neurologist Richard Restak:

> Es muy útil pensar que la creatividad toma más del hemisferio cerebral izquierdo que del derecho, pero semejante esquema no es más que metafórico. Es *el cerebro entero* el que se halla involucrado en la creatividad, con ambos hemisferios comunicándose entre sí mediante más de ochocientos millones de neurofibras.[70]

> [While it is useful to think that creativity draws more from the left cerebral hemisphere than from the right, that paradigm is only a metaphor. The *whole brain* is involved in creativity, with both hemispheres communicating with each other through more than eight hundred million neurofibers.]

These comments by Shlain, Restak and Blanco all show the centrality of metaphoric language to the understanding and explaining of difficult concepts to others, in much the same way that thought experiments explain and make up important foundations of quantum mechanics.

The principles and metaphors of brain lateralization have informed Blanco's poems and essays since his earliest work. In "La ciencia" he writes:[71]

> Se trata, pues, de dos oficios, dos lenguajes, dos tradiciones, dos lógicas y dos visiones del mundo que, más que opuestos, habría que ver como complementarios, y que—ahora lo sabemos—corresponden a los dos modos de funcionar, interdependientes a la vez que bien diferenciados, que se han descubierto,

investigado y asignado a nuestros hemisferios cerebrales: el derecho y el izquierdo.[72]

[It's about two functions, two languages, two traditions, two logics and two visions of the world that, rather than being opposites, must be seen as complements, and that—we now know—correspond to the two ways of functioning, interdependent as well as differentiated, that have been discovered, investigated and assigned to our two cerebral hemispheres: the right and left.]

The poet then uses this idea to describe reading and writing, specifically, as a tension between two separate but interrelated complements, something he elegantly terms the "anhelo polar" [polar longing] of poetry.[73] The writer's fascination with brain lateralization comes out in many ways in his work. We see it in the foreground in an explicit comment like "Phil pinta con las dos manos, con los dos ojos, con ambos lados del cerebro" [Phil paints with his two hands, with his two eyes, with both sides of his brain][74] in the important critical poem "Phil Bragar pinta un retrato" ["Phil Bragar Paints a Portrait"] or in the background, informing every step of "Aforismos" ["Aphorisms"] the key poem about the multitalented Leonardo da Vinci:

"Aforismos"
Que no me lea quien no sea matemático,
porque yo lo soy siempre en mis principios
Leonardo da Vinci

1. El dibujo es la razón y el color es la locura.
2. Se dice que el dibujo requiere de músculos tensos y que el color sólo necesita libertad de acción.
3. El dibujo puede tener la gravedad de un argumento. El color puede tener la ingravidez que distingue a las intuiciones verdaderas. Aquél limita y este otro expande.
4. En el tiempo, el dibujo es una cita a largo plazo. Llega del mundo tridimensional a la ilusión del plano: la pintura. Del mundo bidimensional a la ilusión de las líneas: el dibujo. El color es puntual. Es instantáneo.
5. Cierto que el dibujo puede llegar a disfrutar de esa libertad propia del color, en la misma línea de las emociones; y que el color se puede someter a veces a las necesidades de la construcción, propias de los matices filosóficos, o de los sistemas puramente conceptuales.
6. Pero, en términos generales, podemos decir que el dibujo está del lado derecho de la vida, y el color está del lado izquierdo. Ambos son, obviamente necesarios. Sin ellos no hay armonía ni simetría. Expresan los principios elementales de la creación: sístole y diástole, causa y efecto, potencia y necesidad, contracción y expansión.

7. Para el dibujante racional, las manchas tienen características morales de impureza; para el colorista nato, las líneas duras y rectas tienen características morales de inflexibilidad. Más allá de la moral, baste distinguir los efectos que producen una manera y otra de trabajar, para comprender las cantidades continuas y las discontinuas, pero sobre todo, la calidad.
8. El dibujo lleva de un modo natural a las obras de la imaginación. El color, por su parte, solicita apoyo de la naturaleza para hallar sostén y forma. El dibujo: seres de razón fundados en lo imaginario. El color: seres de imaginación fundados en lo real. Son las dos alas de un mismo pájaro. La gran obra de arte viene a ser, por lo que se ha dicho, un vuelo perfecto donde estos dos principios consiguen un equilibrio precioso e inimitable.[75]

["Aphorisms"
Non mathematicians should probably not read me,
because I am always a mathematician in principle.
Leonardo da Vinci

1. Drawing is reason and color is madness.
2. It is said that drawing requires tensed muscles and that color only needs freedom of action.
3. Drawing can have the gravity of an argument. Color can have the lack of gravity which distinguishes true intentions. The latter expands while the former limits.
4. Drawing is a long-term commitment. It comes from the tridimensional world to the illusion of a flat one: painting. From the bi-dimensional world to the illusion of lines: drawing. Color is punctual. It is instantaneous.
5. It is true that drawing can achieve that same freedom that color enjoys, within the same range of emotions, and that color can yield to the necessities of construction, proper to philosophical subtleties, or to purely conceptual systems.
6. But, in general, we can say that drawing is on the right-hand side of life, and that color is on the left side. Both are, obviously necessary. Without them there is neither harmony nor symmetry. They express the elemental principles of creation: systole and diastole, cause and effect, strength and necessity, contraction and expansion.
7. For the rational artist, smudges on the drawing are characteristic of moral impurity; for the innate colorist, straight and hard lines are characteristic of moral inflexibility. Beyond the moral aspects, it might be enough to distinguish the effects that one manner or another of working produces, to comprehend the continuous and discontinuous quantities, but above all the quality.
8. Drawing is a natural medium for works of the imagination. Color, on the other hand, requires help from nature to find support and form. Drawing:

> beings of reason founded in what has been imagined. Color: imaginary beings founded in reality. They are the two wings of a single bird. The great work of art becomes, it is said, a perfect flight in which these two principles achieve a precious and inimitable equilibrium.][76]

It's clear that this poem from the 1980s contains elements of Blanco's poetics of polarity that will continue to develop over subsequent decades: poetry/prose, time/space, color/form, left/right, etc. As we will explore in our coda, "Aforismos" also contains one of Blanco's main thought experiments with regard to poetry, "las dos alas de un mismo pájaro" [two wings of the same bird]. In "Aforismos," the poet's "poetics of equilibrium," to borrow Bruce Dean Willis's term, resolves in a perfectly balanced synthesis of interdependent functions and processes, something that is not always the case, especially in his later work.[77]

"Coronación" ["Coronation"], another early visual poem from *El corazón del instante*, combines the kind of poles and opposites we see in "Aforismos" into a distinctive mixture of form and content. This visually striking text brings together life and death, days and nights, the powerful and the powerless, black and white, two opponents in a chess match, two lovers, sleep and wakefulness, interior and exterior, and other complements:

> "Coronación"
> Los hombres son la medida de todas las cosas existentes
> Al intentar coronarse al final de sus días y sus noches
> Como un rayo que asciende desde un peón hasta una reina
> O como dos rostros que se aman en el envés de un espejo
> Reunión de los opuestos   con camisas ajedrezadas
> Origen de los alfiles   que al filo del sueño
> No oyen a los caballos   trazando las paralelas
> A los estados de vigilia   a la sombra de una torre
> De dos colores   hacen su juego
> En cada hoja   ambos reinos
> Las emociones   transparentes
> Arman batallas   en el interior
> Crecen las lluvias   cambia la forma
> Ronda el tablero   de vez en cuando
> Entra a la noche   del campo entero
> Al jaque mate   con más razón
> Con mucha paciencia se gana la victoria en la fiera partida
> Imaginando los pétalos humanos sobre las losas alternas
> O tal vez la estrella que nos hace palidecer con su luz
> Nunca salió del ósculo de nuestros hemisferios cerebrales[78]

["Coronation"

People are the measure of all things that exist when trying
to crown themselves at the end of their days and nights
Like a line that runs from a pawn to a queen
Or like faces that love each other in the back of a mirror
Meeting of opposites   with checkered shirts
Origin of the bishops   that at the edge of sleep
Don't hear the horses   moving in parallel lines
To the states of wakefulness   by the shadow of a rook
Of two colors   make their move
On each page   both kingdoms
The emotions   transparent
Wage battles   in the interior
The rains pick up   forms change
Circling the board   from time to time
Entering by night   the whole field
To check mate   with more reason
With great patience one can win the fierce game
Imagining the human petals over the alternating squares
Or perhaps the star that makes us pale with its light
Having never left the kiss of our cerebral hemispheres]

"Coronación" draws it title and imagery from chess, but its central image, its crown, is also essential to its final word: brain. The poem uses words and images, both the concrete and the abstract, to create a unique artistic experience that challenges both of a reader's cerebral hemispheres. Cognitive scientists would surely study which of the text's three main elements the eye races to first when presented with this poem. Regardless of the visual track of the reader's eye, the push and pull of the poem's acrostic, its negatively spaced central visual, and its verbal content give it an uncommon and distinctive texture that, in the words of James A. W. Heffernan, "challenge and stretch our conception of what it means to read anything at all."[79]

Reading is a complex neurological process that engages both lobes of the brain working in tandem, though not symmetrically. Blanco's poems are acutely aware of this process and use it as a central metaphor for poetics. The next two sections of this chapter explore two of the most significant representations of complements in Blanco's work, one visual, one nearly impossible to envision.

Taijitu

In *El llamado y el don*, Blanco reminds us that Einstein's famous comment that "imagination is more important than knowledge" is based on the idea that imagination can bridge the two sides of our brains, sides that he, like Leonard Shlain, sometimes calls, among many other complementary sets, poetry and physics:

> Día y noche, Apolo y Dionisio, masculino y femenino, vigilia y sueño, ciencia y poesía, razón e intuición . . . la metáfora, al optar por el camino de las transformaciones y la ambivalencia no deja lugar a dudas respecto de su filiación. Allí donde el lenguaje duro, lineal, del conocimiento científico, que no admite interpretaciones ni opiniones, nos dice que Pi = 3.1416, y nada más . . . la poesía nos dice otra cosa. La poesía nos recuerda que todo está relacionado y, en última instancia, todo es lo mismo. "Todo es un ojo abierto—observa Roberto Juarroz—y yo formo parte de ese ojo."[80]
>
> [Day and night, Apollo and Dionysus, masculine and feminine, wakefulness and sleep, science and poetry, reason and intuition . . . metaphors, by opting for the road of transformations and ambivalence do not leave room for doubt about their filiation. There where the hard, linear language of scientific knowledge that admits no interpretations or opinions tells us that Pi = 3.1416, and nothing else . . . poetry tells us something else. Poetry reminds us that everything is related and, in the end, everything is the same. "Everything is an open eye"—observed Roberto Juarroz—and I am part of that eye.]

Where the opening ideas of this quote are familiar by now, the last line is central to one of the main metaphors and images in Blanco's poetics—a circle containing two different, though interconnected halves—the same yin/yang or *taijitu* symbol that intrigued Danish physicist Niels Bohr (see chapter 5). As Irma Chávez Robinson notes, the *taijitu* is a powerful sign for Blanco since it represents a unique kind of relationship, one that is constantly in motion.[81] Much like the metaphor of a magnet with two opposite yet connected poles, the *taijitu* challenges traditional dialectical notions of separation and connection and also adds the dynamic element of continual movement.

"Nocturno transfigurado" ["Transfigured Nocturne"] is one of many poems built on the "sentido intermitente" [intermittent way] of the oscillations between light and darkness, space and time, writing and speaking, day and night, life and death, things that endure and things that fade:

> "Nocturno transfigurado"
>
> La tenue luz de las palabras
> débilmente se debate
> con las sombras
>
> No alcanza a rozar los muros
> ni a penetrar en la tiniebla
> sin límites del tiempo

Por el papel avanza
mas no logra abrirse paso
más allá de su reino de sonido

Sentido intermitente
restringido al breve ámbito
de sus oscilaciones

La página escrita
en su blanda trama
de hollín y desamparo

Termina al alba
su duelo con la noche
la astuta tejedora

De su terca vigilia
de su clara batalla
con la sombra sólo queda

La ceniza
de esa luz vencida
la memoria de su vana proeza

Como un pálido aviso
del mundo de los vivos
al mundo de los que van a vivir[82]

[The tenuous light of words
weakly debates
shadow

It is unable to touch the walls
or penetrate the limitless
shadows of time

It passes through paper
but cannot make way for itself
beyond the realm of sound

Intermittent way
limited to the short field
of its oscillations

The written page
in its bland weave
of soot and neglect

Finishes at dawn
its duel with the night
the astute weaver

Of its stubborn sleeplessness
of its clear battle
with the shadows only leaving

ash
from that vanquished light
the memory of its vain feat

Like a pale notice
from the world of the living
to the world of those that have yet to live]

The vibrant relationship between complements takes many forms in Blanco. "Líneas gemelas" ["Twin Lines"], for example, is a love poem textured by spinning dualities in which opposites combine and then dynamically pass to the next strophe to further intertwine and create new metaphors of *concordia discors*:

"Líneas gemelas"

El poder del sueño
radica en la vigilia:
somos el día y la noche
para un mismo mundo.

El poder de la vigilia
radica en el tiempo:
somos dos viajes de ida
y un mismo regreso.

El poder del tiempo
radica en la música:
somos dos flautas
dando la misma nota.

El poder de la música
radica en el silencio:
sístole y diástole
en el mismo pecho.[83]

[The power of sleep
lies in wakefulness:
we are day and night
of a same world.

The power of wakefulness
lies in time:
we are two outbound trips
with one same return.

The power of time
lies in music:
we are two flutes
playing the same note.

The power of music
lies in silence:
systole and diastole
in the same chest.]

We come across the yin/yang symbol in the context of love once again in the metapoetic "Círculo del horizonte" ["Circle of the Horizon"]:

El sueño de un puente
que no separa sino que una
las riberas de la vida
y de la muerte

Dos riberas
y un solo río
dos amantes
y un solo beso

Por una instantánea eternidad
no unidos ni confundidos
simplemente unos
en la indivisibilidad del uno[84]

[The dream of a bridge
that does not separate but unites
the banks of life
and death

Two banks
and only one river
two lovers
and only one kiss

For an eternal instant
neither united nor confused
only ones
in the indivisibility of one]

Only in poetry ("la yoga del lenguaje" [the yoga of language]) can a couple be "unos / en la indivisibilidad del uno."[85] In "Corriente directa" ["Direct Current"] from *El corazón del instante* we read "Aquí te amo / en la dualidad" ["I love you here / in duality],[86] and in *Cuenta de los guías* we see many iterations of the yin/yang in the context of relationships. Near the end, for example, the speaker acknowledges the Buddhist allegory that underpins the complex book's journey:

> Hace diez años vi la luna estremecida en la profundidad del agua . . . yo también tuve mi *satori*. Vi que vida y muerte no están separadas. Vi que tú y yo, la luna y su reflejo, somos lo mismo. . . .
>
> Por eso cuando te digo "te amo," te digo "no estamos separados," "somos lo mismo."[87]
>
> [Ten years ago I saw the moon shimmering in the depths of the water . . . I also had my *satori*. I saw that life and death are not separated. I saw that you and I, the moon and its reflections, are the same. . . .
>
> That's why when I say "I love you," I am saying that "we are not separate," "we are the same."]

The most prominent of Blanco's *taijitu* poems has to be the climatic last stanza of *Cuenta de los guías*. As we explored in chapter 3, its unique use of rhyme blends aural and visual complements that add symbolic depth and dramatic sweep to the book's climax. That final poem, number 260, creates a series of mental *taijitus* that illustrate how poetry embodies convergences through the metaphor of its "cuento" and "canto."[88]

The Third Half

Returning for a moment to the essay "La escritura" from *El llamado y el don*, Blanco suggests the expression "entrar en un poema" [entering a poem] as a possible improvement to "leer un poema" [reading a poem] since "entering" takes both space and time into account. He then likens poetry to those images called "stereograms" that require a viewer to stare at a picture with relaxed eyes while moving it closer and farther from their face until a third dimension suddenly appears within a previously flat image. Next, he observes, "Leer poesía implica una intensidad, un silencio, y una capacidad de observación extraordinarias" [Reading poetry implies an extraordinary intensity, silence, and capacity for observation].[89] When the reader enters a poem under those conditions, there exists the possibility of seeing, just as in a stereogram, "una dimensión más" [another dimension].

Dimension is a polyvalent word and Blanco uses it on purpose. He often calls poetry "el otro lado del lenguaje" [the other side of language] or "otro uso del lenguaje" [another way of using language] because it contains the potential power to transport readers that prose typically does not. Poetry exists in a different time and is fast, instant, not sequential or narrative. This is to say that it can take its reader into another dimension beyond length, width, depth, space, or time.

There are many implications to the idea that poetry can access another dimension. In an essay on the psychology of reading, Alan Kennedy notes the existence of stimuli that, despite being beyond the range of the human sensory organs, are nonetheless very real: "If we were equipped to detect infra-red light directly, objects would take on visual properties related to their temperatures. We would then see a different set of things from those we see at present. In another sense the implications of the proposition are far less obvious. To explore this further we need to consider which aspects of the perceived world arise from the way the brain is constructed and which result from processes of experience and learning."[90]

Blanco's *poesía transformalista* [transformalist poetry] is a means to the end of transcending the reader and writer, but it has other motives too.[91] Rather than just representing light or temperature or dreams, Blanco's poetry also questions the notion of reaching the "universal mind"—a "unified entity in the higher dimension of the spacetime continuum."[92] To illustrate this concept, Leonard Shlain draws on a powerful metaphor credited to Russian philosopher P. D. Ouspensky (1878–1947):

> Observe from one side of a pane of frosted glass the prints made by the tips of someone's fingers touching the opposite side. A two-dimensional investigator, counting five separate circles, would conclude that each fingerprint is a separate entity. But we who can appreciate the third dimension of depth know that the five separate fingerprints belong to one unified object in three dimensions: a hand. We also know that the three-dimensional hand is attached to a being that generates mind when time is added to the vectors of space. By extrapolation, this is exactly the example that illustrates how our separate, individual minds, existing in our limited perceptual apparatus using two coordinates, space and time, could also be part of a *universal mind* that is a unified entity in the higher dimension of the spacetime continuum.[93]

For Blanco, poetry contains a potential gateway to another dimension, one that reveals connections we don't see in everyday life. Stockwell and other cognitive linguists study a text's "graded depth" to uncover "how the process of using and understanding language gives dynamism to figuration," but we are talking about an even more abstract concept here.[94] Blanco's poetry teases readers with glimpses of what this next dimension could be: a magnetic ideal that draws complements together and powers the drive for communion.

"Poema visto en una página en blanco" ["Poem Seen in a Blank Page"] combines the poet's interest in real and implied readers with levels of perception and all the dimensions of poetry: space, time, mental space and time, and "el otro mundo":

> . . . Basta un descuido
> en la realidad de todos los días
> para que el otro mundo se manifieste.
>
> De hecho está sucediendo
> en este mismo instante
> en que lees este poema.
>
> Pero, ¿*quién* está leyendo este poema?
> ¿De *quién* es el poema?
> ¿*Quién* escribe? . . . [95]
>
> [. . . With just one slip
> in everyday reality
> the other world will reveal itself.
>
> In fact, it's happening
> in this very moment
> when you are reading this poem.
>
> But, *who* is reading this poem?
> *Whose* poem is it?
> *Who* is writing? . . .]

The ontological questioning of "Poema visto en una página en blanco" is deepened in "Duermevela" ["Halfsleep"], which moves the discussion in a more spiritual direction and explores what life could be like after a moment of *satori*.

> Vivir simplemente la vida
> sin misterio ni asombro
> allí donde todas las cosas
> son sólo lo que son
> es una tristísima rutina
>
> Hasta que un día se concede
> sin que sepamos por qué
> la capacidad de leer
> el reverso del texto
> en el espejo de los nombres
>
> A partir de ese momento
> la vida vuelve a ser un misterio
> que irradia sin remedio

y vemos todo con asombro
inmersos en lo desconocido

Lo más misterioso de todo
es que tras la transformación
las cosas siguen siendo
tan sólo lo que son

Y la única salida
es vivir simplemente la vida[96]

[To simply live life
without mystery or surprise
there where everything
just is what it is
is a sad routine

Until one day we are given
without knowing why
the capacity to read
the reverse side of the text
in the mirror of words

From that moment
life becomes a mystery again
that shines enigmatically
and we, astonished, see everything
immersed in the unknown

The most mysterious of all
is that through transformation
things keep being
only what they are

And the only escape
is to simply keep living life]

There is a Zen-style inversion in these verses that surprises us—that mystery is a privileged state and life without it is simply prosaic. As Chávez Robinson points out, another of the characteristics Blanco's work shares with the Buddhist koans is the unexpected combination of simplicity of expression and depth of content. Poems such as "Poética" ["Poetics"] showed us that many of Blanco's most persuasive statements on poetry use direct language to express difficult topics. One of the strongest pieces of empirical evidence of the power of poetry is found in a deceptively simple passage from the poem "El hombre":

El hombre: mitad luz
mitad sombra
mitad imaginación[97]
[Humans: half light
half shadow
half imagination]

This text may at first seem ironic, but its highlighting through repetition and sparse verses and its position as the last line of a long poem add weight to its message. Logic tells us there cannot literally be three halves to anything, but poems are able to defy those laws through a clear example and language that suddenly becomes defiantly figurative. Blanco's *vasos comunicantes* and metapoems show us how reading with an eye for the other side of language can reveal moments of communion with new dimensions of perception concealed in the deep textures of his poems.

CHAPTER 5

Metaphysics

In 1947, more than twenty years after winning the Nobel Prize in Physics, Danish physicist Niels Bohr (1885–1962) received his country's highest honor, the Order of the Elephant. Recipients of this award are mostly prominent world politicians, royalty, and a very select group of Danes noted for significant contributions to science or industry. Initiation into the Order of the Elephant brought a unique conundrum for the physicist since the coats of arms of all its knights are proudly displayed in Hillerød's Frederiksborg Castle and Bohr's family, it turned out, did not have one.

Bohr was known as always being a little bit different from the other Copenhagen physicists. Besides being a natural athlete and gifted table tennis player, Bohr has been described as a scientist who always wanted to be a philosopher and was highly aware of the language-bound nature of scientific inquiry.[1] When pressed to design his family's crest, the author of the "theory of complementarity" began with a motto in Latin: *contraria sunt complementa* [opposites are complementary]. For the visual element of the emblem, he chose a bold Asian image that held special meaning for him—a red and black yin/yang symbol. Needless to say, the *taijitu* on Bohr's coat of arms makes it easily identifiable among the field of traditional Danish heraldry that adorns the Chapel of Frederiksborg Castle.

Early in the twentieth century Bohr's revolutionary discovery of the wave/particle duality, when taken together with Werner Heisenberg's Uncertainty Principle and other advances in quantum mechanics by Max Planck, Albert Einstein, and Erwin Schrödinger, helped contribute to the sense of indeterminacy that undermined the bedrock of Newtonian physics. The iconoclastic theories of these scientists contain a mixture of physics and what could be called "metaphysics" since their ideas "went beyond" established limits of understanding of being and matter. Metaphysics is an amorphous philosophical field that contains contradictory subfields each with the potential to cancel out the authority of the larger discipline. Of such paradoxes, Blanco notes: "Es muy cierto que la física, para operar, no requiere en lo más mínimo de la metafísica; también es cierto lo contrario. Pero nosotros, criaturas dobles, los seres humanos, necesitamos de las dos" [It's true that physics, in order to operate, does not require in the least, metaphysics; the opposite is also true. But we, double creatures, human beings, need both].[2]

In his poems, Blanco examines the nature of being (ontology, a branch of metaphysics) through scientific modes but, as in Fritjof Capra's *The Tao of Physics*, at the same time, he includes a cosmological element in his work and what could be called a dose of quantum mysticism. Blanco uses science to classify the natural laws of matter while never losing sight of the possibilities of transcendence into a fourth dimension, something beyond the empirically observable. Like Aristotle's *Metaphysics*, the poetry of Alberto Blanco considers the nature of "first causes" and cosmology's "origins of the universe" from discourses based in both reason and faith. This chapter analyzes the metaphysical relationship of complementarity between empirical and nonempirical knowledge through representations of philosophic, scientific, mathematical, and spiritual discourse in Blanco's poems.

Scientific Methods

In the essay "La ciencia" ["Science"] from *El canto y el vuelo* [*Song and Flight*] Blanco writes, "Tanto la poesía como la ciencia comparten un mismo anhelo: penetrar de lleno en la realidad sin conformarse con lo que nos dicen las apariencias inmediatas para tratar de entenderla mejor, de comprenderla" [Poetry and science share a similar desire: to fully enter reality in order to try to understand it better, to comprehend it, without at the same time conforming to what outside appearances say].[3] "La ciencia" discusses the overlaps in language (specifically metaphor) between science and poetry and the importance of observation to both. Despite similarities between both approaches (and the fact that a large number of poets are also scientists), Blanco notes that poets represent their findings through language, while scientists, on the other hand, are, for the most part, bound to using numbers. Drawing on Albert Einstein's famous adage "Imagination is more important than knowledge" he also notes that great scientists, like great artists, must use their creativity to set a vision for themselves as they delve into the unknown: "Y si algo me enseñó la ciencia es que cuando uno investiga, es porque no sabe" [If I learned one thing as a scientist, it is that when one conducts research, it is because things are unknown]. In a translated interview with poet Jerome Rothenberg, Blanco expounds upon his vision of the complementary nature of poetry and science: "Having been trained as a Chemist, it is not a surprise that I have always been tempted by the poetic possibilities of scientific imagination. Which is a way to speak of the poetics of science. Because, in the long run, both poetry and science work with metaphors of the world. I am not saying that, ultimately, they are the same thing. . . . Science deals with numbers and measurable realities: quantity. Poetry—as all art does—deals with quality and the unmeasurable. But both endeavors deal with the unknown."[4]

One of the most prominent ways in which Blanco's poetry attempts to measure and order his world is through the creation of poetic taxonomies or clusters of poems united by both similarity and difference. These thematic categories can be seasons, points of the compass, months of the year, or, in a poem about baseball, nine poetic innings. "Tras el rayo" [*Afterglow*], from *El corazón del instante* [*The Heart of the Moment*], to take one example, is composed of four sections: "Llaves" ["Keys"], "Las jaulas de la creación" ["Cages of Creation"], "Velas" ["Candles"], and "Tras el rayo" ["Afterglow"].[5] Two of these main sections, "Llaves" and "Velas," are further divided into four subsections (*Norte*, *Sur*, *Este*, and *Oeste* [North, South, East, and West]), each of which has a unique geometric form associated with it (a circle, a square, a triangle, and an upside-down triangle). These directions fall in a different order in each poem, and each direction-section is itself composed of four (or more) movements while "Las jaulas de la creación" and "Tras el rayo," the other two main divisions in the poem, each contain eighteen segments. Perhaps finding inspiration in the *I Ching* or the analogic methods of Leonardo da Vinci, these structures force the reader to consider over and over the place of each part within the whole, both in the particular and in the larger sense of examining the possibilities of wholeness itself.

El libro de las plantas [*A Book of Plants*] from *A la luz de siempre* [*In Constant Light*] contains four sections: "Árboles" ["Trees"], "Flores" ["Flowers"], "Plantas" ["Plants"], and "Alimentos" ["Crops"]. Read in series, we discover that a poem appears in a set because of an initial similarity (being about flowers, for example), but when taken together as a group, these texts are actually exercises in differentiation that the poet compounds through stylistic diversity. "La buganvilla" ["Bougainvillea"] teaches us that the bright red leaves we associate with the plant are really just that, leaves, and not its flowers. "El nenúfar" ["Water Lilies"] spins a series of personal associations the poet has with water lilies (Monet, Yoga, Buddah, Gorostiza) and then subtly likens the form of the plant's different parts (visible and invisible) to the mysterious way it connects with his memories. "La alfalfa" ["Alfalfa"] engages in wordplay with the word "alpha," and so on. These sets are an exercise in both natural history and ontology in that they explore what is in the world and how these similar beings are different from each other.

Blanco's familiarity with scientific discourse comes in part from his education but also from his work as a translator of books like *Plants of the Gods* by Richard Evans and Albert Hofmann and *The Left Hand of Creation* by John D.

Barrow and Joseph Silk.[6] Aside from his poems organized into sets, *Tras el rayo*, and the two sets of *Teorías* [*Theories*] (one from *La raíz cuadrada del cielo* in *El corazón del instante* [*The Heart of the Moment*], one from "Tiempo extra" ["Overtime"] in *La hora y la neblina* [*Time and Mist*]), can be considered Blanco's "science poems" since these texts explicitly deal with scientific ideas and do so in the register of the scientific method. The "Teorías," especially, tend to be more prosaic and conversational than other Blanco poems and privilege observation, measurement, analysis, skepticism, and the formation of hypotheses. These experiments in language address readers' inherent biases or assumptions through logical argumentation and the persuasive exposition of evidence by the voice of a teacher or guide who states a theory, explains it, and then illustrates it with an example:

> "Segunda teoría del tiempo"
>
> Las leyes de la ciencia no distinguen
> entre avanzar o retroceder en el tiempo.
>
> Sin embargo, existen tres flechas
> que sí nos permiten darnos cuenta
> de que el tiempo se mueve hacia adelante.
>
> La flecha termodinámica:
> todo tiende hacia el desorden.
>
> La flecha psicológica:
> recordamos el pasado, no el futuro.
>
> La flecha cronológica:
> el universo no se contrae . . . se expande.
>
> No hay excepciones a la dirección de estas flechas.
>
> Por lo que toca a la flecha termodinámica,
> todo esfuerzo en busca de un cierto orden
> —desde un buen gobierno hasta una obra de arte—
> no es sino una precaria victoria temporal
> en medio de un creciente desorden.
>
> En lo que hace a la flecha psicológica,
> hay que decir que la posibilidad de recordar el futuro
> —salvo entre los profetas, videntes y poetas—
> siempre ha sido puesta en razonable duda.
>
> De la eventual contracción del universo
> no podemos decir nada pues no tenemos la experiencia.
> Solamente podemos soñar.[7]

["Second Theory of Time"

The laws of science do not distinguish
between going forward or going back in time.

Nonetheless, there are three arrows
that help us understand
that time is constantly moving forward

The thermodynamic arrow:
everything moves in the direction of disorder.

The psychological arrow:
we remember the past, not the future.

The chronological arrow:
the universe does not contract . . . it is expanding.

There are no exceptions to the rules of these arrows.

In terms of the thermodynamic arrow,
all effort going toward order
—from good governance to a work of art—
is nothing but a vicarious temporary victory
in the midst of growing disorder.

In terms of the psychological arrow,
we would have to say that the possibility of remembering the future
—except for prophets, seers and poets—
has always been put into reasonable doubt.

Of the eventual contraction of the universe
we can't say anything because we have no experience.
We can only dream.]

In addition to framing scientific hypotheses as metaphors by the simple fact that they appear in a poem, "Segunda teoría del tiempo" ["Second Theory of Time"], like the beam of light that refracts through a prism and then compresses again when returning to a prism, also creates figurative language through deductive reasoning: our efforts to govern or create art, it tells us, are like the theory of thermodynamics. The sum effect of the poem is one of the coexistence of empirical and nonempirical modes of knowing that characterizes metaphysics—that special mixture of what we observe and what lies beyond.

While the scientific method generally employs deductive reasoning, "Poema visto en el ventilador de un motel" ["Poem Seen in a Motel Fan"] is inductive. It begins with the description of a small event that leads to the formation of a hypothesis. It then collects, analyzes, and interprets data, draws conclusions, and even publishes the results so that others may test them:

> "Poema visto en el ventilador de un motel"
>
> Hace un calor endemoniado.
> Enciendo el ventilador
> y empiezan a girar las aspas levemente.
> Pronto se desplaza un suave viento
> y las cortinas comienzan a bailar.
>
> El centro del ventilador
> es un espejo convexo,
> un ojo de pescado,
> un casco de oro.
> Allí vibran los reflejos
> con el ronroneo de la máquina,
> pero no se mueven de su sitio.
>
> Aumento la velocidad y las aspas giran
> hasta volverse casi invisibles
> —sólo una gasa blanquecina—
> pero los reflejos en el centro
> siguen siendo los mismos.
>
> Así ha de ser con todo—me digo—
> las superficies se mueven a gran velocidad
> pero las formas que reflejan no.
>
> Pasan los individuos de una especie,
> pero la especie sigue siendo la misma.
>
> Pasan los hombres de un pueblo,
> pero el pueblo permanece.
>
> Pasan todos los poetas,
> pero queda la poesía.
>
> Pasan nuestros pensamientos,
> pero algo, o alguien,
> está observando.
> Sigue observando.[8]
>
> [It's devilishly hot.
> I turn on the fan
> and the blades begin to revolve slowly.

At once a soft breeze springs up
and the curtains begin to dance.

The center of the fan
is a convex mirror,
a fish-eye,
a golden dome.
The reflections vibrate there
with the purring of the machine,
but do not move from their place.

I turn up the speed and the blades spin
almost turning invisible
—only a whitish gauze—
but the reflections in the center
continue the same.

And so it should be with everything—I tell myself—
the exterior surfaces move at great speed
but not the reflected forms.

The individual of a species pass,
but the species continues the same.

The men and women of a nation pass,
but the nation goes on.

All the poets pass,
but poetry remains.

Our thoughts pass,
but something, or someone,
is observing.
Keeps observing.][9]

At its heart, this poem is a metaphor for life's cycle of permanence and change. Its imagery is dominated by opposites: hot and cool, movement and stasis, visible and invisible, the part and the whole. Each stanza of this meditative and conversational text develops the poet's thesis a bit more: it is hot so the speaker turns on the fan, thinks about the movement of the blades, then notices the reflections in the metallic center dome that unites them. Next, he turns up the fan and the increased speed makes the blades appear to change form while the reflected images in the center stay the same. From this he extracts a hypothesis, that life may also be composed of a fleeting outer shell (the blades) with an unchanging inner core. This constantly spinning center contains reflections of unmoving distant forms such as humanity or poetry. Finally, in short lines that contrast with the tone of the first few stanzas, he considers a few examples.

"Poema visto en el ventilador de un motel" is clearly Platonic. In the allegory of the cave, Plato wrote of forms and their imitation or reflection—the forms we can see are the pale imitation or reproduction of true Forms, just as the forms Blanco's speaker sees in the inner dome of the fan are reflections, not true forms themselves. These shapes, like the puppets that throw shadows onto the wall of Plato's cave, lay beyond his field of vision. In an early passage in the *Republic*, Plato described a two tiered hierarchy of knowledge. In it, intelligible forms, that is, abstract ideas, are above the realm of visible objects. Within the second tier, the visible, reflections are below objects themselves. Blanco's poem supports this conception of reality: poems and poets come and go but Poetry, "La Poesía," remains.

The inner dome of the fan introduces another dimension as well—that of the "ever alert" observer that concludes the text. Like much of Blanco's work, this poem does not avoid Judeo-Christian symbology and introduces it in its very first line with "un calor endemoniado." The poem then closes with the "algo, o alguien" that is always watching us. What is this being? A creator? A demon? The only thing we know for sure is that it is an eye—an image reinforced by a tight visual rhyme with the form of the fan. In fact, "Poema visto en el ventilador de un motel" has another metaimage as well—Plato's ideas are reflected in the text just as the forms are reflected in the fan's dome. So like Velázquez's masterpiece "Las meninas" ["The Ladies in Waiting"], this poem is ultimately about seeing, about representation, about questions and answers. It is ontological and ultimately epistemological due to the mysterious and unnamed someone or something of the conclusion. The poem does not tell us what is ultimately real and what is reflected but instead urges the reader to keep questioning the authenticity of forms. This question, as Carlos Fuentes has noted, "es tan vieja como las sombras de la caverna platónica . . . es parte de nuestra condición viviente: no podemos sentirnos del todo a gusto con ninguna definición de la realidad. Mucho menos convincentes son, en todo caso, las reglas derivadas de estas definiciones" [it is as old as the shadows in the Platonic cave . . . it is a fact of life: we can't feel totally comfortable with any definition of reality. And even less convincing are, in any case, the rules derived from these definitions].[10]

The impulse to create poems with scientific discourse is a constant throughout Blanco's work. About halfway through the dense journey of *Cuenta de los guías*, the poetic voice relates: "Inmerso en el milagro descubro, paso a paso, los fundamentos de una ciencia del alma—quiero decir—un sistema experimental capaz de comprobar objetivamente nuestras más profundas intuiciones. . . . Juego perfecto en el que las reglas se revelan hasta la culminación de la partida" [Immersed in the miracle I discover, step by step, the foundations of a science of the soul—I mean—an experimental system capable of proving objectively our deepest intuitions. . . . A perfect game in which the rules are not revealed until the end of the match].[11] The desire to quantify the unquantifiable resurfaces as well in a much later poem, the elegant "Música química" ["Chemical Music"] that provides a poetics of science and a scientific look at poetics by presenting music and chemistry in a complementary relationship:

"Música química"

Sigue las instrucciones que dictan los átomos y verás
cómo la partitura está lista antes de lo que piensas

El aire que se desliza por el filtro de carbón activado
tarde o temprano llega a la embocadura de la flauta

Allí lentamente destila un coagulado azul de semejanza:
una línea que va desde el tubo de ensayo hasta la tuba

Y cuyos resultados vistos al microscopio
revelan un notable don para la melodía

Una escala temperada que se parece a una tabla
de temperaturas que desafía las estadísticas

Una célula desarrollándose contrapuntísticamente
por su propio acuerdo y dentro de sus limitaciones

Pues en el laboratorio del arte contemporáneo
cada nota es un núcleo dispuesto a dividirse

Hasta que la luz se sublime y luego cristalice
en el vaso de precipitados de la conciencia[12]

[Follow the instructions that govern atoms and you will see
that the score is ready long before you anticipate

The air that slides through the filter of activated carbon
sooner or later arrives at the opening of the flute

There, a blue mixture slowly distills:
a line that runs from the test tube to the tuba

And whose results, when seen beneath a microscope,
reveal a notable gift for melody

A tempered scale that looks like a table
of temperatures that challenges the statistics

A cell growing in counterpoint
by its own accord and within its limitations

Because in the laboratory of contemporary art
each note is a nucleus ready to divide

Until the light sublimates and then crystalizes
in the beaker of consciousness]

In a sense, "Música química" itself is simply "Una célula desarrollándose contrapuntísticamente / por su propio acuerdo y dentro de sus limitaciones" as its empirical description becomes more and more figurative (through synesthesia) in the third, fourth, and fifth stanzas. The last stanza makes clear that the limitations of chemistry and music are the same that govern the world outside the concert hall or lab and the mystery of an un-caused cause underlies both.

"Vapor, agua, hielo" also uses scientific principles to explore being and origins:

I.
El agua cae
en flecos de lluvia y en cascadas

El agua cae
desde el principio de los tiempos

El agua fluye
bajo las capas congeladas

El agua fluye
sobre los huesos de los muertos

El agua pasa
sobre las piedras y las hojas

El agua asciende
con la luna, el sol o el viento

II.
Hielo, agua, vapor
nada ni nadie dirían que son lo mismo

Vapor, agua, hielo
tres formas distintas y un solo elemento

Sólo nada
detiene su incesante ritmo o su tonada

Sólo nadie
remonta el silencioso río del tiempo[13]

[I.
Water falls
in flecks of rain and in waterfalls

Water falls
from the beginning of time

Water flows
beneath the frozen ice caps

Water flows
over the bones of the dead

Water passes
over stones and leaves

Water ascends
with the moon, sun or wind

II.
Ice, water, steam
nothing or nobody would say they are the same

Steam, water, ice
three distinct forms and only one element

Nothing alone
stops its incessant rhythm or tune

Nobody alone
travels upstream in the silent river of time]

The poem posits that ice and steam are still water and that water can move through the air as rain, a cloud, or a waterfall. It also asks us to accept that water can flow beneath a layer of ice, move through the earth, and both rise and fall. If we do indeed accept that matter can exist in all of these states, then the poem opens new dimensions to us that can metaphorically broaden and deepen our appreciation of other aspects of reality. The paradox of the poem's content, and its holy trinity of matter, surfaces in a subtle way in its form through the paradoxical negative phrasings "Sólo nada" [nothing alone] and "Sólo nadie" [nobody alone] that introduce ideas under erasure. In *El corazón del instante,* Blanco posits a "Teoría de la evolución" ["Theory of Evolution"] based on a similar metaphor:

¿Cómo es posible dudar a estas alturas
de la teoría de la evolución?

"El hombre es—dice Shakespeare
y lo repite Milton—una obra maestra."

Pero claro que cuando observamos
que la nube se convierte en lluvia
la lluvia en granizo, y el granizo en lodo,
uno se pone a dudar de todo, seriamente.[14]

[How is it still possible to doubt
the theory of evolution?

"Humans are"—Shakespeare said
and Milton concurs—"a masterpiece."

But of course when we see
that a cloud converts into rain
rain into hail, and hail into mud,
one begins to have one's doubt about everything, seriously.]

As "Teoría de la evolución" shows, creation and evolution exist side by side in Blanco's work in the same way that the tension, perhaps the main tension, of a plurality of theories and a single theory runs through the science poems. In the essay "La ciencia" Blanco notes, "Hay que reconocer que tanto la poesía como la ciencia aspiran a un resultado semejante: reducir la pluralidad multiforme de la realidad a la unidad sintética de una ley o de un poema para tratar de integrar la vida, el mundo, el universo, en eso que Einstein llamaba 'El campo unificado'" [We have to recognize that both poetry and science aspire to similar results: to reduce the multiformed plurality of reality to the synthetic unity of a law or a poem that tries to integrate life, the world, the universe, in that which Einstein called a "unified field"].[15] Like the "sólo nadie" of "Vapor, agua, hielo," science's Holy Grail, as it were, the hypothetical Theory of Everything, is a present absence in Blanco. In the early 1700s, Sir Isaac Newton thought he had discovered a "super theory" with his laws of motion and gravity. In "Teoría de Newton" ["Newton's Theory"] we read:

Hay una sola norma
en el universo que vale
lo mismo para las estrellas
que para las manzanas,
las órbitas de los planetas,
la forma de la luna
y la velocidad del sol.

Hay una sola ley
que lo mismo gobierna

la mente de un físico
que los versos de este poema.[16]

[There is but one law
in the universe that is
the same for the stars
as it is for apples,
the orbit of the planets,
the form of the moon
and the speed of the sun.

There is but one law
that rules both the
mind of the physicist
as the rules of this poem.]

Just as science is searching for a single theory to unify all matter, science also serves Blanco for some engaging metaphors of separation:

"Poema visto al hervir la leche"

Un cielo blanco,
una luna líquida,
un hueso de algodón:
la leche sin hervir
es una sola cosa.

Pero si la ponemos a hervir
entra en acción el fuego . . .

Se verifican primero
cambios físicos
—fácilmente observables—
y luego cambios químicos
que ya no son tan fáciles de ver.

El resultado a final de cuentas
es que una parte de la leche
se separa: sube, flota . . .

Cuando la leche se enfría
nos quedan dos componentes:

La leche líquida y la nata.
Y no se mezclan.

Antes eran una sola cosa.
Ahora ya son dos.

Siguen siendo lo mismo,
pero ya son dos.

Principio de la creación,
de la lucha y el drama:

Lo que antes era uno
—fuego mediante—
es ahora dos.[17]

["Poem Seen While Boiling Milk"

White sky,
liquid moon,
cotton bone:
milk, before boiling,
is whole.

But if we put it on the burner,
the flame starts its work . . .

First, we see
changes in texture
—easily observable—
and later chemical changes
which are less easy to notice.

In the end the final result
is that one part of the milk
separates: rises, floats . . .

When the milk then cools
we are left with two layers:

Milk and cream . . .
Which do not mix.

Before, they were one.
Now, they are two.

They are still the same,
but now they are two.

It's a law of creation,
of struggle and drama:

What once was one
—when passed through fire—
is now two.]

Scientific discourse provides fresh ways for the poet to study the solitude and communion of matter, relationships, and the idea of the soul. The coexistence and juxtaposition of empirical knowledge and the unprovable along with the phantom of a single theory of everything reflects the kinds of struggles that have always fascinated our most gifted scientific and literary minds. Throughout all these explorations, Blanco's science poems, like the wave/particle duality, provide a particularly engaging and innovative way to study opposites as conjoined poles.

Observer Effects

La raíz cuadrada del cielo from *El corazón del instante* opens with Albert Einstein's famous quote that "imagination is more important than knowledge," which, like the book's title, starts the reader thinking about quantum mechanics' blend of science and poetry, of the knowable and the unknowable. Complementary pairs characterize Blanco's science poems, and as Michael Keith Klam has shown, Blanco's poetry shares quantum theory's acceptance of paradox, chaos, and multiple points of view. In "Teoría cuántica" ["Quantum Theory"] the poet notes:

La teoría cuántica nos propone
—a diferencia de la mecánica clásica—
que puede existir movimiento
sin trayectoria, sin recorrido y sin órbita.

Al menos, sin un camino conocido,
y—lo que es más importante—
sin un camino que se pueda conocer.

¿No es esto la poesía?[18]

[Quantum theory teaches us
—as opposed to classical mechanics—
that there can be movement
without trajectory, without direction, and without orbit.

At least, without a known path,
and—most importantly—
without a path that can be known.

Isn't this poetry?]

"Teoría del color" ["Color Theory"] takes both Newton's discoveries related to optics and Bohr's revolutionary theory of complementarity (the wave / particle duality) to another level by considering the invisible spectrum of light, the frequencies beyond our unaided vision:

"Teoría del color"

Cuando todo parecía ya visto,
cuando la revolución de los acontecimientos
tomaba la curva final para entrar a un nuevo ciclo
y el Eterno Retorno daba seguridad al hombre,
¡apareció el Espectro del Visible!

Y se vio entonces que el rojo y el violeta
no cerraban un círculo cromático . . .

Así, pues, resulta que antes del rojo
no está el violeta sino el infrarrojo.

Y que después del violeta
no está el rojo sino el ultravioleta.

De tal manera que no es del todo cierto
aquello de que *en mi final está mi principio*
como tampoco es cierto lo contrario.

Antes del principio están las bandas del Espectro.
Después del final están las bandas del Espectro.

Y quién sabe si las bandas vuelvan a tocarse en algún punto.[19]

[Just when everything appeared to be seen already
when the revolution of events
was entering the home stretch of a new cycle
and the Eternal Return gave security to humanity,
we are told of the Spectrum of the Visible!

And we were shown that red and violet
do not close the chromatic circle . . .

And so it seems that beyond red
is not violet but infrared.

And after violet
isn't red but ultraviolet.

In that way it's not entirely true
the saying that *in my end is my beginning*
just like the opposite is also not true.

There are bands of the Spectrum before the beginning.
And there are bands of the Spectrum after the end.

And who knows if the bands will ever meet up again at some point.]

This text employs both deductive and inductive reasoning to create a hypothesis and metaphor for what lies beyond the visible spectrum and, by extension, beyond the empirical world. In chapter 4 we discussed poems that posited the existence of other dimensions and another powerful text in Alberto Blanco's poetics of light is "El espectro del visible, acaso" ["The Visible Spectrum, Perhaps"], which examines and counterbalances many theories of seeing (Plato, Aristotle, Einstein) and considers their metaphysical dimensions. Statements like " * Bien visto, ningún objeto tiene, en realidad, el color que supuestamente tiene. / * El color de un objeto depende únicamente de su velocidad" [* To be precise, no object has, in reality, the color it supposedly has. / * The color of an object depends solely upon its velocity"][20] make us reexamine our a priori beliefs and consider the possibility that there is more to life that what we can empirically prove. It reminds us that science, like our spiritual mind, is a process, rather than, as in the case of Newtonian physics, a set of monolithic laws.

"Teoría de conjuntos" ["Theory of Combinations"] is an inductive thought experiment on the dialectic of light and shadow:

"Teoría de conjuntos"

En un cuarto a oscuras se enciende una vela.

Todo lo que en ese cuarto existe
se ve de pronto iluminado por un flanco
y proyecta sombra por el otro.

Todo lo que tiene luz tiene sombra.
La luz y la sombra van de la mano.

Pero, si la llama misma no tiene sombra,
¿De veras tiene luz la llama de la vela?[21]

[In a dark room a candle is lit.
Everything that exists in that room
is suddenly lit up on one side
and in shadow on the other.

All that has light has shadow.
Light and shadow go hand in hand.

But, if the flame itself doesn't have shadow,
Does the light of the candle really have light?]

In addition to employing the cryptic tone of the Buddhist Sutras, "Teoría de conjuntos" alludes to the key elements of two of the best-known principles of quantum physics: Schrödinger's Cat and Heisenberg's Uncertainty Principle. In Erwin Schrödinger's famous thought experiment from 1935, the Austrian physicist demonstrates how there would be a moment when an observer would not be able to know whether a cat, when sealed in a box with a deadly toxin, was dead or alive. In order to find out, the observer would have to open the box and thus interfere with the experiment. Until the box is opened, Schrödinger maintained, the cat exists in a dual state. Werner Heisenberg's Uncertainty Principle is related in that it describes the difficulty in measuring objects in motion. In quantum physics it is impossible to reach any conclusions with complete certainty since it has been proven that the presence of a conscious observer in an experiment fundamentally changes its outcome. These theories are examined explicitly in poems like the aforementioned "Teoría cuántica" ["Quantum Theory"]:

> Si observamos al microscopio electrónico
> un átomo de hidrógeno (el más sencillo de todos)
> veremos que la luz misma del instrumento
> provoca que su único electrón absorba energía,
> se excite, y se salga de su órbita . . .
> y esa órbita nunca la conoceremos.[22]

> [If we observe beneath an electron microscope
> an atom of hydrogen (the most basic of all)
> we will see that the very light of the instrument
> will cause its only electron to absorb energy,
> become excited, and leave its orbit . . .
> and that orbit we will never know.]

Blanco's *Teoría* series provides the conscious observer with multiple and complementary principles of gravity, light, movement, the paradoxes of heat conduction, and the secret frequencies of the color spectrum. "Teoría de la luz" ["A Theory of Light"] considers human thought through the lens of the wave/particle duality and arrives at a conclusion colored by the observer effect:

> La brillantez de esta micra imposible
> es lo que vemos;

> La claridad de este inmenso espacio vacío
> es donde vemos;

> Pero la verdadera paradoja somos nosotros:
> los que vemos.[23]

> [The shine of this impossible micron
> is what we see;

> The clarity of this immense open space
> is what we see;

But the true paradox is we;
we who are looking.]

"Teoría de probabilidades" ["A Theory of Probabilities"], the final poem of the *Teorías* series, also acknowledges the observer effect by directly addressing the reader and his or her judgment of the work at hand: "Puede ser que los nueve poemas anteriores / no den en el blanco, pero la esperanza / es que el décimo sea el bueno" [It may be that the nine previous poems / don't hit the mark, but the hope is that the tenth one does].[24] The tenth poem reiterates the poet's belief in possibility over certainty and ends with a nod to Stéphane Mallarmé and, in this context, Albert Einstein's well-known quip that God "does not play dice":

Una golondrina
no hace verano.

Una teoría es sólo
una probabilidad.

Un haz de versos
no ordena el universo.

Un lance de dados
jamás comprobará el azar.[25]

[One swallow
a summer does not make.

A theory is only
a probability.

A bunch of verses
does not order the universe.

A roll of the dice
will never prove chance.]

The negative statements in the first and third couplets are an appropriate technique to talk about dialectics since they force us to consider combinations of images *sous rature* [under erasure] in order to experience the poem. Interestingly, the making of collages also has some parallel ways of thinking to quantum physics through its acceptance of simultaneous positive and negative conditions, its radical reinventions of space and time, and its frequent juxtapositions of what is and what is not. Furthermore, Blanco's poems about the observer effect ask intriguing questions about the implications of the role of the reader as they set the poetic process in motion. As Leonard Shlain notes, Einstein's iconoclastic special theory of relativity, which Blanco referenced above in "El espectro visible, acaso," showed that "the simultaneity or sequence of events, the colors of objects, and the shapes of forms did not solely belong to a world outside human affairs; instead they were also dependent on the speed of the mind hurtling through space that was doing the observing."[26] Cubism, collage, and rhetorical tropes such as *litotes* that present ideas *sous rature* participate in the new physics' desire to embrace contradiction and to appreciate new perspectives by breaking down traditional notions of fixed space and time . . . situations that cannot help but provoke wonder and dreams about origins in thoughtful readers.

Crisis

Philosopher Nikolas Kompridis notes that in the tradition of critical theory, important ideas by thinkers such as Rousseau, Hegel, Habermas, Marx, and Foucault all sprang from the same starting point—the urgent realization that things around them had gone terribly wrong. Kompridis terms such work "crisis thinking," a mode of discourse motivated and necessitated by the drive to "begin anew." Kompridis writes that "modernity induces 'crisis thinking' because it is inherently crisis generating."[27]

In her fascinating book *Poetry, Physics, and Painting in Twentieth Century Spain*, Candelas Gala draws an interesting parallel between Goya's "El sueño de la razón" ["The Sleep of Reason"] and Rafael Alberti's *Sobre los ángeles* [*Concerning The Angels*], two well-known examples of "crisis thinking" in the Spanish canon that arose from personal and artistic catastrophes to critique the excesses of Spanish society. Through the course of her study, Gala demonstrates how poets used science to react to their changing world and how during the twentieth century, "modern physics moved to the forefront in the overall cultural avant-garde, and to a certain extent it could be considered its leading expression."[28]

While Goya and Alberti's work can be seen, as Gala posits, as forerunners to the revolutions of the Copenhagen School, Blanco came to "the New Physics" later, during the cultural crisis of the late 1960s. As we have seen, one of the defining characteristics of Blanco's science poems is that they are explicitly *about science*. They typically quote and paraphrase specific theories and use them as starting points to explore being and origins. Despite the mostly nonpartisan stance of much of Blanco's work, a few of his scientific poems use physics to respond critically to socio-political realities in Mexico.

The series *Teorías* begins with first principles, so "Teoría del espacio" ["Theory of Space"] is followed by "Primera teoría del tiempo" ["First Theory of Time"]. As we noted in chapter 4, "Vamos" ["Let's Go"], the first word of the section and poem "Teoría del espacio," uses the inclusive first-person plural to emphasize the all-encompassing and inescapable scope of these natural laws:

> Unidos por la palabra estamos aquí.
> Al servicio de una voz estamos aquí.

Leyendo entre líneas estamos aquí.
Al pie de la letra estamos aquí.[29]

[United by words we are here.
To serve a voice we are here.
Reading between the lines we are here.
We are literally here.]

We all experience space and all conceive of time in ways that, depending on how we choose to view them, either comfort or disturb us. Blanco draws a clear connection between the temporal concept of the past and human history in these texts. "Primera teoría del tiempo" [First Theory of Time"] states that we all live in time and that time's rules, independent of our relativistic reactions to them, apply equally to individuals, governments, and "civilizaciones" [civilizations]:

Durante la infancia y la juventud
—lo mismo de los hombres
que de las civilizaciones—
priva la imagen del tiempo
como una constante suma:
un añadido que hace crecer la vida
como hace crecer las raíces
o las hojas de una planta.[30]

[During infancy and youth
—of both people
and civilizations—
it's fashionable to think of time
as a constant sum:
an addition that makes life grow
just like it makes roots
or the leaves of a plant grow.]

The all-encompassing nature of these natural laws is highlighted once again in the first movement of "Teoría de la incertidumbre" ["Uncertainty Theory"], which returns to Heisenberg's famous principle and the related observer effect:

"Teoría de la incertidumbre"

I
Heisenberg descubrió
que un investigador
asomado al microscopio
—se de cuenta o no—
es parte del experimento

que está llevando a cabo
porque la misma luz
que utiliza para observar
lo que está pasando
en su experimento
altera fundamentalmente
el orden de lo que observa.[31]

[I
Heisenberg discovered
that a researcher
leaning into the microscope
—whether they realize it or not—
is part of the experiment
they are carrying out
because the same light
that is used to observe
what is happening
in their experiment
fundamentally alters
the order of what they are observing.]

The foundation of Heisenberg's Uncertainty Principle is the idea that an observer's pretense of distance, objectivity, and, ultimately, privilege is invalid since she or he is always physically complicit in an experiment. In light of previous poems that insistently group the individual and society, it's a short allegorical leap to equate Blanco's observer with a citizen who keeps quiet in the face of abusive power or oppression. The poet's next step on the page, his swerve in the next stanza, is to ground his allegory in a rather lighthearted observation about the influence of parents on the behavior of their children. Next, the poem's second movement considers parallels between the Uncertainty Principle and literature, also shying away from social critique. Despite these subtle metaphors, we saw earlier in this chapter that "Segunda teoría del tiempo" reinforces and expands science's domain by introducing three laws that control time, art, and good government:

todo esfuerzo en busca de un cierto orden
—desde *un buen gobierno* hasta una obra de arte—
no es sino una precaria victoria temporal
en medio de un creciente desorden.[32]

[Every effort in search of a true order
—from *good governance* to a work of art—

is nothing but a precarious temporal victory
in the midst of a growing disorder]

Where "Teoría de la incertidumbre" and "Segunda teoría del tiempo" side-step a direct social critique, "Segunda teoría termodinámica" ["Second Thermodynamic Theory"] builds on the connections between scientific law and government in the two previous poems and places its criticism in a Mexican context. The first seven stanzas of the poem describe how the goal of assembling a jigsaw puzzle is to create order out of chaos. Next, the poet states that the likelihood of solving a puzzle simply by shaking its box is extremely improbable. To this he adds the fact that the second law of thermodynamics states that when more effort is spent attempting to solve a puzzle in this strange way, it becomes less likely a solution will be found. This is due to entropy, the buildup of disorder in a system as energy is exerted upon it. Unlike the previous poem, this time Blanco explicitly discloses the target of his allegory, leaving no room for doubt:

Esta es la Segunda Ley de la Termodinámica:
el desorden aumenta porque la entropía
—este es el nombre que los científicos le dan
a la tendencia al desorden—aumenta.
México es el ejemplo perfecto.[33]

[This is the second Law of Thermodynamics:
disorder increases because entropy
—this is the name scientists give
to the tendency toward disorder—increases.
Mexico is the perfect example.]

In the final two stanzas that follow, the poet reinforces the inescapable nature of the laws of thermodynamics with a tone that drives his point home with an air of inevitability and resignation:

Y el desorden aumenta con el tiempo
por la simple y sencilla razón de que medimos el tiempo
en la dirección en que el desorden aumenta.

No puede estar más claro.[34]

[Disorder increases with time
for the simple reason that we measure time
in the direction in which disorder increases.

It could not be more clear.]

Despite these zingers, Samuel Gordon and Evodio Escalante were right that Alberto Blanco essentially does not write poems with plainly spoken social messages.[35] That being said, Blanco's use of physics as a vehicle for this kind of text is particularly innovative. First of all, scientific laws aim for totality and their systemic and inclusive nature thus lends them authority as allegorical tropes. The inexorable scope of "Segunda teoría termodinámica" ["Second Thermodynamic Theory"] adds pessimism and a sense of inescapability to the crisis of disorder, of entropy, in the governmental and economic systems of Mexico.

Critics of using of quantum mechanics in a literary or critical context argue that theories such as Heisenberg's apply only to very specific systems of subatomic particles or, in the everyday world, create quantities so insignificant that they can be disregarded or corrected for. Blanco, on the other hand, sees science, poetry, and spirituality as intertwined modes of inquiry. "¿Qué sería de la ciencia sin metáforas?" [What would science even be without metaphor?][36] the poet notes at one point, and as Einstein insisted, the new physics would not exist without intuition, imagination, and the figurative language that sustains its central language-based, rather than lab-based, "thought experiments."

In the context of Blanco's poetics, the presence of scientific laws is indicative of a greater nostalgia for the possibility of unifying theories.[37] Always aware of the limitations and relative nature of such laws, his work is flavored nonetheless by a longing for all-encompassing theories such as Newton's classical mechanics. As we will explore below, Blanco's depictions of faith are also closely related to this impulse. Basing himself in Chinese philosopher Chuang Tzu and more contemporary Buddhist writer Lama Anagarika Govinda, Fritjof Capra notes that Einstein's notion of a spacetime continuum is the fourth dimension reached by Eastern mystics in which time stops and the connections between separate individuals are revealed.[38] This idea of unity, of the interconnection of all minds, also ties into the observer effect and reminds us that there simply may not be any "others."[39]

The search for another dimension is an additional characteristic of cultural productions in a time of crisis. The new physics represents its own kind of "crisis thinking" and, as such, is an excellent vehicle for poems concerned with the renovation of systems in decline.[40] In his *Teorías*, Alberto Blanco uses the inclusive authority of Heisenberg's Uncertainty Principle and the observer effect to both urge bystanders to action but to also remind us of the unavoidable, even if unintentional, role that privilege plays. Just as scientists such as Bohr, Einstein, and Schrödinger used metaphors to disrupt and overturn Newton, Blanco turns to physics as part of his project to begin anew in language.

Iconoclastic knowledge, however, can bring serious consequences, as the visual poem "La trinidad" ["Trinity"] warns. Here, the white light of this narrative and descriptive poem reminds us of an extreme example of what can happen when science and governments collide. Note the connection to Indian spirituality spoken, ironically perhaps, by Robert Oppenheimer, at the conclusion of this poem:

"La trinidad"

Un día como hoy
hace exactamente 50 años
en un lugar llamado
"La Trinidad"
en Nuevo México
desaparecieron
por un segundo
todos los colores

El palo verde
el árido mezquite
y la hierba del chaparral
se volvieron blancos
blancos
de aquel árbol de fuego
que en unos cuantos minutos
creció hasta alcanzar
15 kilómetros
de altura

Eran las 5 y media
de la mañana
y el paisaje nocturno
del Desierto de Mojave
en esa zona que llaman
La Jornada del Muerto
quedó galvanizado
por una luz
de una intensidad
muy superior
a la del sol de mediodía

Aquel 16 de julio de 1945
amaneció dos veces

Una lluvia de oro
rojo naranja morado
violeta azul y gris
bañó cada uno de los picos
que rodean el valle
como una corona de lágrimas
con tal claridad

y tan terrible belleza
que el joven Oppenheimer
no pudo más que balbucear
aquellos versículos
del Bhagavad Ghita

"Me he convertido en la Muerte:
el Destructor de los Mundos"

Desierto de Mojave
16 de julio de 1995[41]

[A day like today
exactly fifty years ago
in a place called
"La Trinidad"
in New Mexico
for one second
all the colors
disappeared

The green branches
of the arid mesquite
and the grass on the chaparral
glowed white
white
from that tree of fire
that in just a few minutes
grew 15 kilometers
in height

It was 5 thirty
in the morning
and the nocturnal landscape
of the Mojave Desert
that in that zone they call
La Jornada del Muerto
was galvanized
by a light
of an intensity
far greater than
the sun at noon

On July 16th, 1945
dawn came twice

A golden rain
red orange purple
violet blue and gray
bathed each of the peaks
that surround the valley
like a crown of tears
with such clarity
and such terrible beauty
that the young Oppenheimer
could barely mumble
those verses
from the Bhagavad Gita

"I am become death:
Destructor of Worlds"

Mojave Desert
July 16, 1995]

Lessons in Geometry

A famous epigraph from Leonardo da Vinci introduces Blanco's early poem "Aforismos" ["Aphorisms"]: "Que no me lea quien no sea matemático, / porque yo lo soy siempre en mis principios" ["Non mathematicians should probably not read me, because I am always a mathematician in principle"].[42] The same must be considered for Blanco, of course, whose poetic trilogy clearly exhibits a penchant for sequences, repetitions, symmetries, fractals, and employing mathematical concepts and discourse in the service of poetry. "La clave está en los números—el mundo y su reflejo—dos ascuas en el espejo del rostro" [The key is in the numbers—the world and its reflection—two embers in the mirror of the face] he writes in *A la luz de siempre*.[43]

The speaker of "El sueño dorado" ["The Golden Dream"] clearly a poetic "I," uses the analogy of describing a baseball's 108 double stitches as 216 individual ones as a simple example of how relative a point of view can be, even when it has to do with numbers. The poem's titular "golden dream" is symmetry itself even if, as the speaker notes, life's asymmetrical moments are what make things interesting:

Ambos números
(como todos los números)
son redondos y sagrados.

Conozco sus atributos
pues los he utilizado
para estructurar todos mis libros.

Y mejor sería decir:
me los he encontrado
al dilucidar la estructura
de cada uno de mis libros.

En alas de estos números
los poemas vuelan mejor.

Y en este sentido el béisbol
es igual que la poesía. O casi . . .

La bola vuela más
alto, más lejos, más rápido,
si se le quitan una o dos costuras.[44]

[Both numbers
(Like all numbers)
are round and sacred.

I know their attributes
since I have used them
to structure all my books.

And it would be better to say:
I have found them
while explaining the structure
of each of my books.

On the wings of these numbers
poems fly better.

And in this sense baseball
is like poetry. Or almost . . .

The ball flies
higher, farther, faster,
if you remove one or two stitches.]

The speaker is quick to throw doubt into the mix by correcting the statement that he structures all his books with numbers by noting that instead, as we discussed in the passage from *El llamado y el don*, language, not the poet, is the rider in the horse-and-rider relationship of writing poetry. Through poetic experiments with Euclidean geometry, finite mathematics, the possibilities of the Fibonacci sequence (in which each number is the sum of the two preceding ones), and fractals, Blanco's math poems, like his science poems, show a fascination with a fourth dimension and the ontological and metaphysical possibilities of mathematical metaphors.

"Teoría holográfica" ["Holographic Theory"] employs the now familiar voice and register of the science poems to question our assumptions about reality and create allegories of oneness. The poem begins with a description of how the ripples on the surface of a pond created by two thrown stones create an interference pattern and that this pattern, if frozen in time, is like a hologram. When a human-made hologram is shown under the appropriate light, the image takes on a three-dimensional effect. This is where the poet finds two captivating correspondences:

Lo sorprendente es que,
si el holograma se rompe,
cualquier trozo del mismo
conserva toda la información.

¡A partir de cualquiera
de sus fragmentos
es posible reconstruir
la imagen completa!

En la esfera holográfica
cada fragmento u organismo
representa—de alguna forma—
el universo entero.

Cada rizo congelado
en la superficie del estanque
lleva siempre consigo
su espacio y su tiempo:
la historia completa
de las piedras lanzadas.

Y si bien el modelo
de la placa holográfica
no tiene dimensiones en sí mismo
—¡no tiene espacio ni tiene tiempo!—
en cualquier punto de la placa
se encuentra la imagen completa.

Como dice el antiguo Sutra budista:

"En el cielo de Indra
se dice que hay una red de perlas
dispuestas de tal manera
que si miras a una
ves a todas las demás
reflejadas en ella.

Del mismo modo,
cada ser en el mundo
no es solamente él mismo,
sino que implica
a todos los demás seres
y es, de hecho, todos
y cada uno de los demás."[45]

[The surprising thing is that,
if the hologram is broken,
any piece of the original
holds all its information.

From any one
of its fragments
it's possible to reconstruct
the complete image!

In the holographic sphere
each fragment or organism
represents—in some form—
the entire universe.

Each frozen ripple
on the surface of the pond
carries with it
its own space and time:
the whole story
of all the stones thrown.

Even if the model
of the holographic sheet
does not have its own dimensions
—it has neither space nor time—
in any section of the sheet
you can see the whole image.

As the ancient Buddhist Sutra says:

"In Indra's heaven
they say there is a network of pearls
set out in such a way
that if you look at one
you will see all the others
reflected in it.
In the same way,

each being in the world
is not only itself
but is also part of
all the other beings
and is, by the way, all
and every one of the others."]

The first concept at play here is fractals, that is, shapes that are made of parts that reflect the form of its whole (such as making one large triangle by stacking one identical but smaller triangle on top of three similar triangles). Fractals create their own dimensionality and, like holograms, contain miniature versions of the whole within each of their individual parts. In this way, they have their own space and time. The notion of a fractal opens intriguing questions about the relationship between individual people and society, as well as between other parts and their corresponding wholes—the kinds of relationships that fascinated a young Leonardo as he sketched a fetus alongside a geminating seed in search of analogies and correspondences.

The second thematic thread here is from the Buddhist Sutras. In the *Tao of Physics*, Fritjof Capra states emphatically that "the most important characteristic of the Eastern world view—once could almost say the essence of it—is the awareness of the unity and the mutual interrelation of all things and events, the experience of all phenomena in the world as manifestations of a basic oneness."[46] To cite just one of many manifestations of this idea, Lao Tzu, the founder of Taoism in the sixth century BCE, wrote: "Tao gave birth to one, one gave birth to two, two gave birth to three, three gave birth to all the myriad things. All the myriad things carry the yin on their backs and hold the yang in their embrace."[47]

We are reminded here once again of P. D. Ouspensky's metaphor of the unseen connection between fingerprints on a frosty window pane examined in chapter 4 since Blanco's poems that embrace the new physics and mathematics invite the reader to consider other dimensions and the possibilities of unity they contain. They force us to rethink our understanding of logic and our definitions of ideas of terms such as "finite," "infinite," or "chaos." "Teoría de modelos finitos" ["A Theory of Finite Models"], for example, is a logic puzzle in the register of Euclid's Elements of Geometry:

Si A es distinto de B;
B es distinto de C;
C es distinto de D . . .

Entonces,
A, B, C y D
son iguales.[48]

[If A is different than B;
B is different than C;
C is different than D . . .

Therefore,
A, B, C and D
are equal.]

"Primera teoría del caos" ["First Theory of Chaos"] shows how hard it truly is to find chaos in a random selection of numbers. If we start and end with an odd number, there is a symmetry. If we start with an odd digit and end with an even one, we then have a contrast which, the poem notes, is also not chaotic. "'Es que'—como dijo Borges / en una larga entrevista a los 80 años—/ 'quizá el caos sea difícil. / O imposible.'" [It's that—like Borges said / in a long interview in his 80s—/ "maybe chaos is difficult. / Or impossible"].[49] The poet's conclusion is simply "Las cosas tienden a la forma" [things tend toward form].[50]

Perhaps the most prominent poem in this vein is "Declaración de principios" ["Declaration of Principles"] from *La raíz cuadrada del cielo*. In the essay "La ciencia" [Science], Blanco notes that this poem is "una verdadera declaración de principios que, expresando muy bien—creo—mi doble condición de poeta y de científico, me fue concedido, paradójica y significativamente, durante el sueño" [a true declaration of principles that, expresses clearly—I believe—my double condition of poet and scientist, that appeared to me, paradoxically and significantly, in a dream].[51] Even if Blanco does state that he is a chemist below, there can be no doubt that we are reading poetry and that the scientific principles presented within the text are intended to be read both literally as well as metaphorically. "Declaración de principios" uses quantum mechanics' "observer effect" (verse 4) and Niels Bohr's principle of complementarity (that allows dual interpretations such as the wave/particle duality) to create a truly multifaceted and multidimensional poem.

"Declaración de principios"

Señoras, señores:
antes de comenzar esta lectura
quiero confesar aquí, del modo más natural,
un par de cosas de mucha o poca monta (según se vea)
y, muy probablemente, sin importancia alguna.

La primera de ellas es que yo soy un químico.
No quiero decir con esto que es todo lo que soy,
pero sí que mi formación es de científico
y que, por lo tanto, entre nosotros
no será difícil estar de acuerdo en que $1+1=2$.

Claro está que si alguno de ustedes
piensa que $1+1=3$, yo estoy de acuerdo.

O si alguno de ustedes va más lejos
y piensa que $1+1=3.1416$ . . . también.

Todavía más: si alguno muy osado
piensa que $1+1=0$, también lo suscribo.

Aunque debo confesar
—y esta es la segunda cosa que yo quería confesar—
que siento una fuerte inclinación a creer que $1+1=1$.

Pero cada científico tiene las ecuaciones que se merece
(o las ecuaciones que se le parecen) y no pienso
hacer de esta fórmula una proposición universal.[52]

[Ladies, gentlemen:
before I begin this reading
I would like to confess here, in the most natural way possible,
a few things of much or little significance (depending on you you see them . . .)
and, very probably, without any importance whatsoever.

The first of those is that I am a chemist.
This is not all I am,
but yes, I have been trained as a scientist
and so, therefore, between us
it should not be hard to agree that $1+1=2$.

Of course if any of you believe that
that $1+1=3$, I will agree.

Or if any of you takes it one step farther
and thinks that $1+1=3.1416$ . . . that too.

What's more: if anyone boldly
declares that $1+1=0$, I will also endorse that conclusion.

Although I must confess
—and this is the second thing I wanted to confess—
that I feel a strong inclination to believe that $1+1=1$.

But each scientist has the equations that they deserve
(or the equations that resemble them) and I am not planning
on making this formula into a universal proposition.]

First, the speaker connects with the reader by addressing us directly through a conversational tone. He then builds our commonalities through a few simple mathematical equations. After $1+1=2$ we get the more metaphorical $1+1=3$ (which, perhaps, can be understood as when two people join forces, they can accomplish as much as 3 or can, like parents, create a life) and $1+1=3.1416\ldots$ which can refer to the circumference of any circle, and $1+1=0$ can also be correct in certain mathematic contexts, for example, those that allow dividing by zero. His conclusion is that he feels a strong inclination to believe that $1+1=1$, that is, that everything is united through a plurality of theories. This is another example of the notion we explored in chapter 4 of poetry's unique ability to contain a "third half."

Blanco's lessons in geometry are a sequence of four poems that explore the allegorical possibilities of mathematics. "Primera lección de geometría" ["First Geometry Lesson"] informs us of the origins of numbers in a familiar biblical tone, even if it then goes on to describe the concept in Mayan terms:

> En el principio era el uno.
>
> Más cerca del punto de la escritura maya
> que de la raya vertical de nuestro sistema de notación.
>
> El uno no era una cantidad;
> era la pura calidad del Todo indivisible.[53]
>
> [In the beginning was one.
>
> Closer to the period in Mayan writing
> than to the vertical line in our system of notation.
>
> The one was not a quantity;
> it was the pure quality of the indivisible Whole.]

One, the poem contends, gave birth to all the other numbers, and before it, there was nothing. The totality of this one also allows for an Eastern understanding of unity.

> Antes del uno no había más que el uno.
> No el cero del vacío inexistente.
> Ni el cero de la nada absurda.
> El uno nada más.[54]
>
> [Before one there was nothing but the one.
> Not the nonexistent emptiness of the zero.
> Nor the absurd nothingness of the zero.
> Only the one.]

As we read in "Declaración de principios" and "Teoría de modelos finitos," "Segunda lección de geometría" ["Second Geometry Lesson"] asserts the equality of many seemingly unequal forms, even as they expand from one to two to three to four dimensions:

Una línea, por larga o corta que sea,
tiene un número infinito de puntos.

Una superficie, por chica o grande que sea,
tiene un número infinito de puntos.

Un volumen, por inmenso o diminuto que sea,
tiene un número infinito de puntos.

Cualquier cuerpo de cuatro dimensiones
tiene más puntos que un volumen,
una superficie o una línea,
y, simultáneamente,
el mismo número: infinito.[55]

[A line, as long or short as it is,
contains an infinite number of points.
A surface, as small or large as it is,
contains an infinite number of points.

A volume, as immense or diminutive as it is,
contains an infinite number of points.

Any four dimensional body
has more points than a volume,
a surface or a line,
and, simultaneously,
the same number: infinity.]

Once again, the poet draws our attention to a similarity that unites different quantities. As Klam indicates, via Robert Anton Wilson, the multiple definitions we find in poems like "Vapor, agua, hielo," "Declaración de principios," and Blanco's second and third lessons of geometry attack the tyranny of the word "is" or "equals" and such redefinition, like quantum physics itself, is not without a spiritual dimension.[56] "Tercera lección de geometría" ["Third Lesson in Geometry"] provides an ironic conclusion to its proof ("Todas estas series son infinitas / pero algunas son más infinitas que otras" [All these series are infinite / but some are more infinite than others],[57] while "Cuarta lección de geometría" ["Fourth Lesson in Geometry"] moves from a point to a line to a surface to a volume and from there to a more metaphysical definition of space and time:

El volumen es la superficie en movimiento
fuera de sí, por la noche que vemos.
De día es la resistencia de la sombra.
El volumen no es más que la intersección

de dos tiempos completos en un cuerpo:
Aquí se lucha y se sabe, se ama y se calla.[58]

[A volume is a plane in motion,
outside itself, through our shared night.
By day it is the resistance of shadows.
Volume is nothing more than the intersection
of two perfect moments in a body:
Here we fight, we think, we love, and keep still.]

As we saw in the previous chapter, geometry's circles and lines play an important role in Blanco's visual poetry. In "El espectro del visible, acaso" the poet reminded us that sight is, in a sense, circular: "Sol: luz redonda: ojo abierto del cielo. / * El mundo entero cabe en la pupila: luces y sombras, perfumes visuales. / * El mundo está de cabeza en la retina y la tierra está recostada en la mirada" [Sun: round light: open eye in the sky. / * The whole world fits in a pupil: light and shadow, visual perfumes. / * The world is upside down in the retina and the earth is reclined in our sight].[59] Seeing is central to Alberto Blanco because it allows the creation and appreciation of art as well as the rigorous research of science and mathematics. Blanco's geometric metaphors, from the closed circle that represents both wholeness and emptiness, to the poetic line with its ability to both connect and to separate, are intriguing metaphors of unity between reality and imagination, objects and observers, as well as artists and lovers.[60]

Aura

The reader of *El corazón del instante* is convinced that Blanco is a believer in the authenticity of certain forms since the poet does not hesitate to draw a distinction between concepts such as poetry and Poetry. This half of his dialectical worldview, what may be called a belief in archetypes or the sacred, cannot be overlooked. Critics such as Teresa Chapa have noted that Blanco is a mystical, spiritual, or "religious" poet in many senses of the term.[61] In his 2002 interview with Kimberly Eherenman, Blanco calls all art "religious" in the sense that it reconnects us (*re + ligare*) with other dimensions of our experience. In fact, both Álvaro Mutis and Carlos Zamora use the metaphor of prayer, "poesía en oración," to speak of Blanco's work.[62] This is because, in many moments, *El corazón del instante* resists cynical secularism and embraces what Walter Benjamin once called "aura."

In "The Work of Art in the Age of Mechanical Reproduction" Benjamin wrote of the struggle modern artists undergo to preserve authenticity and authority when so much of what they do can be copied and redistributed either by themselves or by other parties. Contemporary society, Benjamin warned back in 1939, is dominated by an urge to "get a hold of an object at very close range by way of its likeness, its reproduction."[63] "Reproduction," he wrote, leads "to a tremendous shattering of tradition" in which an object is yanked from its context and placed in another, a process which both destroys and reenergizes it.[64] The paradox implicit in this cycle of destruction and renewal (the one that powers collage, of course) informs Blanco's interpretation of "religioso" [religious]—the ties that connect us also hold us back, just as the taboos that draw together a community of believers also set it apart from others.

Benjamin extends his thesis of duplication to claim that an original object, whether historical or natural, suffers through multiple reproductions and loses some of its *aura* or uniqueness. For Benjamin, *aura* is partially a "phenomenon of distance."[65] Other critics have defined it as the "unique nimbus that surround(s) a work of art" or the "*hic et nunc* (here and now) giving authenticity to the work."[66] By way of example, the Diego Rivera murals in the Palacio Nacional have more *aura* than their reproductions in an art book or on an Internet website. Criticism has always followed the lead of art and art has always embraced technological change. As new forms of duplication become available, art evolves and adapts by anticipating reproduction and finding out what can be gained in the process.

At its core, *aura* is an essentialist idea in that it privileges certain objects over others based on their innate qualities. Ironically, the members of the Frankfurt School were Marxists whose ideas on art were directly related to their desire for social change. They held that art that was freed from religious authority could better benefit the group and the revolution. Although Benjamin was highly influenced by dialectical materialism (which privileges science over other metadiscourses), he also retained an interest in metaphysics and the role of the spiritual in society. This conflict and interplay between opposing visions of reality and between originals and reproductions is also central in the poetry of Alberto Blanco.

In the essay "La pobreza de la poesía" ["The Poverty of Poetry"], the poet examines the notion of the place and value of poetry within consumer culture. What exactly are we buying, he asks, when we buy a book of poems? "Nada que parezca realmente necesario. Nada que no se pueda copiar a mano o saber de memoria" [Nothing that seems really necessary. Nothing that can't be copied by hand or memorized].[67] Here is the dialectic of original and reproduction—a conflict that haunts art critics in terms of painting versus photography or film. Blanco's home, Mexico City, like all of *El corazón del instante*, is characterized by the combination of consumer culture and objects with *aura*. In the first book of Blanco's trilogy we see original art objects like Mayan and Roman ruins, biblical scenes, the names of specific works of art—things that certainly can be reproduced with words but will never contain the authority of their originals. The role these objects play in Blanco's poetic world is to confer a sense of emotional authority, we might call it sublimity, that contrasts and complements incomplete representations and to thus create a scene of loss, a visible trace or ghost of what might have been.

In "¿Para qué tantas formas?" ["Why so Many Forms"] the poet returns to a Platonic mode to question originality. "¿Quién no quisiera observar las estrellas / a través de un lente pulido por Spinoza?" [Who would not want to observe the stars / through a lens polished by Spinoza?] is one of six questions in the text that posit an impossible wish.[68] We have all looked through a telescope, and today's, of course, are far superior to those of four hundred years ago, and yet to see through one of the lenses crafted and polished by the hand of the Dutch philosopher is the combination of an action and an emotion. In other terms, it is the combination of reason and imagination: two of the faculties traditionally associated with the sublime. Playing a tune on a reed flute made by Krishna may not traditionally be considered sublime, but it, like the poem's other five questions, is given more dramatic force due to its impossibility. In his gloss of Kant's "Critique of Judgment" Jean-François Lyotard contrasts "taste" and the "sublime" in the following way: "Taste promises everyone the happiness of an accomplished subjective unity; the sublime speaks to the few of another unity, much less complete, ruined in a sense, and more 'noble.'"[69] In a similar way, Blanco's poem is unable to reproduce the original experiences it longs for and, conscious of its shortcomings, offers us instead new solutions for "what to make of a diminished thing." The poet's answer is to reproduce objects with unattainable *aura* and thus construct a new experience in the poem we read, as imperfect and seductive as a wish.

The concept of religious *aura* is a constant in the *hacedor* poems of *La parábola de Cromos* [*The Parable of Cromos*]. These texts' coded dialogues with the work of visual artists open up our reading of them significantly, making it even harder to assign the images or readings within to our poet or the artists and works he cites. Some poems evoke the sacred by employing well known Christian images, figures and scenes such as the adoration of the Christ child ("Adoración" ["Adoration"]) or a dialogue between Jesus and Mary Magdalene ("Noli me tangere" ["Touch Me Not"]). "Mientras hay espacio hay tiempo" ["While There is Space There is Time"] repeats its title like a refrain with the cadence of a responsorial psalm and "La primera estrella" ["The First Star"] blends Judeo-Christian themes with the more metaphorical image of a creator as the center, eye, or sun that reappears throughout Blanco's work. The poem's star shines through a romantic landscape evocative of its dedicatee Caspar David Friedrich and lights the way to "la casa del Padre" ["the house of the Father"].[70] In the context of Friedrich, the capitalized "Padre" can only be an overt reference to God the Father (a similar reference can be found in the first poem of *Cuenta de los guías*). Blanco's treatment of God is usually not as explicit and here, the presence of an *hacedor* distances the content from the text's real author. Many Blanco poems are even more abstract and metaphorical in their descriptions of a prime mover or intelligent designer. "En el país de un mejor conocimiento" ["In a More Knowledgeable

Country"] (dedicated to Paul Klee) posits the presence of "el Creador más allá de todo nombre y toda forma" [the Creator above all name and form].[71] This creator is later described as "el que inspira sublimes melodías en los pulmones" [inspiring sublime melodies in the lungs] in the poem "El músico" ["The Musician"][72] and as the center of a compass in "El cuarto de los tres siglos" ["The Room of Three Centuries"].[73] As in "Poema visto en el ventilador de un motel" ["Poem Seen in a Motel Fan"] this last poem uses combined images of movement and stasis to reflect on permanence and change. When Blanco writes "Un ojo inmenso nos ve" [An immense eye is watching us], he grounds the changes that define life itself with something larger than all of us, something that lasts.[74]

Genesis

La hora y la neblina features a number of poems that question what makes a space sacred. In "Oración de Clonmacnoise" ["Clonmacnoise Prayer"] the poet creates a prayer of *ubi sunt* from the stones that remain at the ruins of the famous Irish monastery and "Mi laberinto" ["My Labyrinth"] uses the labyrinth on the floor of the Cathedral of Chartres as a metaphor for life's journey. Like Clonmacnoise, Chartres is also a '"fortaleza . . . libro abierto" [a fortress . . . an open book] a sacred sign waiting for interpretation, and an "inspirational" space with *aura* in the dual sense in which Blanco uses the word.[75] These texts examine the relationship of space to place and ritual to myth, all within the context of time. As Blanco notes in an essay: "El rito es el recuerdo, por medio de símbolos, de aquel hecho primigenio, donde nació un mundo completo, puro, sagrado" [Ritual is memory, through symbols, of that primitive reality, where a whole, pure, sacred world was born].[76] While the experiences of these religious poems are personal, they also hold a collective importance that opens up their significance and makes them more culturally resonant.

Cuando tú y yo ya no seamos
más que un puñado de polvo
disperso en el agua, en el viento
una imagen de un sueño

Pero recuerda:
una vez estuve aquí
    contigo
y estaré contigo siempre[77]

[When you and I have ceased to be
but a handful of dust
scattered upon the wind and water
image of a dream

But remember:
I was here
    here with you
and will be forever][78]

The labyrinth is a natural point of interest for this poet due to its symmetry and numerological richness. John James has done an extensive study on the levels of meaning in the labyrinth of Chartres and its intricate architecture. Its twelve levels of passages relate to both the zodiac and alchemy as well as to Christian symbolism. James notes, "It is not a maze, but a single way. It is not a mindless trick but an ordered track."[79] The labyrinth is a small pilgrimage route and, like the many examples from Western literature, Blanco's poem is really a small allegory of life that begins with "El cielo" [the sky] and ends in "el mar" [the sea]. The "tú" in the poem is once again a partner, a reader, one who shares the fate of the speaker. In a sense, the most interesting passage in "Mi laberinto" ["My Labyrinth"] is the last, in which there is a shift in voice. Where the third section describes the speaker's death ("ahora me llamo polvo" ["my name now is dust"])[80], the fourth section describes yet another transformation, this time into something that transcends time and space, cause and effect:

No temas
si hoy tengo
otra forma

Déjame seguir
el curso del río
de las cosas

De la vida
de la muerte
del espacio
del tiempo

Déjame ser
al fin el río
el manantial
y el mar

Chartres
Agosto del 2000[81]

[Have no fear
if my form
is other

Let me follow
the river's course
the course of things

Of life
of death
of space
of time

Let me be
at the river's end
the flood
and the sea

Chartres
August 2000]

When describing his different understandings of "Poesía" [Poetry] and "poesía" [poetry], Blanco often speaks of Poetry as having a "divine" aspect, such as being "un estado divino de creación pura" [a divine state of pure creation].[82] Blanco's Poetry is the spirit of artistic creation, related to the notions of the sacred and to Benjamin's idea of aura. On the other hand, poetry, like sculpture or painting, can be considered simply "Poesía del lenguaje" [Poetry of language] since poets create their art from words rather than stone or paint.[83]

Blanco writes poems about all aspects of the spiritual experience, from origins to the idea of a personal god (or Gods) to prayer. In *El llamado y el don*, he notes "si algo podemos sacar en claro de una lectura de los primeros versículos del Génesis es que el ser humano, en la justa medida en la que fue creado 'a imagen y semejanza del Creador,' no puede ser otra cosa que un creador" [if something can be gleaned from reading the first verses of Genesis it is that human beings, since they were created "in the image and likeness of the Creator," cannot be anything but creators].[84] In the beginning were the creators who simply reproduced versions of themselves (in the pattern of mathematical fractals). Representing a moment of creation, of genesis, is a serious challenge for a poet, one Blanco rises to in a few different contexts. "Fuego nuevo" ["New Fire"], for example, contains a hermetic, pre-Columbian metaphor of creation and re-creation and "Raíz cuadrada de dos" ["The Square Root of Two"] is a math poem that describes a scene of creation through a big bang and without naming a divine subject.

Blanco's gods, his creators (and his *hacedores*), are plural: "Hay muchos más dioses que máquinas, burgueses y obreros. / Casi no hay más que dioses" [There are many more gods than machines, bourgeoisie or workers. / There are almost more gods than anything] he notes at one point.[85] In addition to these metaphors of sacred presence, Gods are also frequently described through complementary relationships of presence and absence and faith and doubt. In the clever "Radiografía" ["X-Ray"] the poet's characteristic negative phrasing describes how going to church fulfills a certain lack in people's lives:

Ir el viernes por la noche al cine
a ver una película de aventuras
es confirmar que no hay acción
ni misterio en nuestras vidas.

Ir al Museo de Arte Moderno
el sábado por la mañana
es reconocer que vivimos
sin creatividad ni belleza.

Ir el sábado por la noche
a una fiesta a buscar calor
es admitir que estamos solos.

Asistir a la iglesia el domingo
es confesar que brilla
por su ausencia el Creador.[86]

[Going to the movies on a Friday night
to see an adventure film
is confirmation that there is no action
or mystery in our lives.

Going the Modern Art Museum
on a Saturday morning
is recognition that we live
without creativity or beauty.

Going on Saturday night
to a party in search of warmth
is an admission we are alone.

Going to church on Sunday
is a confession that the Creator
shines through absence.]

The title "Radiografía" tells us that this is a poem about visual diagnosis. Each of the stanzas of this sonnet in blank verse describes a typical weekend activity and then displays it in a negative light, much as an x-ray machine creates an image of tissue or bone from the interplay of positive and negative space surrounding it. Going to the movies, a museum, parties, or church highlights things missing in the speaker's life: action, creativity, beauty, and human warmth are out there to be found if we just know where and how to look. The fourth stanza holds the most interest though, since the tension between presence and absence is itself a fundamental issue of its subject, faith. This fact helps explain and justify the poet's use of the lofty form of the sonnet for a poem that features many everyday places and situations.

Numerous Blanco poems describe God as an absent presence that complements the speaker. "El árbol de la vida" ["The Tree of Life"], to cite just one example,[87] relies on scientific discourse to define the speaker's relationship with the divine:

"El árbol de la vida"

Cuando quiero huir del tiempo,
mi refugio es el espacio.

Cuando quiero huir del espacio,
mi refugio es el tiempo.

Cuando quiero huir del espacio
y del tiempo, mi refugio soy yo.

Cuando quiero huir de mí,
el único refugio es Dios.[88]

[When I want to flee time,
my refuge is space.

When I want to flee space,
my refuge is time.

When I want to flee both space
and time, I am my refuge.

When I want to flee myself,
the only refuge is God.]

Like empathy, prayer is one way for a speaker to bridge the gap ("*re+ligare*") between the poles of self and other. Here, the divine half is described as mystery and the speaker expresses appreciation for it:

"Oración del Café Hauptwache"

Que todo lo que vea—sea
en la luz rubia y radiante
del día, o en la cabellera
de la noche—no sea yo.

Frankfurt
Octubre de 1992[89]

["Prayer in Café Hauptwache"

Let all that I see—be
in the blonde and radiant light
of day, or in the flowing hair
of the night—something other than me.

Frankfurt
October 1992]

In a poem inspired by science, Blanco rewrites a familiar Catholic prayer in "El lado izquierdo de la creación" ["The Left Side of Creation"]:

Madre nuestra,
que estás en la tierra,
santificada sea tu imagen;
siga tu amor con nosotros;
extiéndase tu buena voluntad
así en la tierra como en el cielo.

Déjanos gozar el fruto de cada día;
perdona nuestros desatinos descontrolados
así como nosotros perdonamos a los desatinados.
No nos dejes caer en la impaciencia
y concédenos el bien.
Amén.[90]

[Our Mother,
who art on earth,
hallowed be thy image;
let your love be with us;
let your goodwill extend
to earth as it is in heaven.

Let us enjoy the fruit of each day;
forgive us our uncontrollably foolish
mistakes as we forgive uncontrollable fools.

Do not let us fall into impatience
and grant us your good.
Amen.]

Moving in another direction, *The Left Hand of Creation* is the name of a book by astronomers John D. Barrow and Joseph Silk that Blanco translated from English to Spanish. The book describes how the lost paradise of a symmetrical world was destroyed by the Big Bang and gave birth our universe. As in Blanco's poem, Barrow and Silk's book explores cosmology and the search for "naked singularities"—places beyond the rules of physics—that could prove or suggest the existence of a Grand Designer. Blanco's poem that bears the book's name contains a similar blend of the empirical and the mysterious, the everyday and the divine through its contemporary rewriting of the Lord's Prayer.

"Diez aforismos" [Ten Aphorisms] from *A la luz de siempre* uses the direct and conversational tone of Blanco's science poems to posit three aphorisms about God that demonstrate the poet's insistent polar vision. Ironically, in a case of intertextual *litotes*, these poems reflect those of their *hacedor* Edmond Jabès.

> Yo soy un poema en Dios y Dios es en mí el poeta.
> *
> Cuando reconozco que creo en Dios, de inmediato me nacen dudas; cuando creo que reconozco mis dudas, de inmediato me nace Dios.
> *
> Dios ve por ti a través de ti mismo.[91]

> [I am a poem in God and God is in me the poet.
> *
> When I recognize that I believe in God, I suddenly start to doubt; when I believe
> that I recognize my doubts, I suddenly start to see God.
> *
> God looks out for you through you yourself.]

One final instance of a poem that addresses sacred origins is "Teatro de ausencias" ["Theater of Absences"]. The poet's play with positive and negative space here adds visual impact to the text and his insistence on the connection and inseparability of the Gods and his poetic subject lead us to interpret it as a theological inquiry, rather than a purely existential exercise:

"Teatro de ausencias"
Estoy hecho de ausencias
Soy el hueco entre dos yos
Soy el vacío entre dos notas
Soy una vasta red de ausencias
Soy un teatro hecho de ausencias
Pronto no seré sino una ausencia más
Por el momento la razón está de mi lado
Pero tener razón en nada disminuye mi pena[92]

["Theatre of Absences"
I am made of absences
I am the hollow between two Is
I am the pause between two notes

I am an immense network of absences
I am a theater that is made of absences
Soon I will become but one more absence
For now, however, reason is still on my side
But being right does nothing to diminish my pain]

Faith

In the essay "El margen" ["The Margin"] Blanco cites author Thomas Cahill's notion that after the fall of the Roman Empire, the scribes of Ireland saved Western civilization by recording all the history they could find and then redistributing it throughout Europe in ways that greatly influenced the Medieval European mind. Blanco, though, asks an important question—"¿qué fue lo que mantuvo viva esa cultura en una sociedad pequeña y cerrada de eruditos que se refugiaron en islas como Iona y Lindisfarne? La mantuvo de pie, desde luego, la fe" [what kept culture alive in the small and closed society of scholars that sought refuge on islands like Iona and Lindisfarne? What kept it going, of course, was faith].[93] Faith is belief, trust, confidence in something that is ultimately unknowable. In light of the poet's complementary vision of the world, it is no surprise that he would see this complex and most human emotion as the cornerstone of Western culture:

"Fe ciega"

Una paradoja
no es verdadera ni falsa
sino todo lo contrario[94]

["Blind Faith"

A paradox
is neither true nor false
but rather the contrary]

Absence and presence are core concepts to any definition of faith and, consequently, of origins and creation. From Saint Augustine on, Christians have interrogated faith with doubt in order to reach a fuller and more complete understanding of their beliefs. "Un escéptico Noé" ["A Skeptical Noah"] one of Blanco's most heavily anthologized poems, uses Kompridis's mechanism of crisis thinking in the context of a familiar biblical parable as a springboard for creativity.[95] Complements are the very basis of this poem with its scene of creation through destruction, faith and doubt, and life and death. The reader is set apart from the speaker through the use of the second person in a question that calls attention to the number of believers left behind when the waters rose: "En esta soledad que nunca conociste / te preguntas por los que se quedaron" [In this solitude you have never known / you wonder about those that stayed behind].[96] The text also provides allegories of writing: collecting different species in one place (like a book of poems), listening, creating art without knowing why or how it could possibly change the world. Noah is the one who hears God's voice and collects the animals, "la semilla del mundo" [seeds of the world], before the devastating flood. Noah's redeeming characteristic, in this telling of the story, is his faith to believe in life after apocalypse, a message that surely resonated with Mexican readers living through the 1960s, 1970s, and 1980s.

This section and chapter need to end with a discussion of two poems, "Diez apuntamientos" ["Ten Points"] and "Credo" ["Creed"] that address faith in the kind of direct, light, conversational, and more prosaic register that is so common to Blanco's metaphysical poems. If prose, as we have mentioned a number of times, is used to discuss known quantities or preplanned stories, it makes sense that these poems would be more prosaic in that they are attempting to deliver specific messages about the unknown to readers.

The ten sections of "Diez apuntamientos" open by telling us that (1) "God" is a word. A well-worn, if not worn-out, word, and that stories of God, as varied and at times bizarre as they are (2), have value and should be preserved (3)—the Irish monks and Blanco's skeptical Noah being prime examples. "God" is a linguistic sign, he notes later, whose signifier is unknowable (4, 5) and due to the plurality of stories about "God," "los Dioses" [Gods] seems a better descriptor, one that provides an appropriately humble way to recognize one's humanly limitations (7). This humility will not lead the speaker so far as to say that he doesn't know anything, but he is glad to admit that what he knows is very, very small in comparison to all the knowledge out there (8).

Sections 9 and 10 explain new interpretations of Blanco's complementary concept of god and the self, mystery and empirical knowledge:

> IX: Noveno: En este sentido, no es que "crea" en "Dios"; "Dios," en tanto esa realidad inconmensurable que no conozco y que no podré nunca llegar a conocer, existe. Absolutamente. Sin lugar a dudas. Creer o no creer en Dios, me parece pueril, y, a fin de cuentas, lo mismo: fantasía.
>
> X: Reconocer, en cambio, la extensión de mi ignorancia, me parece cuestión evidente y hasta burda, fuera de toda discusión. Dios es. Y a la luz de este décimo punto quedan claros los aforismos y versos que he escrito donde aparece la palabra "Dios," la palabra "Dioses." Creer no es suficiente. Los Dioses saben.[97]
>
> [IX
> Ninth: In this sense, it's not that I "believe" in "God"; "God," if only in that vast reality of what I don't know and will never come to know, exists. Abso-

lutely. Beyond a shadow of a doubt. Believing in God or not, seems childish to me, since, in the end, it's all the same: a fantasy.

X
On the other hand, admitting the breadth of my ignorance is clear to me, almost too obvious, not even worth discussing. God is. And by the light of this tenth point all the aphorisms and verses I have written with the words "God" or "Gods" make sense. Believing is not enough. Only the Gods know.][98]

After using logic to prove a concept outside of the field of logic, section 10 then offers us a poetic version of a super theory, a unified field to classify Blanco's previous declarations of faith, even if it appears under the sign of another artist.

The final poem in *A la luz de siempre*, the third volume of Blanco's massive poetic trilogy, takes up the notion of faith one last time. In his dissertation on Blanco, Carlos Zamora relies on Earl Miner's notion that even if all poetic collections don't create narratives, they all follow a narrative sequence—with first and last poems being particularly important.[99] "Credo" channels the confidence of a mature poet who has spent decades polishing his beliefs and expresses those affirmations in a more concise way than a similar poem like Paz's "Carta de creencia" ["Letter of Testimony"]. While many of its ideas on poetics and its focus on complements may seem familiar, "Credo" ["Creed"] is also uncharacteristic of Blanco's work in that it relies heavily on the first person and addresses romantic love.

"Credo"

I
Creo en la igualdad
de las importancias:
todo es importante
o nada es importante . . .
da igual.
Y aquí radica
toda la diferencia.

II
Creo que con nuestros pensamientos
construimos el mundo;
por eso cuando para nuestro pensamiento,
paramos el mundo.

III
Creo en la mala memoria
porque ayuda a vivir;

creo en la buena memoria
por lo mismo.

IV
Creo en la inconsecuencia
siempre y cuando ésta se ejerza
inconsecuentemente.

V
Creo que nadie
merece homenajes,
ni siquiera después de la muerte.
El que homenajea
siempre se homenajea a sí mismo.

VI
Creo que nada
representa nada
y nadie representa a nadie,
salvo el lenguaje.

VII
Creo que las palabras
no son las cosas,
aunque las palabras
también son cosas.

VIII
Creo que para vivir
se necesita,
por lo menos, creer.

IX
Creo que el amor
es eterno
porque es instantáneo.

X
¿Creo en Dios?
No lo sé . . .
Sólo Dios sabe.[100]

["Creed"

I
I believe in the sameness
of importances:
everything is important
or nothing is important . . .
it's all the same.
And here lies
all the difference.

II
I believe with our thoughts
we construct the world;
that's why when our thoughts stop
the world stops.

III
I believe in having a bad memory
because it helps us live.
I believe in having a good memory
for the same reason.

IV
I believe in inconsistency
as long as it is practiced
inconsistently.

V
I believe that no one
deserves to be paid homage,
not even after death.
Those that perform those tributes
are always just honoring themselves.

VI
I believe that nothing
represents nothing
and that no one represents no one
except language.

VII
I believe that words
are not things they describe,
although words themselves
are also things.

VIII
I believe that in order to live
one must
at least, believe.

IX
I believe that love
is eternal
because it is instantaneous.

X
Do I believe in God?
I don't know . . .
Only God knows.]

And so Alberto Blanco ends his poetic trilogy with one of the most direct and personal questions that can be asked—a question that has weaved in and out of his poems from his earliest verses. Blanco's work borrows deeply from traditional Catholic symbolism which opens it up to these lines of questioning but without studying the context of his poetry, it would be difficult to understand how such a question could be answered or what the answer could mean.[101]

A poem such as "Credo" can be written only after a long spiritual journey punctuated by gnawing questions and puzzling partial answers.[102] In the end, the poetry of Alberto Blanco shows us time and again the complementary nature of faith and doubt but insists that like a skeptical Noah, our only option when staring at the threatening clouds of doubt is to maintain our faith in the light.

Coda

FLIGHT

J'aimerais peindre
comme l'oiseau chante
—Claude Monet

The poetry of Alberto Blanco is a universe of verse—a large and complex body of meticulously structured and interrelated poems in a constant process of transformation. Together with the essays of *El canto y el vuelo* [*Song and Flight*], Blanco's three poetic cycles embody and interpret a meticulously crafted poetics driven by the energy exchanged between complementary poles of meaning. The trilogies *A la luz de siempre* [*In Constant Light*] and *El canto y el vuelo* are creative and critical complements that posit ideas through poetry and then gloss them through prose in such a way that the reader must negotiate new interpretative positions between those positive and negative spaces. This process of working through Blanco's poetic language uncovers distinctive notions of what poetry itself is and contains implications for how we understand and interpret other poets as well.

Mirroring the symbiotic relationship between the two trilogies, Blanco's poems themselves create and exchange energy between polarities of poetic and prosaic discourse. Showing and telling appear in overtly declarative lines (". . . la prosa encadena. / La poesía desencadena" [. . . prose chains things up. / Poetry breaks chains.]),[1] as well as in the explicit metapoems we have analyzed throughout this manuscript. "El fiel de la balanza" ["The Scale's Needle"] from *El corazón del instante* [*The Heart of the Moment*] provides an innovative blend of poetic showing and prosaic telling through a visual metaphor of poetry's unique capacity for expression:

VII

El hombre
mitad luz   mitad sombra

mitad imaginación
La tercera cara
de la moneda
es el canto[2]

[VII

Humans
half light half shadow
half imagination
The third face
of the coin
is its edge]

As we saw in chapter 4, only in poetry can there be a "tercera mitad" [third half] or a "tercera cara / de la moneda" [third face / of a coin]. The insistence on poetry's laws and their distance from the rules of science or linguistics is especially dramatic for Blanco who speaks the language of chemistry, physics, and creative writing as an informed native. When we read poems that transgress those natural laws, it introduces the element of mystery that strong poems require. Indeed, "El fiel de la balanza" may not have even been written if it were not for Albert Einstein's counterintuitive comment that "imagination is more important than knowledge." In Blanco's poem, "la imaginación" [imagination] is the bridge between the polar energies of light and shadow, both in their literal as well as in any of their many figurative meanings (good/evil, knowledge/ the unknown, etc.). While imagination is clearly an important part of the equation, the homonym "canto" [edge/song] is the key word in "El fiel de la balanza" since it participates in at least two metaphors at once: (1) as the edge of a coin ("Extremidad o lado de cualquier parte o sitio") and also (2) as a "song" or "poem" ("Composición poética").[3]

Throughout our study we have returned many times to the idea in *El llamado y el don* [*The Calling and the Gift*] that language drives the writing of poems and therefore is the rider, rather than the horse, in the well-worn metaphor of the poetic act. Blanco's poems, in this sense, are combinations of the ideas he wants to bring to the text (telling—a poem's more prosaic pole) and the sounds and meaning that come through in the words *that chose him*, since "El poeta no utiliza las palabras para decir, sino para ser dicho. El poeta utiliza las palabras para escuchar" [Poets do not use words to say, but rather to be said. Poets use words to listen].[4]

The balance of poetry and prose in "Encore" ["Encore"] provides a clear example of what a Blanco poem strives to accomplish. In spite of its seemingly prosaic definitions of "humankind," "art," "poetry," etc., the poem succeeds because it contains an extra dimension that prose cannot, its "encore":

"Encore"

El hombre:
mitad luz,
mitad sombra,
mitad imaginación.

El arte:
mitad suerte,
mitad ciencia,
mitad misterio.

La poesía:
mitad imagen,
mitad música,
mitad poesía.

El poema:
mitad qué,
mitad cómo,
mitad silencio.[5]

["Encore"

Humans:
half light,
half shadow,
half imagination.

Art:
half luck,
half science,
half mystery.

Poetry:
half image,
half music,
half poetry.

Poem:
half what,
half how,
half silence.]

The fourth stanza provides an excellent statement of the poetics of Alberto Blanco since its three halves embody mystery and therefore communicate a depth of meaning that cannot be attained through simple prose. In addition to the pleasing aural cadence of their repetitions, all the poem's stanzas contain a visual element that adds authority to their message. "Encore" balances sound and sense, visual and verbal forms, and the literal as well as the "other side" of language to both show and tell us what poems can do.

The three halves of the images in "Encore" attempt to translate the untranslatable and transcend their form through Blanco's "transformalismo" [Transformalism]: "la forma es un medio y el fin es trascender la forma. . . . La meta es la transformación del artista y quien disfruta de los frutos del trabajo artístico: el creador lo mismo que el recreador" [Form is a means to the end of transcending form. . . . The goal is the transformation of the artist and those that enjoy the fruit of the artist's work: the creator the same as the re-creator][6] The inspired poet fails if she does not, in turn, inspire her readers. Julio Ortega puts it simply: "Blanco no escribe para probarnos su capacidad de decir sino para demostrarnos nuestra capacidad de ver" [Blanco does not write to prove his capacity to tell us things but rather to show us our capacity to see].[7] We explored this idea in chapter 1, along with the implications of manipulating space and time in poetic collages—the second line of "El fiel de la balanza," for example, is full of temporal tension caused by its nontraditional form: in it, light and shadow exist in a state of "anhelo polar" [polar longing]. Longing for communion between opposite terms is a main trope in *A la luz de siempre*, from the mysterious relationship between a text and its paratext, to the interplay of positive and negative spaces, to loftier hypotheses about universal connections between all human beings.

The cult of form in Blanco's work, from the level of the word to the line, stanza, poem, series, chapter, book, and poetic cycle, organically suggests that the reader approach this poetry through visual metaphors of communion. There are countless examples of visual and thematic *taijitu*s in *A la luz de siempre* that envision dynamic relationships of complementarity and carry the mystical or spiritual dimension we see throughout the poems. In a similar way, the two hemispheres of the human brain and the wave/particle duality also provide useful perspectives on how to understand Blanco's dualities. Through another biological metaphor these poems teach us that the inspired poet's job is to use their work to inspire readers, just as our lungs inhale and then exhale or our hearts pump through the rhythm of systole and diastole.

Let's conclude with one last metaphor of poetry, one so personally important, the poet chose it for the title of his trilogy of essays on poetics.

From his early days with the rock band La Comuna [The Commune] to the final lines of *A la luz de siempre*, there is no poetry for Blanco without "el canto" [song], a concept intimately linked, as in the beating of a heart, to "el vuelo" [flight]. The ancient connections between poetry and songs have lead poets of every tradition to identify with images of birds—the English Romantics had their owls, larks, and nightingales, Baudelaire his albatross, Stevens his blackbirds, and Dickinson her hope, “the thing with feathers.” Poets admire birds for their freedom, their individuality, their songs, their sharp vision, and, above all, their ability to fly. Both in *El libro de los pájaros* [*A Book of Birds*] and beyond, Blanco has numerous poems about the affinities between poets and birds. In “Ascenso de energía” [“Energy Rising”] we read:

El hombre
sintiendo cerca
la hora de su muerte

Se tendió
sobre la página
en blanco de la sábana

Donde
su sombra
formó un pájaro.[8]

[A man
feeling the proximity
of the hour of his death

Laid down
on the blank page
of the sheets

Where
his shadow
formed a bird]

Or:

“El hombre”
El hombre
es una especie de cuervo
que vuela con la tinta de sus plumas

25 de junio de 1996, El Paso[9]

“Man”
A man
is a kind of crow
that flies with the ink of his feathers.

June 25, 1996, El Paso]

“El pelícano” [“The Pelican”] is both self-referential as well as self-sacrificing since it uses a pelican’s ability to open its own stomach to provide sustenance for its chicks as a vehicle for reflections on poetry:

En esto se parece—tal vez—a la poesía
que se saca la verdad del mismo pecho,
y es su propio cuerpo la substancia
que sostiene y que nutre a sus criaturas;
y el ritmo de sus frases no es distinto
al ritmo de su corazón acompasado;
y el aliento del verso es comparable
al íntimo ying-yang de su respiración.[10]

[In this way it is similar—perhaps—to poetry
that pulls the truth from its own chest,
and in its own body the substance
that sustains and nurtures its children;
and the rhythm of its phrases is no different
from the rhythm of its rhythmic heart;
and the sound of its verses is similar
to the intimate yin-yang of its breath]

The dualities and physical symmetries of birds also appear throughout the verbal collage of *Cuenta de los guías*:

Con o sin estoy contigo.
Vengo cantando a medio cielo.
Vivo en la inmensidad correspondida.
Como ya se dijo: todas las almas son gemelas.
La puesta de sol y el alba son las dos alas de este vuelo.[11]

[With or without, I am with you.
I come singing through the midheaven.
I am living in the reciprocated immensity.
As we have already said: all souls are twinned.
Sunset and sunrise are the two wings of this flight.]

Clearly, Blanco, like Leonardo da Vinci, sees a kindred spirit in a bird's well-balanced form. In the poem that gives name to his trilogy of poetics, he uses avian imagery to write his *ars poetica*:

"El canto y el vuelo"

Un poema es como un pájaro:
su ala derecha es la imagen,
su ala izquierda es la música,
y su cuerpo es el lenguaje.

Un pájaro de palabras
para el alma y para el cuerpo:

su ala derecha, el espacio,
y su ala izquierda, el tiempo.

Pero la poesía no es la imagen
ni la música ni el lenguaje;
la poesía es el canto . . .
La Poesía es el vuelo.[12]

["Song and Flight"
A poem is a like a bird:
its right wing, an image,
its left wing is music,
and its body is language.

A bird of words
for the soul and for the body:
its right wing, space,
and its left wing, time.

But poetry is not images
or music or language;
poetry is song . . .
while Poetry is flight.]

The text begins with a simile, an especially complex part of speech in light of the many literal and figurative definitions of poetry we have been considering. In the first stanza, a poem is described as a bird of language whose wings are its images and music. In the next strophe, the bird's wings are further defined as space and time and we are told that the bird sings to both the soul and the body. In the final stanza, the poem takes off, as it were, by means of a negative statement of the kind favored by this poet. Poetry is not a collection of images or sounds or words . . . it is the way in which language *transforms* those forms into an intuitive experience, a process in action, *el canto.* Also implicit in this process is "La Poesía," the art, the poem's gift to the reader that plumbs the mysterious depths of creation.

Birds are apt metaphors for Blanco's poetics since they embody the perfect correspondence of all their parts that Pessoa saw as the essence of poetry.[13] A bird, and this is intentionally any species of bird, is composed of flesh and feathers that alone can neither sing nor fly. The wings of the bird are muscular opposites that must work together in order for it to take to the air.[14] "El canto," the mystery of poetry, like us, is born from silence and ends in silence. "La Poesía" is flight, the unknowable life force Blanco tries to uncover through poems. Flight is movement but it too is silent: "el silencio en la poesía es lo que posibilita el uso mágico de las palabras y su poder de encantar. Y es que entre cantar y encantar no media más que una sílaba. Y entre esta sílaba y el silencio del vuelo nada más un paso. Hay que darlo" [silence in poetry is what makes possible the magical use of words and their power to enchant. In Spanish there is only one syllable between *cantar* and *encantar.* And between that one syllable and the silence of flight there is nothing more than one step. We must take it].[15]

Mirroring the form of his trilogies, "El canto y el vuelo" has three stanzas and twelve verses. It mixes poetry and prose through a deceptively simple sounding tone and lexicon that both reveal and conceal a systematic poetics. The poem's flight is energized by the unknown, the solitary work we do as readers when we explore the textures of a poem in our minds and attempt to separate the "dancer from the dance." In the end, the principles and paradoxes of flight, like those of the wave/particle duality, are what transform both poem and reader.

Notes

INTRODUCTION

1. Alberto Blanco, *La hora y la neblina*, 2nd ed. (Mexico: Fondo de Cultura Económica, 2018), 169–170.

2. Unless otherwise noted, translations are by the author or, in this case, the author and Maria Bartlett.

3. Gérard Genette defines paratexts as the binding, publishing house, prologue and epilogue, epigraphs, dedications, cover art, and other glosses or marginalia that accompany a text—see chapter 2. It is important to note that Blanco's *hacedores* [inspirational creators] appear listed in his appendices rather than beside his poems.

4. "A Carafe That Is a Blind Glass," in Gertrude Stein, *Tender Buttons* (Auckland: Floating Press, 2009).

5. The poem "Altaforte" is about the literary group El Zaguán in Alberto Blanco, *A la luz de siempre*, 1st ed. (Mexico: Fondo de Cultura Económica, 2018), 166.

6. http://www.albertoblanco.com.mx.

7. Miguel Angel Flores notes that in *Tras el rayo*, "Alberto Blanco ha pasado de la nitidez a la oscuridad." Miguel Angel Flores, "*Tras el rayo* de Alberto Blanco," *Vuelta*, May 1986, 43.

8. Elena Poniatowska writes, "Blanco fue el primer mexicano publicado por la editorial City Lights" [Blanco was the first Mexican writer published by City Lights]. Poniatowska, "El poeta Alberto Blanco," *La Jornada*, November 18, 2007.

9. Blanco has held visiting positions at San Diego State University, the University of San Diego, the University of Texas at El Paso, and Middlebury College.

10. Evodio Escalante, "Potencia y hermetismo de Alberto Blanco," *Proceso* 370 (July 18, 1983): 51–52.

11. Sandro Cohen, "Poesía mexicana, 1975–1990: De la abundancia raquítica a la escasez saludable o ¿dónde están los poetas?," in *Perfiles: Ensayos sobre literatura mexicana reciente*, edited by Federico Patán (Boulder, CO: Society of Spanish & Spanish American Studies, 1992), 11.

12. Jesús Gómez Morán, "*La hora y la neblina:* Alberto Blanco," http://www.fondodeculturaeconomica.com/subdirectorios_site/Lecturas/LEC-013607R.pdf.

13. Julio Ortega, "Fronteras de la poesía," *La Jornada Semanal* 217 (1993): 12.

14. The diversity and expansive breadth of Blanco's work defies easy labels and surely contributes to the lack of critical work dedicated to his poetry since the 1990s. In terms of articles, Sandro Cohen's essay in *Perfiles* gives a thorough background to Mexican poetry from 1975 to 1990, particularly the impact of the 1982 debt crisis and its influences on young poets. Escalante's articles are also important for Blanco's earliest work. Other key essays include those by Adolfo Castañón, Julio Ortega, Jorge Fernández Granados, and Jacobo Sefamí as well as the poet's interviews with Kimberly Eherenman.

In terms of theses, Teresa Chapa's dissertation chapter and article on Blanco situate the poems of *Amanecer de los sentidos* [*Dawn of the Senses*] in a generational context. Juan Armando Rojas's master's thesis considers science and the idea of fractals in *Tras el rayo* [*Afterglow*], and his dissertation studies Coral Bracho and Blanco's work until 2000. Irma Chávez Robinson's dissertation (Irma Chávez Robinson, "El budismo Zen, el Yin Yang y la ecología en la Obra de Alberto Blanco" [PhD diss., Florida State University, 2004]) explores the influence of Asian literatures, cultures, and mysticisms in Blanco's work until 2000. Carlos Zamora's "Crítica contextural: *El corazón del instante* de Alberto Blanco: Ensayo de un Método" (PhD diss., University of Kentucky, 2014) centers on the forms and structures of *El corazón del instante.* Michael Klam's master's thesis also studies science, particularly quantum physics, in *La raíz cuadrada del cielo* [*The Square Root of Heaven*] and includes translations of those poems.

15. Juan Armando Rojas, "Pos/modernidad y (multi)forma en la obra de dos poetas mexicanos contemporáneos: Alberto Blanco y Coral Bracho" (PhD diss., University of Arizona, 2002), 88.

16. Samuel Gordon, "Breves atisbos metodológicos para el examen de la poesía mexicana al fin de siglo," *Graffylia* 2, no. 3 (2004): 129–142.

17. See Cohen, "Poesía mexicana," 1–25, for more on publishing.

18. Gordon, "Breves atisbos," 137.

19. Gordon, "Breves atisbos," 139.

20. See the introduction for more on "la generación del desengaño" and chapter 4, dedicated to Blanco of Teresa Chapa, "Contemporary Mexican Poetry: 'La generación' del desengaño" (PhD diss., University of Kansas, 1992).

21. David Harvey, *The Condition of Postmodernity: An Enquiry into the Origins of Cultural Change* (Hoboken, NJ: Blackwell, 1990), 38.

22. Harvey, *Condition of Postmodernity*, 38.

23. See Caren Kaplan's critique of Baudrillard's *America* and *Cool Memories* in *Questions of Travel: Postmodern Discourses of Displacement* (Durham, NC: Duke University Press, 1996), 73.

24. Luis Cortés Bargalló, "Alberto Blanco: las diez mil facetas del instante," *La Jornada Semanal*, September 20, 1998, http://www.jornada.unam.mx/1998/09/20/sem-blanco.html.

25. Gómez Morán, "*La hora y la neblina.*"

26. Evodio Escalante, *Poetas de una generación (1950—1959)* (Mexico: Premiá, 1988), 9.

27. Blanco, *La hora y la neblina*, 218–219.

28. *A la luz de siempre*, 335.

29. *A la luz de siempre*, 205, vv. 1–5.

30. Gordon, "Breves atisbos," 139.

31. Evodio Escalante, "De la vanguardia militante a la vanguardia blanca: Los nuevos trastornadores del lenguaje en la poesía mexicana de nuestros días: David Huerta, Gerardo Deniz, Alberto Blanco y Coral Bracho," in Patán, *Perfiles*, 30.

32. Escalante, "De la vanguardia militante," 31.

33. Alberto Blanco, *El corazón del instante*, 2nd ed. (Mexico: Fondo de Cultura Económica, 2018), 210, vv. 13–14.

34. Jorge Fernández Granados, "Alberto Blanco, escalas," *La Gaceta del Fondo de Cultura Económica*, no. 329 (May 1998): 54.

35. *El corazón del instante* contains four sections with 149 poems about painters and one section with 9 poems about rock musicians. *La hora y la neblina* has 17 texts about musicians, 40 about film directors, 106 about poets, and 60 about visual artists. Finally, *A la luz de siempre* has 114 poems about rock, jazz, and classical performers and composers, 158 about poets, and 44 about visual artists.

36. *A la luz de siempre*, 9–10.

37. See Bruce Dean Willis's *Aesthetics of Equilibrium: The Vanguard Poetics of Vicente Huidobro and Mário de Andrade* (West Lafayette, IN: Purdue University Press, 2006) for more on the desire of equilibrium between poetry and poetics in Mário de Andrade and Vicente Huidobro, two important influences on Blanco.

38. W. J. T. Mitchell, *Picture Theory: Essays on Verbal and Visual Representation* (Chicago: University of Chicago Press, 1994), 152.

39. Mitchell, *Picture Theory*, 156, 163–164.

40. Zamora, "Crítica contextural," 53.

41. Zamora, "Crítica contextural," 173.

42. Email from Alberto Blanco, September 13, 2019.

43. There does not appear to be a discernable pattern among the placement of chapters between the cycles, though, since chapters 9, 10, and 1 of the three books of the trilogy, respectively, bear the titles of the volumes themselves. In drafts, the poet meticulously counts and records the number of verses in each imaginable section of his work.

44. Zamora, "Crítica contextural," 74.

45. Zamora, "Crítica contextural," 15.

46. Email from Alberto Blanco, February 14, 2017.

47. Chávez Robinson, "El budismo Zen," 227.

48. Alberto Blanco, *La poesía y el presente* (Mexico: AUIEO y CONACULTA, 2013), 27.

49. Alberto Blanco, *El canto y el vuelo* (Mexico: Editorial anDante, 2016), 181–182.

50. Octavio Paz, *El arco y la lira* (Mexico: Fondo de Cultura Económica, 1998), 24.

51. The field of relational dialectics identifies "monologic," "dualistic," and "duologic" outcomes in these situations.

52. Linda Hutcheon, *Irony's Edge: The Theory and Politics of Irony* (London: Routledge, 1994), 58.

53. *Encyclopedia Britannica*.

54. These three definitions are from the *Oxford English Dictionary*.

55. Chávez Robinson, "El budismo Zen," 227.

56. *El canto y el vuelo*, 184.

57. Ernst Hans Gombrich, "The Visual Image: Its Place in Communication," in *The Essential Gombrich: Selected Writings on Art and Culture*, ed. Richard Woodfield (New York: Phaidon, 1996), 56.

58. Alberto Blanco, "El llamado del ángel de fuego: Reflexiones en torno a la poesía de Juan Martínez," in *Juan Martínez: Toda la poesía reunida*, ed. José Vicente Anaya, Luis Cortés Bargalló, Alberto Blanco, and Heriberto Yépez, 18, https://www.yumpu.com/es/document/read/14898696/juan-martinez-toda-la-poesia-reunida-circulo-de-poesia.

59. *El canto y el vuelo*, 20.

60. Alberto Blanco, *El llamado y el don* (Mexico: AUIEO, 2011), 27–28.

61. *El llamado y el don*, 36.

62. *El llamado y el don*, 36.

63. Although we consider the entire poetic trilogy throughout this study, we will focus more on *La hora y la neblina* and *A la luz de siempre* than *El corazón del instante*. In the interests of space, some books are analyzed more deeply than others.

CHAPTER 1 — IMAGE

1. "Los collages de Alberto Blanco," interview with Alberto Blanco, *Zeta Tijuana*, February 23, 2015, http://zetatijuana.com/2015/02/los-collages-de-alberto-blanco/.

2. Alberto Blanco, "El *collage*: una historia sin nombre," in *Collage* (Mexico: CONACULTA, 2015), 4.

3. "El *collage*," 2.

4. Peter Stockwell, *Cognitive Poetics: An Introduction* (London: Routledge, 2002), 14.

5. Alberto Blanco, *Las voces del ver: Ensayos sobre artes visuales* (Mexico: Consejo Nacional para la Cultura y las Artes, 1997), 90.

6. *Las voces del ver*, 87.

7. *Las voces del ver*, 90.

8. *Las voces del ver*, 93.

9. In the next chapter we will contrast collage with montage influenced by Russian director Sergei Eisenstein and Walter Benjamin's later work.

10. *A la luz de siempre*, 302, vv. 1–4.

11. *A la luz de siempre*, 303, vv. 29–32.

12. *A la luz de siempre*, 293, vv. 1.

13. *A la luz de siempre*, 293, vv. 11–14.

14. *A la luz de siempre*, 293, vv. 20–23.

15. *A la luz de siempre*, 324.

16. *A la luz de siempre* 325, vv. 37–40.

17. *A la luz de siempre*, 303–304.

18. *The New Princeton Encyclopedia of Poetry and Poetics* (Princeton, NJ: Princeton University Press, 1993), 702.

19. *Princeton Encyclopedia*, 877.

20. *A la luz de siempre*, 15, vv. 1–4.

21. Alberto Blanco, "La poesía y la imagen," *Bric à Brac* 3 (2020): 17.

22. *El corazón del instante*, 376.

23. Blanco, *La hora y la neblina*, 55.

24. *La hora y la neblina*, 56–57.

25. *La hora y la neblina*, 59.

26. Alberto Blanco, "El pozo de Lebab (o de la traducción como un trabajo interior)," *INTI—Revista de Literatura Hispánica* 42 (Autumn 1995): 271.

27. "El pozo de Lebab," 271.

28. Kim Knowles, Anna Katharina Schaffner, Ulrich Weger, and Andrew Michael Roberts, "Reading Space in Visual Poetry: New Cognitive Perspectives," *Writing Technologies* 4 (2012): 77.

29. Knowles et al., "Reading Space in Visual Poetry," 77.

30. See the article "Reading Space" by Kim Knowles et al. for a cognitive study of how the verbal and visual compete for dominance through empirical research that employs eye tracking and data analysis.

31. See the books by E. H. Gombrich, James A. W. Heffernan, and W. J. T. Mitchell for more on our evolving understanding of the interplay of visual and verbal signs.

32. See Alberto Blanco, *Poesía visual* (Mexico: Ediciones del Lirio y Conaculta, 2015), 12.

33. *A la luz de siempre*, 227, vv. 1–2.

34. For the reader interested solely in Blanco's visual poems, *Poesía visual* has selections from all three volumes of the trilogy.

35. *Poesía visual*, 11.

36. *Poesía visual*, 11.

37. *A la luz de siempre*, 205.

38. *A la luz de siempre*, 144.

39. Paz, *El arco y la lira*, 278.

40. *El corazón del instante*, 491.

41. Translating *Antes De Nacer* into English in a way that even approaches the form and sense of the original is a task beyond this translator.

42. Kimberly A. Eherenman, "Las formas del instante: Entrevista con Alberto Blanco," *Fractal: Revista Trimestral* 7, no. 25 (April–June 2002): 151–176.

43. In "De la vanguardia militante" Evodio Escalante critiques the poem's "oscuridad excesiva" [excessive obscurity] (40) and Sandro Cohen observes that the visual aspect dominates all others in the text (12). For Teresa Chapa, *A.D.N.* "produce la sensación de un poema continuo que, como el proceso vital mismo, se altera y sin embargo es interminable, y la circularidad del poema afirma el incesante movimiento de toda materia orgánica" [produces the sensation of a continuous poem that, like life itself, changes and yet is interminable, and the circularity of the poem affirms the incessant movement of all organic matter] (Chapa, "La poesía de Alberto Blanco: innovación y renovación en *Amanecer de los sentidos*," *Revista de literatura mexicana contemporánea* 2, no. 4 (October 1996): 29.

44. Marjorie Perloff, "Refiguring the Poundian Ideogram: From 'Blanco/*Branco*' to the *Galáxias*," in *Transpoetic Exchange: Haroldo de Campos, Octavio Paz, and Other Multiversal Dialogues*, ed. Marília Librandi, Jamille Pinheiro Dias, and Tom Winterbottom (Lewisburg, PA: Bucknell University Press, 2019), 35–37.

45. João Adolfo Hansen, "'Blanco' and *Transblanco*: Modern and Post-Utopic," in Librandi, Dias, and Winterbottom, *Transpoetic Exchange*, 25.

46. *A la luz de siempre*, 242.

47. *La hora y la neblina*, 454, vv. 1–5.

48. Haroldo de Campos, *Novas* (Evanston, IL: Northwestern University Press, 2007), 217.

49. De Campos, *Novas*, 218.

50. De Campos, *Novas*, 236.

51. *La hora y la neblina*, 432, vv. 1–3.

52. *La hora y la neblina*, 365.

53. De Campos, *Novas*, 218.

54. "La poesía y la imagen," 18.

55. *La hora y la neblina*, 536, vv. 59–70.

56. "La poesía y la imagen," 18.

57. *La hora y la neblina*, 462.

58. *La hora y la neblina*, 463.

59. *La hora y la neblina*, 467–468.

60. See Zamora ("Crítica contextural," 88) and Rojas's "Pos/modernidad," chap. 4, on *Cromos*.

61. *El corazón del instante*, 9.

62. James A. W. Heffernan, *Cultivating Picturacy: Visual Art and Verbal Interventions* (Waco, TX: Baylor University Press, 2006), 18.

63. *A la luz de siempre*, 272.

64. Mitchell, *Picture Theory*, 152.

65. Mitchell, *Picture Theory*, 156.

66. Mitchell, *Picture Theory*, 163–164.

67. *El corazón del instante*, 38, vv. 1–4.

68. *El corazón del instante*, 38, vv. 5–8.

69. *El corazón del instante*, 38, vv. 9–12.

70. Mitchell, *Picture Theory*, 164.

71. Wendy Steiner, *The Colors of Rhetoric* (Chicago: University of Chicago Press, 1982), 41.

72. *El corazón del instante*, 126, vv. 35–36.

73. *A la luz de siempre*, 47.

74. Mitchell, *Picture Theory*, 152.

75. *A la luz de siempre*, 260.

76. Linda Hutcheon, *A Theory of Parody: The Teachings of Twentieth-Century Art Forms* (London: Routledge, 1991), 32.

77. Hutcheon, *Theory of Parody*, 4.

78. *La hora y la neblina*, 419.

79. *La hora y la neblina*, 440, vv. 19–30.

80. *La hora y la neblina*, 436.

81. Mitchell, *Picture Theory*, 156, 163.

82. Carlos Zamora, "Poesía en oración: *Cuenta de los guías*," *Revista de Literatura Mexicana Contemporánea* 1, no. 2 (1995): 26.

83. *A la luz de siempre*, 335.

84. For the sake of clarity, we sometimes refer to the poems of *Cuenta de los guías* by number even though they are unnumbered in the text.

85. *A la luz de siempre*, 346.

86. Stockwell, *Cognitive Poetics*, 14.

87. Stockwell, *Cognitive Poetics*, 19.

88. Jacobo Sefamí, "Alberto Blanco. *Cuenta de los guías*," *Revista de Literatura Mexicana Contemporánea* 1, no. 2 (January–April 1996): 142.

89. *A la luz de siempre*, 405.

90. *El llamado y el don*, 83.

91. *El llamado y el don*, 83.

92. *El llamado y el don*, 48–49.

93. *El llamado y el don*, 48.

94. *A la luz de siempre*, 335.

95. *A la luz de siempre*, 377.

96. *A la luz de siempre*, 429.

97. *A la luz de siempre*, 393.

98. *A la luz de siempre*, 407.

99. *A la luz de siempre*, 336.

100. *A la luz de siempre*, 363, 381, 375.

101. *A la luz de siempre*, 372, 377, 380.

CHAPTER 2 — SPACE

1. *La hora y la neblina*, 9–10.

2. Gérard Genette, *Paratexts: Thresholds of Interpretation*, trans. Jane E. Lewin (Cambridge: Cambridge University Press, 1997), 135.

3. Genette, *Paratexts*, 136.

4. Genette, *Paratexts*, 158.

5. Definition of exergue from the Oxford English Dictionary.

6. Genette, *Paratexts*, 158.

7. Eric Prieto, *Listening In: Music, Mind, and the Modernist Narrative* (Lincoln: University of Nebraska Press, 2002), 41.

8. Gombrich, "Visual Image," 59.

9. Genette, *Paratexts*, 149.

10. Genette, *Paratexts*, 144.

11. "Dedicatoria," which borrows from the dedication to Robert Graves's *The White Goddess*, is currently uncollected.

12. Genette, *Paratexts*, 134–135.

13. Genette, *Paratexts*, 156.

14. *El corazón del instante*, 151–152.

15. Lucio Fontana, publication excerpt from *MoMA Highlights: 375 Works from the Museum of Modern Art, New York* (New York: Museum of Modern Art, 2019), https://www.moma.org/collection/works/37812.

16. *A la luz de siempre*, 51, vv. 1–4.

17. *A la luz de siempre*, 54, vv. 1–4.

18. *A la luz de siempre*, 51.

19. *A la luz de siempre*, 54.

20. *La hora y la neblina*, 148.

21. *La hora y la neblina*, 71.

22. *OED*.

23. *OED*.

24. Eric Prieto, *Literature, Geography, and the Postmodern Poetics of Place* (London: Palgrave Macmillan, 2013), 93.

25. *La hora y la neblina*, 72–73.

26. *La hora y la neblina*, 75.

27. *La hora y la neblina*, 87.

28. Hutcheon, *Theory of Parody*, 2.

29. In *The Practice of Everyday Life* de Certeau explains that "a place is the order (of whatever kind) in accord with which elements are distributed in relationships of coexistence"; a place is thus "an instantaneous configuration of positions. It implies an indication of stability" (117). Space, on the other hand, "is composed of intersections of mobile elements . . . space is a practiced place" (117). *The Practice of Everyday Life*, trans. Steven Rendall (Berkeley: University of California Press, 1984).

30. *La hora y la neblina*, 380.

31. *La hora y la neblina*, 390.

32. *La hora y la neblina*, 405–406.

33. Paul Fussell, *Abroad: British Literary Writing Traveling between the Wars* (Oxford: Oxford University Press, 1980), 43.

34. *La hora y la neblina*, 400.

35. De Certeau, *Practice of Everyday Life*, 117.

36. Mary Louise Pratt, *Imperial Eyes: Travel Writing and Transculturation* (London: Routledge, 1992), 6.

37. *La hora y la neblina*, 384, vv. 4–5.

38. *La hora y la neblina*, 385, vv. 15–18.

39. *La hora y la neblina*, 385, v. 23.

40. *La hora y la neblina*, 408.

41. *La hora y la neblina*, 385.

42. Gombrich, "Visual Image," 51.

43. Carlos Zamora sees in "Mapas" the allusions to the Tao Te Ching and Stephen Spender ("Crítica contextural," 144) and notes that the poems are a journey with instructions (what I call "directives") that examine space and time.

44. Gombrich, "Visual Image," 52.

45. *El corazón del instante*, 462, vv. 1–8.

46. Almost all of my translations of "Mapas" are taken from Michael Klam, "Quantum Theory in the Poetry of Alberto Blanco and Translation of *La raíz cuadrada del cielo*" (MA thesis, San Diego State University, 1998).

47. *El corazón del instante*, 462, vv. 10–12.

48. *El corazón del instante*, 462, v. 3; 458; 461, v. 3.

49. *El corazón del instante*, 460, v1.

50. *El corazón del instante*, 461, v. 2.

51. *El corazón del instante*, 461, v. 4.

52. Jean Baudrillard, "Simulacra and Simulations," in *Selected Writings*, ed. Mark Poster (Redwood City, CA: Stanford University Press, 1988), 166.

53. *El corazón del instante*, 461, v. 1.

54. *El corazón del instante*, 462, vv. 4–7.

55. Gombrich, "Visual Image," 52.

56. *El corazón del instante*, 462, vv. 9–10.

57. *El corazón del instante*, 463, v. 8.

58. *El corazón del instante*, 463, v. 10.

59. *El corazón del instante*, 463, vv. 2–3.

60. *El corazón del instante*, 464, vv. 5–6.

61. *El corazón del instante*, 460, vv. 9–11.

62. *El corazón del instante*, 464, vv. 5.

63. Baudrillard, "Simulacra and Simulations," 166.

64. "A mathematically conceived curve such that any small part of it, enlarged, has the same statistical character as the original" (*OED*).

65. See chapter 5 for more on *aura*.

66. Walter Benjamin, *The Arcades Project*, trans. Howard Eiland and Kevin McLaughlin (Cambridge, MA: Belknap, 2002), xi.

67. Benjamin, *The Arcades Project*, xi.

68. Cathy L. Jrade, "Modernist Poetry," in *The Cambridge History of Latin American Literature*, vol. 2, ed. Roberto González Echevarría and Enrique Pupo-Walker (Cambridge: Cambridge University Press, 1996), 16.

69. *A la luz de siempre*, 259–260.

70. During the process of revising *La hora y la neblina* for the 2018 Feria Internacional del Libro in Guadalajara, the poet removed a section of poems about animals titled "Medio cielo" that was in the first edition. In homage and reference to that collection, he named his book of film poems "Medio Cine" to play off the name "Medio Cielo."

71. *La hora y la neblina*, 154.

72. Translations from *Medio Cine/Cinemap* were done by Maria Bartlett and the author.

73. *La hora y la neblina*, 158.

74. Sergei Eisenstein, "A Dialectic Approach to Film Form," in *Film Form: Essays in Film Theory*, ed. and trans. Jay Leyda (New York: Harcourt, Brace, Jovanovich, 1977), 4.

75. *La hora y la neblina*, 155.

76. Stockwell, *Cognitive Poetics*, 14.

77. *La hora y la neblina*, 172.

78. See Eugen Gomringer's notion of a constellation: "The constellation is the simplest possible kind of configuration in poetry which has for its basic unit the word, it encloses a group of words as if it were drawing stars together to form a cluster. The constellation is an arrangement, and at the same time a play-area of fixed dimensions. The constellation is ordered by the poet. He determines the play-area, the field or force and suggests its possibilities. The reader, the new reader, grasps the idea of play, and joins in. In the constellation something is brought into the world. It is a reality in itself and not a poem about something or other. The constellation is an invitation." Gomringer, "From Line to Constellation," in *Concrete Poetry: A World View*, ed. Mary Ellen Solt (Bloomington: Indiana University Press, 1968), 67.

79. Gilles Deleuze, *Cinema 1: The Movement-Image*, trans. Hugh Tomlinson and Barbara Habberjam (Minneapolis: University of Minnesota Press, 1986), 29.

80. Eisenstein, "Dialectic Approach," 15.

81. Eisenstein, "Dialectic Approach," 15.

82. *La hora y la neblina*, 158.

83. Zamora, "Poesía en oración," 27.

84. Ulalume González de León, "*El largo camino hacia Ti* de Alberto Blanco," *Vuelta*, July 1980, 39–40.

85. Ortega, "Fronteras de la poesía," 12–13.

86. Marc Augé notes that journeys are "punctuated by the mention of the places resulting from them or authorizing them." Augé, *Non-Places: An Introduction to Supermodernity*, trans. John Howe (New York: Verso, 2008), 66. To use Eric Prieto's term, Blanco "de-territorializes" places as well as texts by providing individual and particular responses to them (*Literature, Geography*, 99).

87. For de Certeau, spaces take "into consideration vectors of direction, velocities, and time variables . . . intersections of mobile elements" (*Practice of Everyday Life*, 117).

88. De Certeau contrasts totalizing maps with fragmented itineraries, tours, and travel stories (*Practice of Everyday Life*, 119–120).

89. *A la luz de siempre*, 341.

90. *A la luz de siempre*, 347.

91. *El corazón del instante*, 463, vv. 1–2.

92. *A la luz de siempre*, 343.

93. Paz, *El arco y la lira*, 284.

94. Fussell, *Abroad*, 16.

95. Alberto Blanco, *Dawn of the Senses*, ed. Juvenal Acosta, prologue by José Emilio Pacheco (San Francisco: City Lights, 2001), xiv.

96. De Certeau, *Practice of Everyday Life*, 121; Augé, *Non-Places*, xiv.

97. *A la luz de siempre*, 438.

98. *A la luz de siempre*, 438.

99. In *Postmodern Geographies*, Edward Soja argues that "the organization, and meaning of space is a product of social translations, transformations, and experience" (80). He coined the term "spatiality" to capture the dynamic nature of space. Soja, *Postmodern Geographies: The Reassertion of Space in Critical Social Theory* (New York: Verso, 1989).

100. Fussell, *Abroad*, 36.

101. *A la luz de siempre*, 438. Carlos Zamora notes that "*Cuenta de los* guías esboza un tiempo mexicano horizontal, mientras el tiempo norteamericano es vertical" ("Poesía en oración," 28).

102. Augé, *Non-Places*, ix.

103. *A la luz de siempre*, 451–452.

104. *A la luz de siempre*, 402.

105. *A la luz de siempre*, 454.

106. *A la luz de siempre*, 410.

107. *A la luz de siempre*, 420.

108. *A la luz de siempre*, 421.

109. *A la luz de siempre*, 434.

110. *A la luz de siempre*, 448.

111. Zamora, "Poesía en oración," 26–27.

112. *A la luz de siempre*, 435.

113. Interview with the author in México DF, March 6, 2018.

114. *A la luz de siempre*, 395.

115. Augé, *Non-Places*, xiv.

116. *A la luz de siempre*, 443.

CHAPTER 3 — SOUND

1. *La poesía y el presente*, 90.

2. *La poesía y el presente*, 90.

3. See Eric Zolov's excellent *Refried Elvis: The Rise of The Mexican Counterculture* (Berkeley: University of California Press, 1999) for much more on the music, culture, fashion and sexual mores of "La Onda."

4. Interview with the author, in México DF, March 6, 2018.

5. See Zolov's chapter "La Onda in the Wake of Tlatelolco." The cultural history of the years leading up to and following Tlatelolco have been extensively documented and analyzed by Zolov, Carlos Monsiváis, and many others.

6. *A la luz de siempre*, 315.

7. Prieto, *Listening In*, 25.

8. The reader should also consult the essays "La música," and "La forma" from *La poesía y el presente* and "El silencio" from *El canto y el vuelo*.

9. *El canto y el vuelo*, 183.
10. *A la luz de siempre*, 315.
11. Following Ezra Pound's definition.
12. The introduction to Eric Prieto's *Listening In* provides an informative background and review of approaches to and essays in musico-literary studies. The bulk of his book focuses more on narrative than on poetry.
13. Benoît Santini, "Entrevista al poeta chileno Raúl Zurita: 'Todo poema, toda poesía, son pequeñas islas en el océano infinito del silencio,'" http://www.cervantesvirtual.com/obra-visor/entrevista-al-poeta-chileno-raul-zurita—todo-poema-todo-poesia-son-pequenas-islas-en-el-oceano-infinito-del-silencio/html/06bf3c4b-126a-461a-970e-2be9a969420c_2.html.
14. Prieto, *Listening In*, 7.
15. Prieto, *Listening In*, 7.
16. Prieto, *Listening In*, 1.
17. George Steiner, *Language and Silence: Essays on Language, Literature and the Inhuman* (New York: Athenaeum, 1967), 41. There is a large body of critical literature dedicated to studying the interarts, from T. S. Eliot to Paz, Jean Hagstrum, and Blanco himself.
18. *A la luz de siempre*, 316.
19. *El canto y el vuelo*, 95.
20. *El canto y el vuelo*, 184, emphasis added.
21. *La hora y la neblina*, 444.
22. *La hora y la neblina*, 444.
23. *La hora y la neblina*, 482.
24. Marjorie Perloff, *The Poetics of Indeterminacy: Rimbaud to Cage* (Princeton, NJ: Princeton University Press, 1981), 338.
25. *La hora y la neblina*, 459–460.
26. Listening is prominent in many of Blanco's metapoems. For just one example, see the first section of "Virgo" that, like "Cuando la tierra sueña," references the music of the spheres (*A la luz de siempre*, 29).
27. *La hora y la neblina*, 487.
28. Leonard Shlain, *Art and Physics: Parallel Visions in Space, Time, and Light* (New York: Perennial, 2001), 285.
29. *El corazón del instante*, 60–61.
30. *A la luz de siempre*, 142, vv. 1–3.
31. *A la luz de siempre*, 142, vv. 21–24.
32. *A la luz de siempre*, 154.
33. *La poesía y el presente*, 103.
34. *La hora y la neblina*, 80.
35. *La hora y la neblina*, 76.
36. Prieto, *Listening In*, 10.
37. Steiner, *Language and Silence*, 43.
38. *A la luz de siempre*, 323.
39. *A la luz de siempre*, 461.
40. De Campos, *Novas*, 283.
41. *A la luz de siempre*, 125.
42. *Antimetabole* is "word repetition in reverse," such as, "What is Hecuba to him, or he to Hecuba?" (*Hamlet*). *Princeton Encyclopedia*, 79.

43. *A la luz de siempre*, 509–510.
44. *La hora y la neblina*, 480.
45. *La hora y la neblina*, 459.
46. *La hora y la neblina*, 181.
47. Translation by Friis and Bartlett.
48. *La hora y la neblina*, 459.
49. Genette, *Paratexts*, 135.
50. *A la luz de siempre*, 483, 1–4.
51. *A la luz de siempre*, 483, 5–12.
52. *La hora y la neblina*, 103–104.
53. *A la luz de siempre*, 158, 4–8.
54. See Prieto, *Listening In*, 28–42.
55. Prieto, *Listening In*, 34–36.
56. Prieto, *Listening In*, 41.
57. *A la luz de siempre*, 159.
58. Genette, *Paratexts*, 158.
59. Genette, *Paratexts*, 158.
60. Adolfo Castañón, "De la vocación (Gaos-Paz-Blanco)," *Revista Crítica* 157 (January–February 2014): 22.
61. *La hora y la neblina*, 99–100.
62. *El corazón del instante*, 214.
63. *El corazón del instante*, 213.
64. *El corazón del instante*, 213.
65. *El corazón del instante*, 226.
66. *El corazón del instante*, 228.
67. Adolfo Castañón and Marcela Pimentel write, "Su verso es anchuroso, pausado, como el de algunos poetas usamericanos de la nombrada Generación Beat. Su idioma: cifrado e innumerable, llano y directo, ávido de una transparencia tanto más lúcida cuanto menos visible en el horizonte" [His verses are spacious, deliberate, like that of a few American poets from the so-called Beat Generation. His idiom: coded and innumerable, flat and direct, striving for a transparency that becomes more lucid the less visible it is on the horizon]. See Adolfo Castañón and Marcela Pimentel, "Alberto Blanco, *El corazón del instante*," *Reforma*, September 7, 1998, 4.
68. *La hora y la neblina*, 316, 14.
69. Blanco's connections to the Beats, particularly Gary Snyder, is the subject of a forthcoming article by the author.
70. *La hora y la neblina*, 310–311.
71. Paz, *El arco y la lira*, 282.
72. *El canto y el vuelo*, 167.
73. *El canto y el vuelo*, 169–170.
74. See chapter 1 for more on *A.D.N.* and Kimberly A. Eherenman, "Las formas del instante: Entrevista con Alberto Blanco," *Fractal: Revista Trimestral* 7, no. 25 (April–June 2002): 151–176.
75. See Javier Galindo Ulloa, "El silencio en la poesía de Alberto Blanco," *Tema y Variaciones de Literatura*, UAM–Azcapotzalco, no. 48 (2017): 85–98, for a reading of silence in *Antes De Nacer*.
76. *A la luz de siempre*, 83.

77. *A la luz de siempre*, 507.

78. See Perloff's *Poetics of Indeterminacy*, 306, for more on Cage and Gertrude Stein.

79. Johanna Drucker, "Not Sound," in *The Sound of Poetry / The Poetry of Sound*, ed. Marjorie Perloff and Craig Dworkin (Chicago: University of Chicago Press, 2009), 237.

80. Orlando White, "Functional White: Crafting Space and Silence," *Poetry Foundation*, 2015, https://www.poetryfoundation.org/harriet/2015/11/functional-white-crafting-space-silence.

81. *A la luz de siempre*, 320.

82. White, "Functional White."

83. *A la luz de siempre*, 555–556.

84. John Cage, *Silence: Lectures and Writings of John Cage* (Middletown, CT: Wesleyan University Press, 1960), 275.

85. Kay Larson, *Where the Heart Beats: John Cage, Zen Buddhism, and the Inner Life of Artists* (London: Penguin, 2012), 270.

86. Larson, *Where the Heart Beats*, 271.

87. *La hora y la neblina*, 153.

88. *La hora y la neblina*, 182.

89. See Steiner, *Language and Silence*, 49–54, for more on politics and silence.

90. *El corazón del instante*, 210.

91. Galindo Ulloa, "El silencio en la poesía de Alberto Blanco," 90.

CHAPTER 4 — TEXTURE

1. *El llamado y el don*, 188.

2. De Certeau, *Practice of Everyday Life*, 169.

3. De Certeau, *Practice of Everyday Life*, 169.

4. Stockwell, *Cognitive Poetics*, 168.

5. Stockwell, *Cognitive Poetics*, 151.

6. Stockwell, *Cognitive Poetics*, 167.

7. Stockwell, *Cognitive Poetics*, 107.

8. *La hora y la neblina*, 318, vv. 1–3.

9. *La hora y la neblina*, 318.

10. *El llamado y el don*, 155.

11. *El llamado y el don*, 155.

12. *A la luz de siempre*, 264.

13. *La hora y la neblina*, 83.

14. *El llamado y el don*, 40.

15. *El llamado y el don*, 43.

16. *A la luz de siempre*, 561–562, vv. 1–7.

17. *A la luz de siempre*, 245.

18. *El llamado y el don*, 39.

19. *El llamado y el don*, 156.

20. Julio Ortega, ed., *Antología de la poesía hispanoamericana actual*, 8th ed. (Madrid: Siglo Veintiuno Editores, 2001), 9.

21. *La hora y la neblina*, 244.

22. Hutcheon, *Theory of Parody*, 101.

23. *La hora y la neblina*, 303–304.

24. *A la luz de siempre*, 183, vv. 1–7.

25. *A la luz de siempre*, 184, vv. 8–22.
26. *El llamado y el don*, 156.
27. *A la luz de siempre*, 184, vv. 23–30.
28. *A la luz de siempre*, 184–185, vv. 31–42.
29. *A la luz de siempre*, 185, vv. 43–51.
30. Stockwell, *Cognitive Poetics*, 42.
31. Mitchell, *Picture Theory*, 163.
32. *La hora y la neblina*, 58.
33. *La hora y la neblina*, 373, vv. 1–7.
34. *La hora y la neblina*, 373, vv. 18–24.
35. *La hora y la neblina*, 373–374, vv. 25–34.
36. *La hora y la neblina*, 374, 35–40.
37. Marco Antonio Campos, "*El largo camino hacia Ti*, de Alberto Blanco," *Proceso* (1981), http://www.proceso.com.mx/130411/el-largo-camino-hacia-ti-de-alberto-blanco.
38. I borrow the term "directive" from the Robert Frost poem of the same name that asks its reader to visit "a house that is no more a house" by letting "a guide direct you / Who only has at heart your getting lost."
39. *A la luz de siempre*, 342.
40. *A la luz de siempre*, 359.
41. *A la luz de siempre*, 383.
42. *A la luz de siempre*, 423. Previous versions of the poem included this third verse: "Y sé que estamos juntos como la misma nota tocada por dos instrumentos."
43. *La hora y la neblina*, 61.
44. *La hora y la neblina*, 515.
45. *El corazón del instante*, 209, vv. 25–33.
46. *El canto y el vuelo*, 31. See also "El tiempo del poema."
47. Bruce Dean Willis sees five functions of description and prescription in poetics: "(1) differentiation, (2) exemplification, (3) establishment, (4) idealization, and (5) prophecy." See Willis, *Aesthetics of Equilibrium*, 179.
48. *El llamado y el don*, 104.
49. *El llamado y el don*, 25.
50. *A la luz de siempre*, 402.
51. *A la luz de siempre*, 402.
52. *El llamado y el don*, 104.
53. *El llamado y el don*, 142.
54. *El llamado y el don*, 184.
55. *La hora y la neblina*, 39.
56. *La hora y la neblina*, 414.
57. *El llamado y el don*, 142.
58. *A la luz de siempre*, 257.
59. *A la luz de siempre*, 553.
60. *A la luz de siempre*, 324.
61. *A la luz de siempre*, 451.
62. On "the middle way," see S. B. Dasgupta, *An Introduction to Tantric Buddhism* (Calcutta: University of Calcutta, 1958), 14.
63. *A la luz de siempre*, 553.
64. *La hora y la neblina*, 473.

65. *El llamado y el don*, 142.
66. Shlain, *Art and Physics*, 410.
67. Shlain, *Art and Physics*, 400.
68. Shlain, *Art and Physics*, 397. See also Reuven Tsur, "Deixis and Abstractions: Adventures in Space and Time," in *Cognitive Poetics in Practice*, ed. Joanna Gavins and Gerard Steen (London: Routledge, 2003), 53–46.
69. Shlain, *Art and Physics*, 388–389.
70. *El canto y el vuelo*, 35.
71. Consult the essays "La polaridad" and "El cerebro" from *La poesía y el presente* for an in-depth discussion of brain lateralization and research into the concepts of the reptilian, mammal, and human brain, as well as Pound's Melopea, Fanopea, and Logopea and Freud's ego, superego, and id.
72. *El canto y el vuelo*, 35.
73. *La poesía y el presente*, 27.
74. *La hora y la neblina*, 444.
75. *El corazón del instante*, 79–80.
76. Translation by Robert L. Jones in *Dawn of the Senses*.
77. See the introduction to Willis's *Poetics of Equilibrium* for more on this tendency in Vicente Huidobro and Mário de Andrade.
78. *El corazón del instante*, 95.
79. See James A. W. Heffernan's "Reading Pictures," *PMLA* 134, no. 1 (2019): 32.
80. "La poesía y la imagen," 16.
81. See chapter 5 of Chávez Robinson, "El budismo Zen."
82. *La hora y la neblina*, 312–313.
83. *La hora y la neblina*, 494.
84. *A la luz de siempre*, 329.
85. *El llamado y el don*, 89. "Revelado," "El cardo y la estrella polar," and "Conspiración" are three more of the countless examples of such two-in-one imagery in Blanco.
86. *El corazón del instante*, 416.
87. *A la luz de siempre*, 439.
88. Poem 260 is cited in chapter 3.
89. *El llamado y el don*, 156–157.
90. Alan Kennedy, *The Psychology of Reading* (London: Routledge, 1984), 45.
91. "La forma es un medio, y el fin es trascender la forma. En este sentido el poema es sólo un vehículo, una herramienta, una hipótesis de trabajo. La meta es la transformación del artista y quien disfruta de los frutos del trabajo artístico: el creador lo mismo que el recreador" [Form is a means, and the end is to transform form. In this way, a poem us only a vehicle, a tool, a working hypothesis. The goal is the transformation of the artist and the person who enjoys the fruits of the artistic labor: the creator and the recreator] (*El llamado y el don* 36).
92. Shlain, *Art and Physics*, 387.
93. Shlain, *Art and Physics*, 386–387.
94. Stockwell, *Cognitive Poetics*, 22.
95. *La hora y la neblina*, 51, vv. 8–16.
96. *A la luz de siempre*, 79.
97. *A la luz de siempre*, 179.

CHAPTER 5 — METAPHYSICS

1. See Henry Folse, *The Philosophy of Niels Bohr: The Framework of Complementarity* (New York: North-Holland, 1985).

2. See the essay "El conocimiento," from *El llamado y el don*, 126. Blanco here is quoting Fritjof Capra's influential best-seller *The Tao of Physics: An Exploration of the Parallels between Modern Physics and Eastern Mysticism* (Boulder, CO: Shambhala, 2000).

3. *El canto y el vuelo*, 23.

4. See Jerome Rothenberg, "Alberto Blanco: 'Three Theories' from 'The Square Root of Heaven,'" *Jacket* 2, December 31, 2012, https://jacket2.org/commentary/alberto-blanco-three-theories-square-root-heaven.

5. See Jennifer Rathbun's *Afterglow* for an English translation of the challenging *Tras el rayo*.

6. Richard Evans Schultes and Albert Hofmann, *Plantas de los dioses: orígenes del uso de los alucinógenos*, trans. Alberto Blanco (Mexico: Fondo de Cultura Económica, 1982); John D. Barrow and Joseph Silk, *El lado izquierdo de la creación*, trans. Alberto Blanco (Mexico: Fondo de Cultura Económica, 1991). See Rojas, "Pos/modernidad," 160.

7. *La hora y la neblina*, 518.

8. *El corazón del instante*, 486–487.

9. Translation by John Oliver Simon in *Dawn of the Senses*.

10. Carlos Fuentes, *Viendo visiones* (Mexico: Fondo de Cultura Económica / Fundación Bancomer, 2003), 24.

11. *A la luz de siempre*, 414.

12. *A la luz de siempre*, 264–265.

13. *El corazón del instante*, 351–352.

14. *El corazón del instante*, 457–458, vv. 7–14.

15. *El canto y el vuelo*, 24.

16. *El corazón del instante*, 519–520, vv. 30–41.

17. This is the version from the first edition of *El corazón del instante* (43–44). The same poem, essentially, is reworked into "Poema visto al hervir y servir el café" (*El corazón del instante*, 2nd ed., 481–482).

18. *El corazón del instante*, 455, vv. 18–25.

19. *El corazón del instante*, 453–454.

20. *La hora y la neblina*, 429, vv. 11–12.

21. *El corazón del instante*, 456.

22. *El corazón del instante*, 455–456, vv. 11–16.

23. *El corazón del instante*, 452, vv. 14–19.

24. *El corazón del instante*, 458–459, vv. 20–22.

25. *El corazón del instante*, 459, vv. 1–8.

26. Shlain, *Art and Physics*, 136.

27. Nicholas Kompridis, *Critique and Disclosure: Critical Theory between Past and Future* (Cambridge, MA: MIT Press, 2006), 3–4.

28. Candelas Gala, *Poetry, Physics, and Painting in Twentieth Century Spain* (London: Palgrave Macmillan, 2011), 205.

29. *La hora y la neblina*, 515, 4–7.

30. *La hora y la neblina*, 516, vv. 11–18.

31. *La hora y la neblina*, 526, 1–12.

32. *La hora y la neblina*, 518, vv. 14–17, emphasis added.

33. *La hora y la neblina*, 523, vv. 24–28.

34. *La hora y la neblina*, 524, vv. 29–32.

35. Gordon, "Breves atisbos" and Escalante, "De la vanguardia militante."

36. *El canto y el vuelo*, 26.

37. In his doctoral dissertation, Juan Armando Rojas shows how Blanco's work exhibits what Edward O. Wilson calls "consilience," or the idea of a united field of knowledge that includes both science and the humanities.

38. Capra, *Tao of Physics*, 185–186.

39. See chapter 4.

40. In *Physics for Poets*, Robert H. March writes that relativity and quantum mechanics "were conceived, at least in part, in much the same spirit—that of critical evaluation of the process by which a physicist actually observes the world in which he lives." March, *Physics for Poets* (New York: McGraw-Hill, 1970), 3.

41. *La hora y la neblina*, 380–381.

42. *El corazón del instante*, 79.

43. *A la luz de siempre*, 406.

44. *La hora y la neblina*, 466, vv. 11–27.

45. *La hora y la neblina*, 538, vv. 27–64.

46. Capra, *Tao of Physics*, 130.

47. Tara Macisaac, "3 Concepts Ancient Chinese Science Grasped, Modern Physics Is Just Learning." *Epoch Times*, June 11, 2014, https://www.theepochtimes.com/3-concepts-ancient-chinese-science-grasped-modern-physics-just-learning_726622.html.

48. *La hora y la neblina*, 529.

49. *La hora y la neblina*, 525, vv. 10–13.

50. *La hora y la neblina*, 526, v. 32.

51. *El canto y el vuelo*, 36.

52. *El corazón del instante*, 447.

53. *El corazón del instante*, 448, vv. 1–5.

54. *El corazón del instante*, 448, vv. 12–15.

55. *El corazón del instante*, 448, 5–15.

56. Klam, "Quantum Theory," 19–21.

57. *El corazón del instante*, 450, 19–20.

58. *El corazón del instante*, 450, 19–24.

59. *La hora y la neblina*, 429, 1–3.

60. Blanco's lines are often related to games and rules. See "Nubes" (*El corazón del instante*, 106) based on the I Ching, "La vida en el diamante" ["Life in the Diamond"] (*El corazón del instante*, 322), about baseball, or "Damas chinas" ["Checkers"] (*El corazón del instante*, 57).

61. Chapa, "La poesía de Alberto Blanco," 29.

62. Alberto Blanco, *Amanecer de los sentidos*, Antología personal precedida por una presentación de Alvaro Mutis, Lecturas Mexicanas, Tercera Serie, Num. 79 (Mexico: CONACULTA, México, 1993), 26.

63. Walter Benjamin, "The Work of Art in the Age of Mechanical Reproduction," in *Illuminations*, trans. Harry Zohn (New York: Schocken Books, 1969), 223.

64. Benjamin, "Work of Art," 221.

65. Benjamin, "Work of Art," 223.

66. Martin Jay, *The Dialectical Imagination: A History of the Frankfurt School and the Institute of Social Research 1923–1950* (Berkeley: University of California Press, 1996), 210.

67. Alberto Blanco, "La pobreza de la poesía," *Graffylia* 2, no. 3 (2004): 8.

68. *El corazón del instante*, 97, vv. 6–7.

69. Jean-François Lyotard, *Lessons on the Analytic of the Sublime* (Stanford, CA: Stanford University Press, 1994), 25.

70. *El corazón del instante*, 104, v. 21.

71. *El corazón del instante*, 130, 34.

72. *El corazón del instante*, 173.

73. *El corazón del instante*, 95.

74. *El corazón del instante*, 95.

75. *La hora y la neblina*, 402, v. 13.

76. *El llamado y el don*, 67.

77. *La hora y la neblina*, 403, vv. 30–37.

78. Translations from "Mi laberinto" are by Joan Lindgren in *A Cage of Transparent Words*, ed. Paul B. Roth, trans. Judith Infante, Joan Lindgren, Elise Miller, Edgardo Moctezuma, Gustavo V. Segade, Anthony Seidman, John Oliver Simon, and Kathleen Snodgrass (New York: Bitter Oleander Press, 2007), 130–135.

79. John James, "The Mystery of the Great Labyrinth, Chartres Cathedral," *Studies in Comparative Religion* 11, no. 2 (Spring 1977), http://www.studiesincomparativereligion.com/Public/articles/browse_g.aspx?ID=311.

80. *La hora y la neblina*, 403, v. 50.

81. *La hora y la neblina*, 403, vv. 50–64.

82. *El llamado y el don*, 40.

83. Blanco is relying on books by Karl Shapiro and W. H. Auden here in the essay "Poesía y poesía" from *El llamado y el don*.

84. *El llamado y el don*, 40.

85. "Los dioses" in *La hora y la neblina*, 277, vv. 6–7.

86. *La hora y la neblina*, 58–59.

87. See also "Cosmogonía" ["Cosmogony"] (*La hora y la neblina*, 86–87) or "Dios" ["God"] (*La hora y la neblina*, 82).

88. *La hora y la neblina*, 176.

89. *La hora y la neblina*, 378.

90. *La hora y la neblina*, 437.

91. *A la luz de siempre*, 220, vv. 8–10.

92. *A la luz de siempre*, 503.

93. *El canto y el vuelo*, 80.

94. *A la luz de siempre*, 270.

95. For Juan Armando Rojas it is "quizá el poema que mejor describe el canto poético inaugural de Blanco y en el cual se observan algunas de sus características básicas: el uso de la tradición poética para buscar la ruptura posterior, la musicalidad de la canción, la oración, los rasgos bíblico-históricos que funcionan a manera casi profética y la estructuración por medio de estrofas de dos o tres versos tan común en mucha de su obra" [perhaps the poem that best describes Blanco's inaugural poetic song and in which some of his fundamental characteristics are seen: the use of the poetic tradition to break with the past, the musicality of song, prayer, the biblical-historical touches that work in

an almost prophetic way and the structure by means of stanzas of two or three lines than is so common in much of his work]. "Pos/modernidad," 89.

96. *El corazón del instante*, 45, vv. 11–12.

97. *La hora y la neblina*, 166.

98. Translated by the author and Maria Bartlett.

99. Zamora, "Crítica contextural," 15.

100. *A la luz de siempre*, 464–466.

101. Interestingly, the important last three words of *A la luz de siempre* are the same three that appear in poem 5 of "Diez apuntamientos" ["Ten Points"]: "En este sentido, el quinto punto es evidente: cada vez que digo 'sólo Dios sabe,' quiero decir: 'yo no lo sé . . . pero tal vez en lo que no sé esté la solución o la respuesta. En todo caso me queda claro que la respuesta no la sé yo, ni la puedo saber yo, ni tiene que ver con yo'" [In this sense, the fifth point is evident: each time I say 'only God knows,' I mean to say: 'I don't know' . . . but maybe the answer or solution lies in what I don't know. In any case, it's clear to me that I don't know the answer, I can't know the answer, and that it has nothing to do with me] (*La hora y la neblina*, 165).

102. Three other poems that follow this archetype, "Duermevela" [*Halfsleep*], "Círculo del horizonte" ["Circle of the Horizon"], and *Cuenta de los guías*, also offer ideas on how to persist toward and after a moment of epiphany. The speaker of the chaotic swirl of *Cuenta de los guías* implores us: "Siempre hay que tener presente la posibilidad de un naufragio, pero entre todas las opciones, escogemos la mejor: creer" [We always have to keep the possibility of a disaster in mind but, among all these options, we choose the best one: to believe] (*A la luz de siempre*, 346).

CODA

1. *A la luz de siempre*, 405.

2. *El corazón del instante*, 430.

3. Definitions from the *Diccionario de la Real Academia Española.*

4. *El llamado y el don*, 49.

5. "Encore" is currently uncollected.

6. *El llamado y el don*, 36.

7. Ortega, "Fronteras de la poesía," 12.

8. *La hora y la neblina*, 490.

9. *La hora y la neblina*, 179.

10. *El corazón del instante*, 253, vv. 9–16.

11. *A la luz de siempre*, 460.

12. *A la luz de siempre*, 558.

13. *El canto y el vuelo*, 39.

14. See the essay "La polaridad" from *La poesía y el presente* and "El canto y el vuelo" from the book of the same name.

15. *El canto y el vuelo*, 187.

Bibliography

Acosta, Juvenal, ed. *Light from a Nearby Window: Contemporary Mexican Poetry*. San Francisco: City Lights, 2001.

Augé, Marc. *Non-Places: An Introduction to Supermodernity*. Translated by John Howe. New York: Verso, 2008.

Bachelard, Gaston. *The Poetics of Space*. Translated by Maria Jolas. Boston: Beacon, 1994.

Barrow, John D., and Joseph Silk. *El lado izquierdo de la creación*. Translated by Alberto Blanco. Mexico: Fondo de Cultura Económica, 1991.

———. *The Left Hand of Creation*. New York: Oxford University Press, 1994.

Baudrillard, Jean. *Cool Memories IV: 1995–2000*. Translated by Chris Turner. New York: Verso, 2003.

———. "Simulacra and Simulations." In *Selected Writings*, edited by Mark Poster, 166–184. Redwood City, CA: Stanford University Press, 1988.

Benjamin, Walter. *The Arcades Project*. Translated by Howard Eiland and Kevin McLaughlin. Cambridge, MA: Belknap, 2002.

———. "The Work of Art in the Age of Mechanical Reproduction." In *Illuminations*, translated by Harry Zohn, 217–251. New York: Schocken Books, 1969.

Blanco, Alberto. *Afterglow / Tras el rayo*. Translated by Jennifer Rathbun. New York: Bitter Oleander Press, 2011.

———. *A la luz de siempre*. 1st ed. Mexico: Fondo de Cultura Económica, 2018.

———. *Amanecer de los sentidos*. Antología personal precedida por una presentación de Álvaro Mutis. Lecturas Mexicanas, Tercera Serie, Num. 79. Mexico: CONACULTA, México, 1993.

———. *A Cage of Transparent Words*. Edited by Paul B. Roth. Translated by Judith Infante, Joan Lindgren, Elise Miller, Edgardo Moctezuma, Gustavo V. Segade, Anthony Seidman, John Oliver Simon, and Kathleen Snodgrass. New York: Bitter Oleander Press, 2007.

———. *Cinemap*. Translated by Ronald J. Friis and Maria Bartlett. Forthcoming.

———. *Cuenta de los guías*. Mexico: Ediciones Era, 1992.

———. *Dawn of the Senses*. Edited by Juvenal Acosta. Prologue by José Emilio Pacheco. San Francisco: City Lights, 2001.

———. *De vierkantswortel van de hemel*. Translated by Bart Vonck. Holland: Wagner & Van Santen, 2002.
———. *El canto y el vuelo*. Mexico: Editorial anDante, 2016.
———. "El *collage*: una historia sin nombre." In *Collage*, 4–9. Mexico: CONACULTA, 2015.
———. *El corazón del instante*. 1st ed. Mexico: Fondo de Cultura Económica, 1998.
———. *El corazón del instante*. 2nd ed. Mexico: Fondo de Cultura Económica, 2018.
———. *El eco de las formas, 64 ensayos sobre artes visuales*. México: Teoría y Práctica del Arte, Consejo Nacional para la Cultura y las Artes, México, 2012.
———. *El largo camino hacia Ti*. Mexico: Cuadernos de Poesía, UNAM, 1980.
———. "El llamado del ángel de fuego: Reflexiones en torno a la poesía de Juan Martínez." In *Juan Martínez: Toda la poesía reunida*, edited by José Vicente Anaya, Luis Cortés Bargalló, Alberto Blanco, and Heriberto Yépez. https://www.yumpu.com/es/document/read/14898696/juan-martinez-toda-la-poesia-reunida-circulo-de-poesia.
———. *El llamado y el don*. Mexico: AUIEO, 2011.
———. *El origen y la huella / The Origin and the Trace*. Images by Alberto Dilger. Translated by Julian Palley. San Diego: Circa, 2000.
———. "El poeta mexicano Alberto Blanco con Jordi Batallé en El invitado de RFI." May 19, 2017. https://www.youtube.com/watch?v=GQkEk5gm9Lk&t=41s.
———. "El pozo de Lebab (o de la traducción como un trabajo interior)." *INTI—Revista de Literatura Hispánica* 42 (Autumn 1995): 265–275.
———. *Feu nouveau / Fuego Nuevo*. Translated by Stéphane Chaumet. Paris: L'Oreille du Loup, Paris, 2009.
———. http://www.albertoblanco.com.mx/. Personal website.
———. *La hora y la neblina*. 2nd ed. Mexico: Fondo de Cultura Económica, 2018.
———. "La pobreza de la poesía." *Graffylia* 2, no. 3 (2004): 7–11.
———. "La poesía y la imagen." *Bric à Brac* 3 (2020): 9–18. http://www.arteoutsider.com/revista/numero-3-2020/.
———. *La poesía y el presente*. Mexico: AUIEO y CONACULTA, 2013.
———. *Las voces del ver: Ensayos sobre artes visuales*. México: Consejo Nacional para la Cultura y las Artes, 1997.
———. "Los collages de Alberto Blanco." Interview with Alberto Blanco. *Zeta Tijuana*, February 23, 2015. http://zetatijuana.com/2015/02/los-collages-de-alberto-blanco/.
———. *Medio cine*. Mexico: Ediciones Sin Nombre y Conaculta, 2014.
———. *Poesía visual*. Mexico: Ediciones del Lirio y Conaculta, 2015.
Cage, John. *Silence: Lectures and Writings of John Cage*. Middletown, CT: Wesleyan University Press, 1960.
Campos, Marco Antonio. "*El largo camino hacia Ti*, de Alberto Blanco." *Proceso*, 1981. http://www.proceso.com.mx/130411/el-largo-camino-hacia-ti-de-alberto-blanco.
Cansigno, Yvonne. *La voz de la poesía en México*. Mexico: Universidad Autónoma de Tlaxcala, 1993.
Capra, Fritjof. *The Tao of Physics: An Exploration of the Parallels between Modern Physics and Eastern Mysticism*. Boulder, CO: Shambhala, 2000.
Castañón, Adolfo. "*El canto y el vuelo*, de Alberto Blanco." *Literal: Latin American Voices: Voces latinoamericanas*, June 27, 2017. http://literalmagazine.com/el-canto-y-el-vuelo-de-alberto-blanco/.
———. "De la vocación (Gaos-Paz-Blanco)." *Revista Crítica* 157 (January–February 2014): 20–24.

Castañón, Adolfo, and Marcela Pimentel. "Alberto Blanco, *El corazón del instante*." *Reforma*, September 7, 1998.

Chapa, Teresa. "Contemporary Mexican Poetry: 'La generación' del desengaño." PhD dissertation, University of Kansas, 1992.

———. "La poesía de Alberto Blanco: innovación y renovación en *Amanecer de los sentidos*." *Revista de literatura mexicana contemporánea* 2, no. 4 (October 1996): 27–32.

Chávez Robinson, Irma. "El budismo Zen, el Yin Yang y la ecología en la obra de Alberto Blanco." PhD dissertation, Florida State University, 2004.

———. "Ciencia y poesía en Tras el rayo de Alberto Blanco." MA thesis, University of Texas at El Paso, 1996.

Chouciño Fernández, Ana. *Radicalizar e interrogar los límites: Poesía mexicana 1970—1990*. Mexico: UNAM, 1997.

Cohen, Sandro. "Poesía mexicana, 1975–1990: De la abundancia raquítica a la escasez saludable o ¿dónde están los poetas?" In *Perfiles: Ensayos sobre literatura mexicana reciente*, edited by Federico Patán, 1–25. Boulder, CO: Society of Spanish & Spanish American Studies, 1992.

Cortés Bargalló, Luis. "Alberto Blanco: las diez mil facetas del instante." *La Jornada Semanal*, September 20, 1998. https://www.jornada.com.mx/1998/09/20/sem-blanco.html.

Dasgupta, S. B. *An Introduction to Tantric Buddhism*. Calcutta: University of Calcutta, 1958.

de Campos, Haroldo. *Novas*. Evanston, IL: Northwestern University Press, 2007.

de Certeau, Michel. *The Practice of Everyday Life*. Translated by Steven Rendall. Berkeley: University of California Press, 1984.

Deleuze, Gilles. *Cinema 1: The Movement-Image*. Translated by Hugh Tomlinson and Barbara Habberjam. Minneapolis: University of Minnesota Press, 1986.

Domínguez Michael, Christopher, ed. *Diccionario crítico de la literatura mexicana (1955–2011)*. Mexico: Fondo de Cultura Económica, 2012.

Drucker, Johanna. "Not Sound." In *The Sound of Poetry / The Poetry of Sound*, edited by Marjorie Perloff and Craig Dworkin, 237–248. Chicago: University of Chicago Press, 2009.

Eherenman, Kimberly A. "El corazón instantáneo de un poeta: una entrevista con Alberto Blanco." Interview by Kimberly A. Eherenman. *Bitter Oleander* 8, no. 2 (2002): 45–75.

———. "Las formas del instante: Entrevista con Alberto Blanco." *Fractal: Revista Trimestral* 7, no. 25 (April–June 2002): 151–176. https://www.wasafiri.org/article/interview-with-mexican-poet-alberto-blanco/.

Eisenstein, Sergei. "A Dialectic Approach to Film Form." In *Film Form: Essays in Film Theory*, edited and translated by Jay Leyda, 1–16. New York: Harcourt, Brace, Jovanovich, 1977.

Escalante, Evodio. "De la vanguardia militante a la vanguardia blanca: Los nuevos trastornadores del lenguaje en la poesía mexicana de nuestros días: David Huerta, Gerardo Deniz, Alberto Blanco y Coral Bracho." In *Perfiles: Ensayos sobre literatura mexicana reciente*, edited by Federico Patán, 27–45. Boulder, CO: Society of Spanish & Spanish American Studies, 1992.

———. *Poetas de una generación (1950–1959)*. Mexico: Premiá, 1988.

———. "Potencia y hermetismo de Alberto Blanco." *Proceso* 370 (July 18, 1983): 51–52.

Evans Schultes, Richard, and Albert Hofmann. *Plantas de los dioses: orígenes del uso de los alucinógenos*. Translated by Alberto Blanco. Mexico: Fondo de Cultura Económica, 1982.

———. *Plants of the Gods: Origins of Hallucinogenic Use*. New York: McGraw-Hill, 1979.

Fernández Granados, Jorge. "Alberto Blanco, escalas." *La Gaceta del Fondo de Cultura Económica*, no. 329 (May 1998): 54–55.

Flores, Miguel Angel. "*Tras el rayo* de Alberto Blanco." *Vuelta*, May 1986, 43.

Folse, Henry. *The Philosophy of Niels Bohr: The Framework of Complementarity*. New York: North-Holland, 1985.

Fontana, Lucio. Publication excerpt from *MoMA Highlights: 375 Works from the Museum of Modern Art, New York*. New York: Museum of Modern Art, 2019. https://www.moma.org/collection/works/37812.

Fraistat, Neil, ed. *Poems in Their Place: The Intertextuality and Order of Poetic Collections*. Chapel Hill: University of North Carolina Press, 1986.

Friis, Ronald J. "Las trinidades poéticas de Alberto Blanco." *Este País: Tendencias y Opiniones*, Sección Cultura, 143 (August 2017): 10–11. https://anterior.estepais.com/articulo.php?id=1140&t=las-trinidades-poeticas-de-alberto-blanco.

———. "*Una telaraña de constelaciones*: Alberto Blanco's Poetry of Communion." *Revista de Literatura Mexicana Contemporánea* 56 (2013): 45–60.

Fuentes, Carlos. *Viendo visiones*. Mexico: Fondo de Cultura Económica / Fundación Bancomer, 2003.

Fussell, Paul. *Abroad: British Literary Writing Traveling between the Wars*. Oxford: Oxford University Press, 1980.

Gala, Candelas. *Poetry, Physics, and Painting in Twentieth Century Spain*. London: Palgrave Macmillan, 2011.

Galindo Ulloa, Javier. "El silencio en la poesía de Alberto Blanco." *Tema y Variaciones de Literatura*, UAM–Azcapotzalco, no. 48 (2017): 85–98.

Gavins, Joanna, and Gerard Steen, eds. *Cognitive Poetics in Practice*. London: Routledge, 2003.

Genette, Gérard. *Paratexts: Thresholds of Interpretation*. Translated by Jane E. Lewin. Cambridge: Cambridge University Press, 1997.

Gombrich, Ernst Hans. *The Image and the Eye: Further Studies in the Psychology of Pictorial Representation*. New York: Phaidon, 1994.

———. "The Visual Image: Its Place in Communication." In *The Essential Gombrich: Selected Writings on Art and Culture*, edited by Richard Woodfield, 41–64. New York: Phaidon, 1996.

Gómez Morán, Jesús. "*La hora y la neblina:* Alberto Blanco." http://www.fondodeculturaeconomica.com/subdirectorios_site/Lecturas/LEC-013607R.pdf.

Gomringer, Eugen. "From Line to Constellation." In *Concrete Poetry: A World View*, edited by Mary Ellen Solt, 67. Bloomington: Indiana University Press, 1968.

González de León, Ulalume. "*El largo camino hacia Ti* de Alberto Blanco." *Vuelta*, July 1980, 39–40.

Gordon, Samuel. "Breves atisbos metodológicos para el examen de la poesía mexicana al fin de siglo." *Graffylia* 2, no. 3 (2004): 129–142.

———. *Poéticas mexicanas del siglo XX*. https://www.scribd.com/document/314641430/Poesia-mexicana-de-medio-siglo.

Hansen, João Adolfo. "'Blanco' and *Transblanco*: Modern and Post-Utopic." In *Transpoetic Exchange: Haroldo de Campos, Octavio Paz, and Other Multiversal Dialogues*, edited by Marília Librandi, Jamille Pinheiro Dias, and Tom Winterbottom, 17–29. Lewisburg, PA: Bucknell University Press, 2019.

Harvey, David. *The Condition of Postmodernity: An Enquiry into the Origins of Cultural Change*. Hoboken, NJ: Blackwell, 1990.

Heffernan, James A. W. *Cultivating Picturacy: Visual Art and Verbal Interventions*. Waco, TX: Baylor University Press, 2006.

———. "Reading Pictures." *PMLA* 134, no. 1 (2019): 18–34.

Huerta, David. "Alberto Blanco: Poesía e imágenes enlazadas en 'Cromos' y 'Un año de bondad.'" Interview. *Proceso* 582 (December 28, 1987).

Hutcheon, Linda. *Irony's Edge: The Theory and Politics of Irony*. London: Routledge, 1994.

———. *A Theory of Parody: The Teachings of Twentieth-Century Art Forms*. London: Routledge, 1991.

James, John. "The Mystery of the Great Labyrinth, Chartres Cathedral." *Studies in Comparative Religion* 11, no. 2 (Spring 1977). http://www.studiesincomparativereligion.com/Public/articles/The_Mystery_of_the_Great_Labyrinth-Chartres_Cathedral-by_John_James.aspx.

Jay, Martin. *The Dialectical Imagination: A History of the Frankfurt School and the Institute of Social Research 1923–1950*. Berkeley: University of California Press, 1996.

Jrade, Cathy L. "Modernist Poetry." In *The Cambridge History of Latin American Literature*, vol. 2, edited by Roberto González Echevarría and Enrique Pupo-Walker, 7–68. Cambridge: Cambridge University Press, 1996.

Kaplan, Caren. *Questions of Travel: Postmodern Discourses of Displacement*. Durham, NC: Duke University Press, 1996.

Kennedy, Alan. *The Psychology of Reading*. London: Routledge, 1984.

Klam, Michael Keith. "Quantum Theory in the Poetry of Alberto Blanco and Translation of *La raíz cuadrada del cielo*." MA thesis, San Diego State University, 1998.

Knowles, Kim, Anna Katharina Schaffner, Ulrich Weger, and Andrew Michael Roberts. "Reading Space in Visual Poetry: New Cognitive Perspectives." *Writing Technologies* 4 (2012): 75–106. https://www.ntu.ac.uk/__data/assets/pdf_file/0029/827093/Kim-Knowles,-Anna-Schaffner,-Ulrich-Weger,-Andrew-Roberts-Reading-Space-in-Visual-Poetry-New-Cognitive-Perspective.pdf.

Kompridis, Nicholas. *Critique and Disclosure: Critical Theory between Past and Future*. Cambridge, MA: MIT Press, 2006.

Labrada Aguilera, Agustín. "Entrevista con Alberto Blanco." *Graffylia* 2, no. 3 (2004): 11–16.

La Charité, Virginia. *The Dynamics of Space: Mallarmé's* Un coup de dés jamais n'abolira le hasard. Philadelphia: French Forum, 1987.

Larson, Kay. *Where the Heart Beats: John Cage, Zen Buddhism, and the Inner Life of Artists*. London: Penguin, 2012.

López Colomé, Pura. "Tiro al Blanco [*Antes De Nacer*]." *Casa del Tiempo* 36 (December 1983–January 1984): 69–71.

Lyotard, Jean-François. *Lessons on the Analytic of the Sublime*. Stanford, CA: Stanford University Press, 1994.

Macisaac, Tara. "3 Concepts Ancient Chinese Science Grasped, Modern Physics Is Just Learning." *Epoch Times*, June 11, 2014. https://www.theepochtimes.com/3-concepts-ancient-chinese-science-grasped-modern-physics-just-learning_726622.html.

March, Robert H. *Physics for Poets*. New York: McGraw-Hill, 1970.

Martínez, Juan. "Toda la poesía reunida." Investigación, recopilación, prólogo y notas de José Vicente Anaya; ensayos de Luis Cortés Bargalló, Alberto Blanco y Heriberto

Yépez. https://www.yumpu.com/es/document/read/14898696/juan-martinez-toda-la-poesia-reunida-circulo-de-poesia.

Mitchell, W. J. T. *Iconology: Image, Text, Ideology*. Chicago: University of Chicago Press, 1987.

———. *Picture Theory: Essays on Verbal and Visual Representation*. Chicago: University of Chicago Press, 1994.

———. *What Do Pictures Want: The Lives and Loves of Images*. Chicago: University of Chicago Press, 2004.

Mitchell, W. J. T., and Louis A. Renza (reply). "Going Too Far with the Sister Arts." In *Space, Time, Image, Sign: Essays on Literature and the Visual Arts*, edited by James A. W. Heffernan, 11–15. New York: Peter Lang, 1987.

Mondragón, Sergio, ed. *República de poetas*. México: Martin Casillas Editores, 1985.

Monsiváis, Carlos. "Confluencia de poesía: Alberto Blanco." *RUAL*, 1981.

———. *La poesía mexicana del siglo XX*. México: Empresas editoriales, 1966.

The New Princeton Encyclopedia of Poetry and Poetics. Princeton, NJ: Princeton University Press, 1993.

Ortega, Julio, ed. *Antología de la poesía hispanoamericana actual*. 8th ed. Madrid: Siglo Veintiuno Editores, 2001.

———. "Fronteras de la poesía." *La Jornada Semanal* 217 (1993): 12–13.

Paz, Octavio. *El arco y la lira*. Mexico: Fondo de Cultura Económica, 1998.

———. *Los hijos del limo*. Barcelona: Seix Barral, 1993.

Perloff, Marjorie. *The Poetics of Indeterminacy: Rimbaud to Cage*. Princeton, NJ: Princeton University Press, 1981.

———. "Refiguring the Poundian Ideogram: From 'Blanco/*Branco*' to the *Galáxias*." In *Transpoetic Exchange: Haroldo de Campos, Octavio Paz, and Other Multiversal Dialogues*, edited by Marília Librandi, Jamille Pinheiro Dias, and Tom Winterbottom, 30–40. Lewisburg, PA: Bucknell University Press, 2019.

Poniatowska, Elena. "El poeta Alberto Blanco." *La Jornada*, November 18, 2007. https://www.jornada.com.mx/2007/11/18/index.php?section=opinion&article=a04a1cul.

Pratt, Mary Louise. *Imperial Eyes: Travel Writing and Transculturation*. London: Routledge, 1992.

Prieto, Eric. *Listening In: Music, Mind, and the Modernist Narrative*. Lincoln: University of Nebraska Press, 2002.

———. *Literature, Geography, and the Postmodern Poetics of Place*. London: Palgrave Macmillan, 2013.

Ramírez, Josué. "*La hora y la neblina*, de Alberto Blanco." *Letras Libres*, September 2006. http://www.letraslibres.com/mexico/libros/la-hora-y-la-neblina-alberto-blanco.

Ricoeur, Paul. *The Rule of Metaphor: Multi-disciplinary Studies of the Creation of Meaning in Language*. Translated by Robert Czerny with Kathleen McLaughlin and John Costello. Toronto: University of Toronto Press, 1993.

Rojas, Juan Armando. "La 'eternidad' en *El corazón del instante*, de Alberto Blanco." *Solar* (Chihuahua, México) 9, no. 33 (July 2001).

———. "The Lightning Bolt: The Allegory of Creation in Alberto Blanco's *Afterglow*." In *De Aztlán al Río de la Plata: Studies in Honor of Charles M. Tatum*, edited by Sergio Martínez, 307–324. Newark, DE: Juan de la Cuesta Hispanic Monographs, 2016.

———. "Pos/modernidad y (multi)forma en la obra de dos poetas mexicanos contemporáneos: Alberto Blanco y Coral Bracho." PhD dissertation, University of Arizona, 2002.

Rothenberg, Jerome. "Alberto Blanco: 'Three Theories' from 'The Square Root of Heaven.'" *Jacket* 2, December 31, 2012. https://jacket2.org/commentary/alberto-blanco-three-theories-square-root-heaven.

Santí, Enrico Mario. "On the Presence of Absence: Octavio Paz's 'Blanco.'" In *Transpoetic Exchange: Haroldo de Campos, Octavio Paz, and Other Multiversal Dialogues*, edited by Marília Librandi, Jamille Pinheiro Dias, and Tom Winterbottom, 9–16. Lewisburg, PA: Bucknell University Press, 2019.

Santini, Benoît. "Entrevista al poeta chileno Raúl Zurita: 'Todo poema, toda poesía, son pequeñas islas en el océano infinito del silencio.'" http://www.cervantesvirtual.com/obra-visor/entrevista-al-poeta-chileno-raul-zurita—todo-poema-todo-poesia-son-pequenas-islas-en-el-oceano-infinito-del-silencio/html/06bf3c4b-126a-461a-970e-2be9a969420c_2.html.

Sefamí, Jacobo. "A la luz de Blanco." *La Orquesta* 3, no. 11 (January–February 1988).

———. "Alberto Blanco. *Cuenta de los guías.*" *Revista de Literatura Mexicana Contemporánea* 1, no. 2 (January–April 1996): 142.

———, ed. *Contemporary Spanish American Poets: A Bibliography of Primary and Secondary Sources.* Westport, CT: Greenwood, 1992.

———, ed. *Medusario. Muestra de poesía latinoamericana.* Edited by Roberto Echavarren, José Kozer, and Jacobo Sefamí. México: Fondo de Cultura Económica, 1996.

Sheridan, Guillermo. "*Giros de faros* de Alberto Blanco." *Vuelta* 33 (September 1979): 33–36.

Shlain, Leonard. *The Alphabet versus the Goddess: The Conflict between Word and Image.* New York: Viking, 1998.

———. *Art and Physics: Parallel Visions in Space, Time, and Light.* New York: Perennial, 2001.

Soja, Edward. *Postmodern Geographies: The Reassertion of Space in Critical Social Theory.* New York: Verso, 1989.

Stein, Gertrude. *Tender Buttons.* Auckland: Floating Press, 2009.

Steiner, George. *Language and Silence: Essays on Language, Literature and the Inhuman.* New York: Athenaeum, 1967.

Steiner, Wendy. *The Colors of Rhetoric.* Chicago: University of Chicago Press, 1982.

Stockwell, Peter. *Cognitive Poetics: An Introduction.* London: Routledge, 2002.

Tsur, Reuven. "Deixis and Abstractions: Adventures in Space and Time." In *Cognitive Poetics in Practice*, edited by Joanna Gavins and Gerard Steen, 53–46. London: Routledge, 2003.

Ulacia, Manuel. *La Sirena en el espejo: Antología de Poesía, 1972–1989.* Edited by Manuel Ulacia, Víctor Manuel Mendiola, and José María Espinasa. Mexico: Ediciones El Tucán de Virginia, 1990.

Valenzuela Navarrete, Gabriela. "Alberto Blanco, *La hora y la* neblina, FCE, México, 2005." *La Jornada Semanal*, September 4, 2005, 548.

White, Orlando. "Functional White: Crafting Space and Silence." *Poetry Foundation*, 2015. https://www.poetryfoundation.org/harriet/2015/11/functional-white-crafting-space-silence.

Willis, Bruce Dean. *Aesthetics of Equilibrium: The Vanguard Poetics of Vicente Huidobro and Mário de Andrade.* West Lafayette, IN: Purdue University Press, 2006.

Xirau, Ramón. *Palabra y silencio.* México: Siglo XXI Editores, 1968.

Zaid, Gabriel, ed. *Asamblea de poetas jóvenes de México.* México: Siglo XXI Editores, 1980.

Zamora, Carlos. "Crítica contextural: *El corazón del instante* de Alberto Blanco: Ensayo de un método." PhD dissertation, University of Kentucky, 2014.

———. "Poesía en oración: *Cuenta de los guías.*" *Revista de Literatura Mexicana Contemporánea* 1, no. 2 (1995): 26–29.

Zolov, Eric. *Refried Elvis: The Rise of the Mexican Counterculture.* Berkeley: University of California Press, 1999.

Index

About the Author

Ronald J. Friis is a professor of Spanish at Furman University in Greenville, South Carolina. He is the author of *José Emilio Pacheco and the Poets of the Shadows* and coauthor of the conversation textbook *Doble vía: Comunicación en español.* His articles on Latin American poetry appear in journals such as *Hispania*, *Latin American Literary Review*, *Revista de Estudios Hispánicos*, *Este país*, *MIFLC Review*, *Revista de Literatura Mexicana Contemporánea*, and *La Torre*. His poetry translations, many coauthored with students, appear in *Cagibi*, *Ezra*, the *Bhubaneswar Review*, and other literary journals.